CULTURAL EXCHANGE AND THE COLD WAR

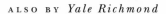

ALSO BY *Yale Richmond*

Soviet-American Cultural Exchanges: Ripoff or Payoff?

Hosting Soviet Visitors: A Handbook

U.S.-Soviet Cultural Exchanges, 1958–1986: Who Wins?

From Nyet to Da: Understanding the Russians

From Da to Yes: Understanding the East Europeans

Into Africa: Intercultural Insights (with Phyllis Gestrin)

CULTURAL EXCHANGE & THE COLD WAR

RAISING THE IRON CURTAIN

YALE RICHMOND

The Pennsylvania State University Press

University Park, Pennsylvania

Library of Congress Cataloging-in-Publication Data

Richmond, Yale.
    Cultural exchange and the Cold War : raising the iron
    curtain / Yale Richmond.
           p.   cm.
    Includes bibliographical references and index.
    ISBN 0-271-02302-3 (cloth : alk. paper)
    1. United States—Relations—Soviet Union.
    2. Soviet Union—Relations—United States.
    3. Cold War.
    4. Cultural relations.
    I. Title.

E183 .R53 2003
303.48'273047'09045—dc21   2002154506

It is the policy of The Pennsylvania State University Press
to use acid-free paper. Publications on uncoated stock
satisfy the minimum requirements of American National
Standard for Information Sciences—Permanence of Paper
for Printed Library Material, ANSI Z39.48–1992.

TO HANIA AND SAM,

who always wanted to know what their daddy did at the office.

It was *man* who ended the Cold War in case you didn't notice. It wasn't weaponry, or technology, or armies, or campaigns. It was just *man.*

—JOHN LE CARRÉ, *The Secret Pilgrim*

CONTENTS

ABBREVIATIONS AND ACRONYMS

ACLS	American Council of Learned Societies
ACTR-ACCELS	American Councils for International Education
ACYPL	American Council of Young Political Leaders
AFSC	American Friends Service Committee
CCI	Center for Citizen Initiatives
CIA	Central Intelligence Agency
CSCE	Conference on Security and Cooperation in Europe
CYO	Committee on Youth Organizations of the U.S.S.R
FBI	Federal Bureau of Investigation
GARF	Gosudarstvennyi Arkhiv Rossiiskoi Federatsii
GRU	Chief Directorate of Military Intelligence
IPPNW	International Physicians for the Prevention of Nuclear War
IMEMO	Institute of World Economy and International Relations
IREX	International Research and Exchanges Board
ISKAN	Institute for U.S. and Canadian Studies
IUCTG	Inter-University Committee on Travel Grants
JRL	Johnson's Russia List
KGB	Committee on State Security
KOR	Committee for Workers' Defense
MSU	Moscow State University
NASA	National Aeronautics and Space Administration
NGO	nongovernmental organization
OSCE	Organization for Security and Cooperation in Europe
S&T	Science and Technology
SCI	Sister Cities International
SPLEX	Special Exchange
TOEFL	Test of English as a Foreign Language
UNA	United Nations Association
USIA	United States Information Agency

PREFACE

Recent research on the collapse of communism and the end of the Cold War has focused, not on the U.S.-Soviet power relationship, but rather on the emergence of ideas that led to Mikhail Gorbachev's "new thinking." Jeffrey Checkel has shown how international political change is driven by ideas.[1] Thomas Risse-Kappen has described how arms controllers in the United States, and peace researchers and left-of-center political parties in Western Europe formed transnational networks with new thinkers in the Soviet Union.[2] Matthew Evangelista has written a history of transnational activism and how it shaped the policies of both the Soviet Union and the United States.[3] And Robert English has written about the westernization of Soviet political and academic elites.[4]

But the ideas behind Gorbachev's new thinking, as well as the westernization of Soviet elites, did not emerge suddenly in the 1980s. They had been gestating slowly in the minds of many members of the Soviet intelligentsia as a result of their contacts and exchanges with the West over the years following the death of Stalin in 1953.

"One of the most important reasons for the victory in Russia of Boris Yeltsin and the pro-Western reform movement," maintains Russian political analyst Sergei Markov, "is that a Western-oriented reform movement developed here during the Soviet period."[5] As Markov explains, "The exchange of scholars and other exchanges played a very important role in Soviet politics because through these exchanges Russian intellectuals were westernized."[6]

This book describes some of those Soviet contacts and exchanges with the West, and with the United States in particular, that influenced Soviet elites and the public at large and helped prepare the way for the ideas that formed the basis of Soviet new thinking. Many Western countries conducted exchanges with the Soviet Union, but the United States had the largest program, and it was specifically designed to bring about changes there.

1. Jeffrey T. Checkel, *Ideas and International Political Change: Soviet/Russian Behavior and the End of the Cold War* (New Haven: Yale University Press, 1997).

2. Thomas Risse-Kappen, "Ideas Do Not Float Freely: Transnational Coalitions, Domestic Structures, and the End of the Cold War," in Richard Ned Lebow and Thomas Risse-Kappen, eds., *International Relations Theory and the End of the Cold War* (New York: Columbia University Press, 1995).

3. Matthew Evangelista, *Unarmed Forces: The Transnational Movement to End the Cold War* (Ithaca: Cornell University Press, 1999).

4. Robert D. English, *Russia and the Idea of the West: Gorbachev, Intellectuals, and the End of the Cold War* (New York: Columbia University Press, 2000).

5. Sergei Markov, in *Moscow Times*, June 23, 1998.

6. Sergei Markov, author's interview, Washington, D.C., November 23, 1998.

I worked on U.S.-Soviet exchanges for many years—at the State Department, U.S. Information Agency, and American Embassy Moscow—and this book is a recounting of several of the major exchanges based on my own experience, readings of the scholarly literature, research in Russian archives, and interviews with many Americans and Russians who were also witnesses or warriors on the cultural front of the Cold War.

Thanks are due all those who gave so generously of their time to contribute recollections of their experiences.

Yale Richmond
Washington, D.C.

ACKNOWLEDGMENTS

Many people have contributed comments, counsel, and encouragement for this book. To all of them, my deep thanks and appreciation: Mikhail D. Afanasyev, Raymond Anderson, Leonard J. Baldyga, Jeffrey Barrie, Raymond E. Benson, Svetlana Boym, E. Willis Brooks, Hodding Carter III, Michael Cole, E. David Cronon, Nicholas Daniloff, Dan E. Davidson, James Dearlove, George J. Demko, Paul Doty, William Edgerton, Herbert J. Ellison, Terence Emmons, Alexander Etkind, Matthew Evangelista, Martin Feinstein, Murray Feshbach, Ralph T. Fisher, Wesley A. Fisher, Catherine Fitzpatrick, Max Frankel, Arnold Frutkin, Toby T. Gati, Thomas W. Gittins, Valery Golovskoy, Alexander R. Gorev, Loren R. Graham, Thomas Graham, Bernard Gwertzman, Mark Von Hagen, Jeffrey W. Hahn, Roald Hoffmann, Nick Holonyak Jr., William H. Hopkins, Oleg D. Kalugin, Edward Keenan, Oleg Kharkhordin, Aleksei R. Khokhlov, Mark Kramer, Marie Lavigne, Wallace W. Littell, Edward Luck, Glynn S. Lunney, Peter B. Maggs, Martin Manning, Everett Mendelsohn, Gerald E. Mikkelson, James R. Millar, George I. Mirsky, James E. Muller, Max Okenfuss, R. Spencer Oliver, Pavel Palazchenko, Arthur E. Pardee, James Pasquill, Mark N. Poole, Alexander Radovinsky, Donald J. Raleigh, George W. Rathjens, Alfred J. Rieber, Roald Z. Sagdeev, Jonathan Sanders, Harold H. Saunders, David M. Schoonover, Ephraim Schulman, Robert Sharlet, Gerson S. Sher, George Sherry, Emilia and Maxim Shrayer, František and Larisa Silnicky, Elbert B. Smith, S. Frederick Starr, Mikhail and Oleg Sulkin, Eugene Trani, Vladimir G. Treml, Vladimir I. Tropin, Benjamin Tua, James Voorhees, Peter Walker, Irwin Weil, Aleksandr N. Yakovlev, Miron Yampolsky, Boris N. Yuzhin, Victor Zablotsky, and Igor Zevelev.

Special thanks to Richard T. Davies, Robert English, Allen H. Kassof, Daniel Matuszewski, and an anonymous reviewer, who read the entire manuscript and made helpful suggestions. And appreciation goes to my copyeditor, Andrew Lewis, whose eagle eye caught several things I had missed.

Any errors or omissions are my own.

INTRODUCTION

Soviet visits to the West persuaded them to trust us more and fear us more, while Western visits there persuaded us to trust them less and fear them less.

—JEREMY J. STONE, former president, Federation of American Scientists

What caused communism to collapse and the Cold War to come to a close?

Some say it was Ronald Reagan who sullied the Soviet Union with his "evil empire" speech. Others point to Pope John Paul II and his visits to Catholic Poland, which challenged Soviet rule in Eastern Europe and ultimately the entire Soviet bloc. Still others recognize the role of the U.S. military buildup, the threat of "Star Wars," and the simple solution that we spent the Soviets into submission. Also credited are international radio broadcasts—the Voice of America, BBC, and Radio Liberty—that exposed the fabrications of the Soviet media.

There are also Western Sovietologists who maintain that the Soviet Union brought about its own demise through mismanagement at home, overextension abroad, an unwise intervention in Afghanistan, failure to cope with the Chernobyl nuclear disaster, and suppression of innovation in politics, economics, and the arts. As former U.S. ambassador to Moscow Jack Matlock has put it, "The Communist dictatorship collapsed under the weight of its own contradictions and irrationality."[1]

Also given credit for the Soviet demise is *glasnost*—the end of state control over the media—and the resultant information explosion in the Soviet Union that exposed the horrors of the past and the realities of the present. Yet another notion credits the abatement of fear among the Soviet people and the emergence of a dissident movement encouraged by the Helsinki Accords on human rights that challenged the authority of the Communist Party. There is even a theory that rock and roll, a Western import, seduced Soviet youth and eroded the authority of the Party's ideologists. And finally, many Russians tell us that glasnost and perestroika, and much that followed, were purely domestic developments that resulted from a reform movement within the Communist Party of the Soviet Union.

There is a grain of truth is some of these explanations, and more than a grain in others. But in the following pages readers will find many grains of another explanation—that the end of the Cold War and the collapse of communism were

---

1. Jack F. Matlock Jr., "The Poor Neighbor," *New York Times Book Review*, April 11, 1999, 11.

consequences of Soviet contacts and exchanges with the West, and with the United States in particular, over the thirty-five years that followed the death of Joseph Stalin in 1953. Moreover, those exchanges in culture, education, information, science, and technology were conducted by the United States openly, for the most part, under agreements concluded with the Soviet government, and at a cost that was minuscule in comparison with U.S. expenditures for defense and intelligence over the same period of time. The result was an increase in Western influence among the people in Russia who count—the intelligentsia.

As U.S. political scientist Michael Mandelbaum wrote in 1988: "Western values have been incubating for two decades. Changes took place under the surface of events during the Brezhnev period. In private conversations, in technical and specialized journals, and in more general publications couched in Aesopian language, controversy, debates, and Western themes began to appear. . . . [T]he intelligentsia of today are certainly better attuned to Western values than were their predecessors a generation ago."[2] The reach of the West was delineated by Vasily Aksyonov, the renowned Russian writer who now divides his time between Russia, France, and the United States: "Far behind the indestructible iron curtain we had somehow managed to develop a pro-Western mentality—and what could be farther West than America?"[3]

Official Washington, however, tended to downgrade the importance of the West's attractions during the Cold War, focusing instead on the Soviet Union's missiles and ground forces. Concerned mainly with Moscow's ability to project its power abroad, Washington underestimated its ability to influence the Soviet intelligentsia, and through them the entire nation.

How all that came about is the theme of this book.

2. Michael Mandelbaum, "Western Influence on the Soviet Union," in Seweryn Bialer and Michael Mandelbaum, eds., *Gorbachev's Russia and American Foreign Policy* (Boulder, Colo.: Westview Press, 1988), 375.

3. Vassily Aksyonov, *In Search of Melancholy Baby,* trans. Michael Henry Heim and Antonina W. Bouis (New York: Random House, Vintage Books, 1989), 17.

1 | RUSSIA AND THE WEST

Russian history is marked by the drama of trying to catch up with the West and then falling back. . . . Humiliated by some military defeat or provoked by some travel experience, leader after leader in what was once Russia and subsequently the Soviet Union determined that his or her mission in life was to transform that backward country into a modernized society equal to those in the West.

—MARSHALL I. GOLDMAN, *What Went Wrong with Perestroika*

For most of its history Russia has been isolated from other major centers of world civilization. Vast distances separated it from Western Europe, the Middle East, and China. In an age when transportation was primitive and hazardous, a trip by horse-drawn coach from Moscow to Western Europe could take three months or more.

At the end of the seventeenth century, for example, before roads were improved, a Russian named Pyotr Tolstoi departed Moscow on January 11 and arrived in Venice on May 22 after several major stopovers. When ordered to return to Moscow, he left Venice on November 1 and arrived in Moscow on January 27, a mere three-month journey because travel in winter over snow and ice was much faster.[1]

Russia's isolation from the West, however, was also self-imposed. Its temporal leaders saw the West as hostile; and after Mongol rule of Muscovy ended in the fifteenth century, Russia was indeed invaded many times from the West—from Sweden and Poland in the seventeenth century, France in the nineteenth, and Germany twice in the twentieth. Russia's religious leaders, moreover, saw the Catholic and Protestant West as threats to their Orthodox Christian beliefs and traditions. *Pravoslaviye,* the Russian translation of *Orthodoxy,* literally means "right praising" and implies that other forms of worship are wrong. Russia's communist leaders demonstrated the same deportment toward any departure from their "party line." Indeed, the Russian word for dissidents, *inakomysliashchi,* literally means "people who think differently."

A big question for Russia over the centuries has been whether it could borrow and learn from the more advanced West and still preserve Russia's *samobytnost'*

---

1. For the details of Tolstoi's travel, I am indebted to Max Okenfuss of Washington University, St. Louis.

(distinctiveness). Differences over the answer to this question has given rise to two rival schools of thought—Westernizers and Slavophiles—a division that has persisted in Russian history from the time of Tsar Peter the Great to the present.

Westernizers, recognizing Russia's backwardness, have sought to borrow from the West in order to modernize. They have regarded Russia as a political entity that would benefit from Western enlightenment, rationalism, rule of law, technology, and manufacturing and the growth of a Western-style middle class. Among the Westernizers have been political reformers, liberals, and socialists.

Slavophiles have also sought to borrow from the West but have been determined to protect and preserve Russia's unique cultural values and traditions. They have rejected individualism, and regarded the Orthodox Church, rather than the state, as Russia's leading historical and moral force. As admirers of agricultural life, they were critical of urban development and industrialization. Slavophiles, moreover, sought to preserve the *mir*, the traditional Russian agricultural commune, in order to prevent the growth of a Russian proletariat. They preferred Russian mysticism to Western rationalism. Among the Slavophiles have been philosophical conservatives, nationalists, and the Church.

The controversy between Westernizers and Slavophiles has surfaced many times in Russian history. As Hugh Seton-Watson has pointed out, it split Russian socialism between Marxists and Populists, Russian Marxism between Mensheviks and Bolsheviks, and Bolsheviks between opponents and followers of Stalin.[2] The controversy, which continues in Russia today, has been between those who believe in Europe and those who believe in Russia.[3]

For an early Russian Westernizer we turn to Tsar Peter the Great.

Peter the Modernizer

In Russian history, modernization has been achieved—notably by Peter the Great—through the process of copying selected features of more advanced Western countries while keeping other spheres of social life unchanged.

—ZDENĚK MLYNÁŘ, *Can Gorbachev Change the Soviet Union?*

Russia's cultural exchanges with the West began in the late sixteenth century when Tsar Boris Godunov sent thirty Russians to study in Western Europe at places like Paris, London, Oxford, Cambridge, Eton, and Winchester. But as historians like to point out, only two returned; the others became Russia's first defectors to the

2. Hugh Seton-Watson, *The Decline of Imperial Russia, 1855–1914* (New York: Frederick A. Praeger, 1952), 24.

3. These paragraphs on Westernizers and Slavophiles are from my book *From Nyet to Da: Understanding the Russians* (Yarmouth, Maine: Intercultural Press, 1996), 61–62.

West.[4] Four hundred years later, another "Tsar Boris" (Yeltsin) sent his grandson and namesake, also a Boris, to study at Winchester, one of the great English "public" schools, founded in 1382 and noted for its academic excellence.

In the late seventeenth century, Tsar Peter the Great, the first of Russia's great modernizers, gave impetus and direction to his country's glacial pace of modernization. With his energy, vision, optimism, and ruthless determination, Peter, who reigned from 1682 to 1725, laid the foundations for an imperial Russia that lasted almost two centuries after his death.

At age twenty-five, Peter, in 1696, undertook an eighteen-month "Grand Embassy," as it was called, to Western Europe to seek assistance for his campaign against the Turks. But he had another objective as well—to study shipbuilding and navigation for the navy he planned to build.

Modernization in Russia was sorely needed, and not only for its ships. In the early years of Peter's reign, when all major European countries had universities, Russia had none. As British historian Lindsey Hughes points out, Russia had not participated in the scientific revolution that had given the West the discoveries and inventions of Leibnitz, Boyle, Pascal, Newton, Galileo, Kepler, and Copernicus. During the entire seventeenth century, the only press in Moscow was run by the Church and published fewer than ten books whose contents were not wholly religious. As Hughes has it: "However hard one tries . . . to find compensating factors in the greater spirituality of Russians, their closeness to nature, or refined aesthetic sense, the 'intellectual silence' of Old Russia was deafening indeed. . . . Foreign learning was still equated with 'guile' and 'deception' even during Peter's childhood."[5]

Peter sought to change that, and his 270-man mission to Western Europe included twenty Russian noblemen and thirty-five "volunteers," many of them friends whom he had designated to study shipbuilding, navigation, and other naval arts and sciences. (More than three hundred years later, in another example of le plus ça change . . . , the first Russian exchange students sent to the United States in 1958 were also "designated" by their government to study abroad.)

Holland was one of the leading maritime powers of the time, and during Peter's almost five months in Amsterdam, he worked as a simple carpenter under a Dutch master shipwright, arriving at a shipyard each morning at dawn carrying his own tools on his shoulder. At the end of his stay in Holland, Peter received a certificate attesting that he had worked four months in the shipyard and was an able and competent shipwright.

Outside the shipyard, Peter's curiosity knew no bounds, and he wondered how the Dutch, in their small country, had been able to accumulate more wealth than

4. Hans von Eckhardt, *Ivan the Terrible* (New York: Knopf, 1949), 49.
5. Lindsey Hughes, *Russia in the Age of Peter the Great* (New Haven: Yale University Press, 1998), 298–99.

Russians in their vast, resource-rich expanse. (Three hundred years later, the economy of Russia was still smaller than that of the Netherlands.)

After Amsterdam, Peter spent four months in London, where he also studied shipbuilding and delved into everything else he encountered. He recognized, as did many Russians who followed him to the West in later years, that Russia was decades, perhaps centuries, behind the West in its development.

By the end of his travels, Peter had recruited some 750 skilled Europeans—shipwrights, naval officers, engineers, technicians, physicians, and others—to return with him to Russia. Most were Dutch but among them were Englishmen, Scots, Venetians, Germans, and Greeks, many of whom remained in Russia for years and helped to modernize the country. In exchange, Peter in the following years sent hundreds of young Russians to study in Holland, Venetia, and England. And in 1725, he established Russia's first scientific forum, the Imperial Academy of Sciences, staffed initially by Western Europeans until Russia could train its own scientists.

In contrast to the students sent to Western Europe by Tsar Boris a century earlier, most of those sent by Peter returned to Russia, where they were instrumental in building a modern Russian navy and schools of naval warfare. But as Max J. Okenfuss has pointed out, the sending of students abroad also influenced Russian cultural life in ways not anticipated by Peter, notably in literature and art. Dmitri M. Golitsyn, one of those sent abroad in 1797 to study seamanship, became an active patron of literature and was responsible for the translation of many Western works into Russian. Ivan Nikitin and Andrei Matveyev, sent to study ship decoration, later became the best of Russia's portrait painters in the first half of the nineteenth century.[6]

In England, Peter encountered the Quakers, who also aroused his curiosity. He attended several of their meetings and met one of their leaders, William Penn, with whom he conversed in Dutch, thus beginning a long Quaker association with Russia that has continued to our own day, and which will be discussed later in these pages.

Peter's reforms were many, and wherever one looks in Russia today, the results of his work can be seen. He is considered the founder of the modern Russian army and navy. Following Western models, he reformed central and local government, established a senate, introduced a head (poll) tax, developed industry and stimulated private enterprise, began the publication of books and newspapers, reformed the alphabet and introduced Arabic numerals, opened new schools of many types, and founded a museum of natural science and a general library open to the public. And in lasting memory of his name, he built St. Petersburg, Russia's first modern European city.

6. Max J. Okenfuss, "Russian Students in Europe in the Age of Peter the Great," in J. G. Garrard, ed., *The Eighteenth Century in Russia* (London: Oxford University Press, 1973), 131–45.

Peter's reforms also opened a long and impassioned debate over how Russia should relate to a Europe that had much to offer a remote and backward country but which also threatened to dilute its distinct culture and way of life.

Post Peter

The eighteenth century in Russia . . . was an age of apprenticeship and imitation par excellence. It has been said that Peter the Great, during the first decades of the century, borrowed Western technology, that Empress Elizabeth, in the middle of the period, shifted the main interest to Western fashions and manners, and that Catherine the Great, in the course of the last third of the century, brought Western ideas into Russia.

—NICHOLAS V. RIASANOVSKY, *A History of Russia*

Many are asking what perestroika was, where it has taken us. . . . The answer is simple; it is yet another Russian march to the West, but on a much greater scale than all those before. Peter only opened a window on Europe, but we're knocking down the walls. Both those that divided us from Europe, and those that cut us off from America and Japan.

—GEORGI SHAKHNAZAROV, *Tsena svobody*

Contact with Europe increased in the eighteenth century under another strong and resolute ruler, Catherine the Great, who reigned from 1762 to 1796. A German princess with a good grounding in French language and literature, Catherine knew well the writings of Voltaire and other luminaries of the Enlightenment, and she brought to the realities of ruling Russia her French reasoning and German work ethic. As Nicholas V. Riasanovsky, professor of history at Berkeley, describes her: "For the first time since Peter the Great, Russia acquired a sovereign who worked day and night, paying personal attention to all kinds of matters, great and small."[7]

The debate over Russia's relationship to Europe came to a head in 1825 with the revolt of the Decembrists, a movement led by army officers, many of them from aristocratic families and elite regiments, who had spent time in the West during the Napoleonic Wars and had been westernized to some extent. As Russia's first liberals, they sought to establish a constitutional state, protect civil rights, and abolish serfdom. But their December revolt failed and its leaders were executed or exiled to the fringes of the empire. By that time, however, Russia's contacts with the West had produced a French-speaking nobility and, in the following decades, a flowering of creativity in art, literature, and music, as well as endless debate over reform and how Russia should relate to Europe.

7. Nicholas V. Riasanovsky, *A History of Russia,* 2d ed. (New York: Oxford University Press, 1969).

The transition, however, was not without turmoil, as Hans Kohn, a foremost authority on nationalism, has described it, in words that could also be used to describe the Russia of our time:

> The most various and daring European ideas, all the conflicting and turbulent currents of the first half of the nineteenth century, poured suddenly into the entirely different Russian society. . . . Neither the political nor the social conditions existed for any practical application of the new ideas, the discussion of which became ever more heated the more it moved in a vacuum. . . . Yet this whole intense intellectual life of Russia between the uprising of the Decembrists and the Crimean War, these unreal discussions leading only to endless talk and a few significant essays—books and deeds were equally rare—illumined the face of Russia as she struggled to gain consciousness of herself through contact with the alien world of Europe.[8]

Modernization and reform continued in the late nineteenth and early twentieth centuries, although in fits and starts, as Russia became increasingly involved with that "alien world of Europe," with Russians traveling there for study, pleasure, or taking the waters at their favorite spa.

When the Bolsheviks seized power in 1917, the ideology they brought with them, Marxism, was yet another Western import, the work of a German scholar who had done his research at the British Museum. The Bolsheviks touted their Marxism as "scientific socialism," a Western product that would bring rationalism to Russia. But Lenin, Trotsky, and Stalin chose technological America as their model, as Thomas P. Hughes has pointed out:

> One of the momentous and almost forgotten chapters of modern history concerns the Bolsheviks' fierce determination between the two world wars to adopt the industrial legacy of the United States: to recreate the steel mills of Gary, Indiana, behind the Urals; to duplicate Ford's River Rouge plant in Nizhni Novgorod; to erect a copy of the great dam and generators of Muscle Shoals, Alabama, on the falls of the Dnieper River—all using American methods and American engineers, planners, and managers.[9]

The welcome mat was out for American know-how, and by 1930 the Soviet Union had agreements on technical cooperation with more than forty of the

8. Hans Kohn, *Pan-Slavism: Its History and Ideology* (Notre Dame: University of Notre Dame Press, 1953), 109–10.

9. Thomas P. Hughes, "How America Helped Build the Soviet Machine," *American Heritage,* December 1988, 56–58.

largest American corporations, including Ford, General Electric, and Dupont, whose efforts contributed to the success of the First Five-Year Plan.[10] And in a repeat of Peter's recruitment of Western experts, on the eve of recognition by the United States in 1933, some fifteen hundred American technical personnel were working in the Soviet Union.[11]

"The initial American banner-bearers in the cultural penetration of the Soviet Union," wrote Harrison Salisbury,

> were not diplomats nor jazz musicians nor even organizers of reading rooms and photo-montage displays. They were rugged capitalist entrepreneurs like Henry Ford, Hugh Cooper, Thomas Campbell, the International Harvester Co., and David Wark Griffith. These men, and their like, were the creators of an American culture which was superior to any the world had ever seen up to that time. It was an industrial and technological culture. And it penetrated Russia as it penetrated almost every corner of the earth without a nickel of appropriations from the federal treasury and without a single government specialist to contrive directives or program a series of consultations of interest agencies in an effort to arrive at agreed decisions.[12]

American technology and efficiency were indeed highly regarded by the Soviets. As Stalin himself said: "We would like the scientific and technical people in America to be our teachers in the sphere of technique, and we their pupils."[13] In a 1948 meeting with Eric Johnston, then president of the American Chamber of Commerce, Stalin acknowledged the Soviet Union's debt to Henry Ford: "He helped build our tractor and automobile industries."[14] Indeed, many of the early Soviet automobiles that one sees today in Russian museums look like carbon copies of the early Fords.

Nevertheless, Russia's age-old fear of contamination by the West resurfaced and even increased during Stalin's "Great Terror" of the late 1930s. Soviet citizens who had been abroad or had had relations with foreigners were arrested and executed or given harsh sentences. After World War II, those who had fought in the Spanish civil war of the 1930s were rewarded with long terms in the *gulag* for their service in Spain, which had been sanctioned by the Soviet government. Sent to

10. Nikolai V. Sivachev and Nikolai N. Yakovlev, *Russia and the United States: U.S.-Soviet Relations from the Soviet Point of View,* trans. Olga Titelbaum (Chicago: University of Chicago Press, 1980), 89.

11. Ibid., 102.

12. Harrison E. Salisbury, "Warfare with Folkways," *Saturday Review of Literature,* November 19, 1960, 25.

13. Ibid., 88.

14. Eric Johnston, *We're All in It* (New York: E. P. Dutton, 1948), 81.

concentration camps were some 1.5 million Soviet military personal who had been German prisoners of war during World War II and were repatriated, many of them forcibly, to the Soviet Union after the war.[15] And in the anti-Semitic campaigns of the 1940s and 1950s, Soviet Jews were labeled *kosmopoliti* (cosmopolitans), an implication that being culturally at home in another country was somehow a threat to the Soviet state.

The major manifestation of Soviet fear of the West was Stalin's Iron Curtain, which as Winston Churchill so eloquently put it, "from Stettin in the Baltic to Trieste in the Adriatic . . . descended across the Continent."

With few exceptions, Soviet citizens could not travel beyond the limits of the Soviet bloc, and for the few foreigners who were able to visit the Soviet Union, large parts of the country were closed, including many of its major cities, effectively cutting them off from contacts with the outer world. When I visited Saratov in 1991, a formerly closed industrial city on the Volga with a population of more than a million, I met with a group of university teachers of English who told me that I was the first native speaker of English they had ever encountered. Moreover, with control of the press, radio, and later, television in the firm hands of the Communist Party, the Soviet public was given a very one-sided view of the outer world.

Zdeněk Mlynář, a Czech communist who studied law in Moscow in the early 1950s, has noted how isolation caused the Soviet people to be woefully misinformed about living conditions in the rest of the world: "Countless occasions convinced us that a vast majority of the Soviet people genuinely believed that elsewhere in the world, in the capitalist states, working people live far worse than they do in the USSR—and in the material sense of the word, as consumers. At the same time, however, they had no actual knowledge of the rest of the world on which this conviction was based."[16]

Nor did the West, when the exchanges began, have an accurate knowledge of the Soviet Union.

Russia and America

The Russians took their art and religion from Byzantium in the tenth century and their first modern governmental institutions from the Swedes in the eighteenth, though only after fighting each for many decades. The United States in the late twentieth century replaced the Germany of the late nineteenth and early twentieth (and the France of the

15. Aleksandr Yakovlev, in "Memorial Mooted for Soviet POWs Imprisoned by Stalin," JRL 5316, June 22, 2001.

16. Zdeněk Mlynář, *Nightfrost in Prague: The End of Humane Socialism*, trans. Paul Wilson (New York: Karz Publishers, 1980), 14.

late eighteenth and early nineteenth centuries) as the essential "West" that Russians must both publicly confront and privately learn from.

—JAMES H. BILLINGTON, *Russia Transformed*

Despite their suspicion and fear of the West, Russians in our time have regarded the United States as the country they seek to be compared with, to emulate and overtake. As Vladimir Mayakovsky, the celebrated Russian poet, wrote when he visited the United States in 1925:

> You bourgeois, go ahead and marvel at the communist shore—
> we will not only overtake but will surpass
> your fleet-footed celebrated America
> at work, in the air, in the railway coach.[17]

Mayakovsky's musings about Russia overtaking and surpassing America presaged Nikita Khrushchev's exhortation, in a 1957 speech to agricultural workers in Leningrad (now St. Petersburg), to catch up with and overtake America in per capita production of meat, milk, and butter. In the following years local party secretaries urged workers to catch up with and surpass America in any number of fields. Two years later, in his famous "kitchen debate" with Vice President Richard Nixon while viewing a model American home at the U.S. National Exhibition in Moscow, Khrushchev colorfully predicted that the Soviet Union would soon surpass the United States in technology. "When we catch you up," he blustered, "in passing you by, we will wave to you."[18]

The United States is indeed the country with which Russians wish to be compared. As a former British ambassador to Moscow has described Russia's fascination with America: "The foreign country in which the majority of Russians . . . are most interested is America. It is the goal they are constantly , or urging themselves, to 'catch up and overtake.' They share many tastes with it—love of gadgets, technology, massive scale. . . . America is their favorite foreign country."[19] Even when Russian public opinion had turned against the United States in the late 1990s because of NATO's expansion to the east, NATO action in Kosovo, and Western criticism of the Russia's war in Chechnya, public opinion polls showed that Russians still had a favorable attitude toward the United States and its people. A public

17. Mayakovsky, quoted in Sivachev and Yakovlev, *Russia and the United States*, 93.

18. Nikita Khrushchev, in *New York Times*, July 25, 1959 (translation by the *Times*). A Soviet joke had it that the part about overtaking the Americans was eventually dropped from the slogan, leaving only the "catch up" part, because if the Soviets passed the Americans, it would be evident that their behinds were bare.

19. Sir William Hayter, *The Kremlin and the Embassy* (London: Hodder and Stoughton, 1966), 133.

opinion poll taken in February 2000 showed that two-thirds of Russians liked the United States, and three-quarters of Russians liked Americans in general.[20]

U.S. efforts to establish cultural exchanges with the Soviet Union began while World War II was still in progress. After the Moscow conference of October 1943, the U.S. ambassador to the Soviet Union, Averell Harriman, in a note to Foreign Minister Vyacheslav Molotov, Stalin's lieutenant, proposed a program of cultural exchanges that included the distribution in the Soviet Union of two bimonthly magazines designed to explain to the Soviet public the nature of the American war effort and aspects of American life. Also included were proposals for direct contact with Soviet news editors and the distribution of American films. Molotov's response was positive, but Soviet follow-up to specific American proposals was hesitant and sporadic, and it was only after another five months that he gave approval for one of the magazines.[21] After the war, several similar American overtures for cultural exchange went unacknowledged or were met with a cool and noncommittal response.[22]

After the death of Stalin in 1953, the Soviet Union began to reach out cautiously to Western countries, including the United States. In 1955, Soviet pianist Emil Gilels and violinists David Oistrakh and Leonid Kogan performed in the United States. A U.S. company of *Porgy and Bess,* which was touring Western Europe, was invited by the Soviet Union to perform for six weeks in Leningrad, Moscow, and Kiev, where they were a smash hit. The Boston Symphony Orchestra followed, as did delegations of the U.S. Congress, medical specialists, religious leaders, scientists, engineers, and business executives. American scholars also began to visit the Soviet Union but as tourists, the only way they could get Soviet visas in those years.[23] Cracks in Stalin's Iron Curtain were opening; and in 1957, through one of those cracks, tens of thousands of Western youth descended on Moscow.

20. The poll was conducted by the All-Russia Public Opinion Research Center (VtsIOM), and reported in *Trud,* March 7, 2000.

21. For more on the U.S. magazine, see "*Amerika* Magazine," in Chapter 13.

22. For details of the U.S. proposals, see Department of State, Office of Public Affairs, "Cultural Relations Between the United States and the Soviet Union: Efforts to Establish Cultural-Scientific Exchange Blocked by U.S.S.R.," Department of State Publication 3480, International Information and Cultural Series 4 (Washington, D.C.: U.S. Government Printing Office, 1949).

23. These exchanges are discussed in some detail in Frederick C. Barghoorn, *The Soviet Cultural Offensive* (Princeton: Princeton University Press, 1960).

2 | THE MOSCOW YOUTH FESTIVAL

... the 1957 World Youth Festival—a great turning point in cultural history.

—RICHARD STITES, *Russian Popular Culture*

When the Soviet Union made plans to host the Sixth World Youth Festival in Moscow, its intent was to demonstrate to the world the changes that had taken place since the death of Stalin four years earlier. Previous such festivals had been held in other countries, where they had been well managed by local communist groups and produced propaganda successes. The results of the Moscow festival, however, were quite different, and the consequences unintended. The tens of thousands of Soviet youth who attended the festival were infected with the youth styles of the West—jeans, jazz, boogie-woogie, rock and roll, and free speech—and the Soviet Union was never the same again.

For two weeks in July-August 1957, 34,000 foreign and 60,000 Soviet delegates descended on Moscow for what Max Frankel of the *New York Times* described as "a dizzying round of games, conferences, parties, and carnivals."[1] But also witnessing those events and observing them with interest and astonishment were the five million residents of Moscow and the thousands of other Soviet citizens who had come to the Soviet capital to see the spectacle. Also in attendance was a British delegation of more than 1,600 and about 160 Americans of various political persuasions who had come against the misguided advice of the State Department.[2]

Political bias was evident in many of the events, and some of the Americans learned that not all of their conversations were faithfully translated by the Russians. Other Americans were shocked to hear vehement denunciations of the United States at meetings where it was thought Americans were not present "There is no doubt," reported Frankel, "that the total effect of the festival pleased the Soviet Government. It has been armed with months' worth of propaganda about the friendship and fellowship demonstrated in Moscow by the visitors."[3]

1. *New York Times,* August 12, 1957.
2. The U.S. government appears to have changed its position by 1959 when the next World Youth Festival was held in Vienna. According to the *New York Times* (February 21, 1967), Gloria Steinem said that the CIA had supported a foundation, established in 1958 and where she was a full-time employee, that sent hundreds of Americans to World Youth Festivals in Vienna in 1959 and Helsinki in 1962.
3. Ibid.

But seeds of protest were also planted that would plague the Soviet government in future years. "There is erratic debate, polyglot conversation and heated argument everywhere," wrote Frankel, and he compared the Moscow festival scene to Union Square, New York City's open-air debating site, as Soviet youth surrounded foreign visitors and peppered them with questions about their home countries and lifestyles.[4] It was the first unstructured contact with foreigners for what would later be called the Gorbachev generation. "After toasts and shouts of peace and friendship," continued Frankel, "there are equally genuine demands from Soviet youths for descriptions of life in the West."[5] Much of the talk was leftist, but some Americans cited the United Nations report on the Hungarian revolution, which had been roundly denounced by the Soviets but never quoted in Moscow. Soviet Jews flocked to the Israeli delegates as well, eager to learn more about a country much maligned in the Soviet press. Flora Lewis, reporting for *Life* magazine, recalled that the 1955 Youth Festival, held in Warsaw, Poland, had unleashed sparks of protest in the communist world, and she wondered who was influencing whom at the Moscow Festival.[6]

Modern art also came to the Soviet Union by way of the festival. Young artists from all over the world had been invited to bring their works and compete for prizes, and an exhibition of their art was staged in Moscow's Gorky Park, the first exhibition of modern "bourgeois" painting to be seen in the Soviet Union. Most Russians, however, brought up on the traditions of socialist realism, were puzzled and shocked by the discordant colors and abstract figures exhibited by the foreign artists, but others defended the new art, and some were encouraged to emulate the experimental Western paintings.

"What is amazing," wrote Frankel, "is that there should be so many defenders of the new and the radical. They speak openly and frankly in this capital which during the festival is getting its first mass demonstration of the blessings of free speech."[7]

Other Western art forms—jazz, and rock and roll—also came to Moscow. "The government's inability to regulate the musical fare at the Sixth World Youth Festival," wrote rock historian Timothy W. Ryback, "highlighted the cultural dilemma that plagued Soviet officials for the next decade. With jazz ensembles thriving in every city, from Tallinn to Odessa, from Moscow to Vladivostok, officials found it impossible to control the wave of Western music sweeping the Soviet republics."[8]

Along with the jazz groups invited to the festival from Eastern and Western Europe, there were also a few of the early rock and roll groups from Britain, with

4. *New York Times*, August 2, 1957.
5. Ibid.
6. Flora Lewis, "USSR Teaches—and Is Taught," in *Life*, August 12, 1957, 23–26.
7. *New York Times*, August 9, 1957.
8. Timothy W. Ryback, *Rock Around the Bloc: A History of Rock Music in Eastern Europe and the Soviet Union* (New York: Oxford University Press, 1990), 30.

their electric guitars, which were new to the Soviet Union. Because rock was not known in the Soviet Union, Soviet officials did not know what to expect and were surprised when it took the festival by storm. Despite later efforts to stem the tide, rock continued to roll on, and with devastating consequences for the ideologists of the communist parties of the Soviet Union and Eastern Europe.

As Ryback wrote:

> The unifying force among the youth of Eastern Europe and the Soviet Union did not emerge from a carefully engineered socialist education: it came through the speaker of a gramophone, blaring the latest boogie woogie or rock and roll. . . . Rock music, despite the claims of Communist leaders, was, for Soviet and East European youths, a visceral rather than political experience. The "heated rhythms" of rock and roll elevated them among the mundane; it allowed them to escape, not engage in, political activity.[9]

9. Ibid., 34.

3 | THE CULTURAL AGREEMENT

If we are going to take advantage of the assumption that all people want peace, then the problem is for people to get together and to leap governments—if necessary to evade governments—to work out not one method but thousands of methods by which people can gradually learn a little bit more of each other.

—DWIGHT D. EISENHOWER, *Waging Peace, 1956–1961*

President Dwight D. Eisenhower envisioned a people-to-people exchange, with people indeed bypassing their governments to learn more about each other. But that was not to be for many years, and in the interim, exchanges had to be negotiated and carried out by governments with their cumbersome bureaucracies and political and security considerations, and under agreements laboriously negotiated and implemented.

Soviet ignorance of the United States was abysmal. Isolated from the outside world and continually told by their media of all the achievements of the Soviet state, the Soviet people believed that they were far better off than those who lived in the capitalist West. American knowledge of the Soviet Union was not much better.

"It is hard for us now to imagine how distant we were from each other and how little we understood each other," writes Sergei Khrushchev, son of Nikita Khrushchev, in describing his father's meeting with Dwight Eisenhower at the July 1955 Four-Power Summit Conference in Geneva.[1] "Living on either side of the iron curtain," he explains, "we knew nothing about each other. Diplomats and intelligence agents supplied their leaders with information, of course, but that was not enough to gain an understanding of the other side. We had to look into each other's eyes."[2]

Eisenhower and Khrushchev did look into each other's eyes at Geneva; and they must have liked what they saw, although it took another three years before the two governments were able to forge a cultural agreement that would enable thousands of American and Soviet citizens to meet face to face.

At the Foreign Ministers' Conference in Geneva in October 1955, the United States, together with Britain and France, proposed a seventeen-point program to

1. Sergei Khrushchev, " The Cold War Through the Looking Glass," *American Heritage,* October 1999, 37.
2. Ibid.

remove barriers to normal exchanges in the information media, culture, education, books and publications, science, sports, and tourism.[3] The initiative was rejected by Molotov, who accused the West of interference in Soviet internal affairs. But the Soviets did show interest in some of the proposals, and Molotov suggested that they might wish to conclude bilateral or multilateral agreements that "could reflect what is of particular interest to the countries concerned."[4]

Further developments had to await the Twentieth Congress of the Communist Party of the Soviet Union in 1956 where Khrushchev criticized Stalin and signaled changes in Soviet policy that included peaceful coexistence and increased contacts with the West.

After the congress, the Soviets moved swiftly to initiate exchanges with the West. Cultural agreements were signed with Norway and Belgium later that year, and with France and the United Kingdom in 1957. Negotiations with the United States began on October 29, 1957, and a U.S.-Soviet agreement on exchanges was signed on January 27, 1958.[5]

This "Agreement Between the United States of America and the Union of Soviet Socialist Republics on Exchanges in the Cultural, Technical, and Educational Fields"[6] included exchanges in science and technology, agriculture, medicine and public health, radio and television, motion pictures, exhibitions, publications, government, youth, athletics, scholarly research, culture, and tourism. Commonly called the Lacy-Zarubin Agreement, it was named after its two chief negotiators, William S. B. Lacy, President Eisenhower's Special Assistant on East-West Exchanges, and Georgi Z. Zarubin, Soviet ambassador to the United States. As an executive agreement rather than a treaty, it did not require ratification by the U.S. Senate, which avoided a prolonged and perhaps bitter debate in a forum that had only recently witnessed the challenges of McCarthyism.

The initial agreement was for a two-year period, but it was periodically renegotiated and, during détente, when both sides felt more comfortable with exchanges, its validity was extended to three years. The final agreement in the series, signed by Ronald Reagan and Mikhail Gorbachev at their 1985 Geneva Summit, was to have been in force until December 31, 1991, but the Soviet Union ceased to exist on

---

3. For the seventeen points, see the author's *U.S.-Soviet Cultural Exchanges, 1958–1986: Who Wins?* (Boulder, Colo.: Westview Press, 1987), 138–39.

4. *New York Times*, November 15, 1955.

5. "Agreement Between the United States of America and the Union of Soviet Socialist Republics on Exchanges in the Cultural, Technical, and Educational Fields," in *United States Treaties and Other International Agreements* (TIAS 3975) vol. 9, 1958, 13–39.

6. The following paragraphs discussing the agreement are from the author's *U.S.-Soviet Cultural Exchanges, 1958–1986*, 2–9.

December 25, and the agreement, no longer necessary, was not renewed with the new Russia.[7]

Signing a cultural agreement was a new departure for the United States. After World War II, the United States, determined to democratize its former enemies, had large exchange programs with Germany and Japan, but those were mostly one-way exchanges, from Germany and Japan to the United States, and they were administered and funded by the United States alone.[8]

Also new for the U.S. government was its partnership with the private sector in funding and carrying out exchanges under the agreement. Many of the activities under the cultural agreement were the responsibility of the U.S. private sector—science and technology, radio and television, motion pictures, publishing, youth, education, performing arts, athletics, and tourism—and governmental participation in many of those fields was only peripheral. In the Soviet Union, by contrast, all of the activities were governmental. Here, at the start, was one of the many difficulties that would emerge as two diametrically different societies attempted to establish contacts and exchanges over a wide range of activities.

On the U.S. side there was no precedent for such an agreement. Thousand of foreign students come to the United States each year without intergovernmental agreements, as well as specialists in technology, science, culture, performing arts, athletics, and other fields covered by the agreement. Why then, was such an agreement necessary? How could the federal government agree to regulate, in its relations with another government, the international activities of U.S. universities, industry, the media, and its many and varied cultural institutions?

The simple answer is that the Soviet leaders wanted an agreement and made it a condition to having exchanges. They were accustomed to putting things on paper, signed by their political authorities at an appropriately high level. In a country where the government and the Party controlled practically everything, it would have been inconceivable to conduct exchanges with another country, particularly the leader of the capitalist West, without a formal agreement that spelled out exactly who and what would be exchanged, under what conditions, and how the costs would be shared. Moreover, with their highly centralized government and

7. The cultural agreement was replaced in 1998 by a "Memorandum of Understanding Between the Government of the United States of America and the Government of the Russian Federation on the Principles of Cooperation in the Fields of Culture, the Humanities, the Social Sciences, and the Mass Media," signed September 2, 1998, in Moscow. The memorandum encouraged exchanges and cooperation in the aforementioned fields but did not provide limiting quotas or conditions for the exchanges.

8. For U.S.-German exchanges, see Henry J. Kellermann, *Cultural Relations as an Instrument of U.S. Foreign Policy: The Educational Exchange Program Between the United States and Germany, 1945–1954* (Washington, D.C.: U.S. Government Printing Office, 1978), and his interview with the Foreign Affairs Oral History Project, conducted by Hans Tuch, January 30, 1989, Lauinger Library, Georgetown University, box 1, folder 247.

bureaucratic planning procedures, the Soviets needed an agreement to enable their participating ministries and agencies to budget in advance for exchanges and to make plans for the agreed activities. But as many governments and private organizations would learn in the following years, signing an exchange agreement with the Soviets was one challenge; implementing it was another and far more difficult task.

For the Americans, however, having an agreement ensured that the exchanges would be conducted on a reciprocal basis and that the Soviet Union would be open to American participants. An East-West Contacts Staff, established at the State Department in 1957, had been sending scientific, technical, and cultural delegations and individuals to the Soviet Union even before the cultural agreement was signed. But the exchange traffic was increasing rapidly in both directions, and the United States needed an agreement to ensure that the principles of equality, reciprocity, and mutual benefit would be observed. Without the cultural agreement, it is questionable how much reciprocity there would have been in the exchanges.

The Soviet agencies responsible for the exchanges, as well as the officials who conducted them, also needed the protective cover of an agreement to justify their exchanges with the United States. The cultural agreement was signed only five years after the death of Stalin, and no one in the Soviet Union could say then whether Soviet policy might again change. Finally, the Soviets, in general, liked bilateral agreements with the United States, believing that they lent legitimacy to their regime and implied equality between the superpowers.

To a great extent, the initial agreement was the result of interest by President Eisenhower in encouraging people-to-people exchanges. As Eisenhower put it, he had long advocated "this kind of direct people-to-people exchange as one fine, progressive step toward peace in the world. In September of 1956 I initiated a broad-scale People-to-People program—an effort to stimulate private citizens in many fields (the arts, education, athletics, law, medicine, business) to organize themselves to reach across the sea and national boundaries to their counterparts in other lands."[9]

U.S. objectives, as stated in a National Security Council directive (NSC 5607), were, among others, to broaden and deepen relations with the Soviet Union by expanding contacts between people and institutions; involve the Soviets in joint activities and develop habits of cooperation with the United States; end Soviet isolation and inward orientation by giving the Soviet Union a broader view of the world and of itself; improve U.S. understanding of the Soviet Union through access to its institutions and people; and obtain the benefits of long-range cooperation in culture, education, and science and technology.[10]

9. Dwight D. Eisenhower, *Waging Peace, 1956–1961* (New York: Doubleday, 1965), 410.
10. For the full text of NSC 5607, see *Foreign Relations of the United States, 1955–1957* (Washington, D.C.: U.S. Government Printing Office, 1958), 24: 220–23.

The Soviet objectives in the exchanges were not openly stated; but from a study of how they conducted the exchanges, they can be presumed to have included the following: to obtain access to U.S. science and technology and learn more about the United States; support the view that the Soviet Union was the equal of the United States by engaging Americans in bilateral activities; promote the view of the Soviet Union as a peaceful power seeking cooperation with the United States; demonstrate the achievements of the Soviet people; give vent to the pent-up demand of Soviet scholars, scientists, performing artists, and intellectuals for foreign travel and contacts; and earn foreign currency through performances abroad of Soviet artists and athletes whose fees and honoraria went, not to the participating individuals, but to the Soviet state.

These differences in objectives were to create difficulties in administering the exchanges. As Nikita Khrushchev later pointed out: "The Americans wanted a much broader exchange of tourists, scientists and students. . . . Many of their suggestions were clearly intended to make us open our borders, to increase the flow of people back and forth. They were also trying to pressure me into permitting stores to be opened in the Soviet Union where our citizens could buy American literature; in exchange they would allow us to open outlets in America where we could sell our books."[11]

Georgi A. Arbatov, a leading Soviet Americanologist and supporter of exchanges, also questioned the motives behind American efforts to foster exchanges. But Arbatov had it right when he made the following statement in 1969, after eleven years of the exchanges:

> Underlying U.S. policy is the so-called "erosion" of our social system. As a professional student of the United States I feel that this is a basic United States policy line and that it distorts all good proposals, including those regarding contacts. Professor [Zbigniew] Brzezinski speaks of promoting evolutionary changes in the Soviet Union. This is what underlies United States policy of promoting cultural contacts and trade. The Republican Party platform speaks of the Soviet system as something abnormal which can yield to the normal and refers to trade as a wedge for this purpose. This is how influential people in the United States *do* regard their policy and we must remain cognizant of this strategy as the framework within which exchanges are conceived. This is the *main* obstacle to contacts and cannot be ignored.[12]

11. Nikita Khrushchev, *Khrushchev Remembers: The Last Testament,* trans. and ed. Strobe Talbott (Boston: Little, Brown, 1974), 409–10.

12. Rapporteur's Notes, Fifth Dartmouth Conference, Rye, New York, January 13–19, 1969, translated from the Russian, emphasis in the original. Quoted in James Voorhees, *Dialogue Sustained: The*

Among the basic tenets of the exchanges, as noted previously, were the principles of equality, reciprocity, and mutual benefit. The two sides were to treat each other as equals, approximate reciprocity was to be the sought in the various exchanges, and the benefits to the two sides should be comparable. To maintain these principles, the periodic renegotiations of the cultural agreement and its annexed program of exchanges were often long and laborious. In 1962, for example, negotiations in Moscow for the third agreement in the series lasted three months before concord was reached on all its provisions. Reaching agreement on the general provisions of the cultural agreements was relatively easy but agreement on the specific exchanges to be conducted was difficult. One continuing difficulty over the years was the exchange of large exhibitions, which will be discussed in Chapter 12. Performing arts was another difficult exchange where the Soviets often resisted accepting American productions or art forms it believed were too avant-garde or even modern.

Another feature of the exchanges conducted under the agreement, as noted above, was the partnership between the U.S. federal government and the private sector. The scholarly exchanges, in their early years, were supported largely by the Ford Foundation and the participating American universities that waived tuition, housing, and other fees for the Soviet students and scholars they received.[13] U.S. industry covered many of the costs of the exchanges of technical delegations. The tours of Soviet performing arts groups and individual artists in the United States were conducted on a commercial basis through American impresarios such as the legendary Sol Hurok and Columbia Artists Management. Likewise, the exchange of athletic teams was the responsibility of U.S. sports associations, and the exchange (actually, sale) of films was arranged, on the U.S. side, through the Motion Picture Association of America.

This unique sharing of costs was useful in two respects. For the State Department and the U.S. Information Agency (USIA), it reduced the costs of the exchanges. It also brought private sector exchanges under the umbrella of an agreement that was a government-to-government initiative. And for the participating U.S. private organizations, it provided State Department approval for their exchanges with the leading country of the communist world.

The cultural agreement and the exchanges conducted within its framework enjoyed broad public support. There was little or no opposition in the Congress, and the exchanges, for the most part, had the support of what constitutes civil

Multilevel Peace Process and the Dartmouth Conference (Washington, D.C.: United States Institute of Peace and Charles F. Kettering Foundation, 2002), 74.

13. Over the years, Ford Foundation funding for U.S.-USSR scholarly exchanges was gradually reduced and replaced by funding from the State Department, the U.S. Office of Education, and the National Endowment for the Humanities.

society in America—academia, the media, science, churches, sports associations, industry, and the public in general.

Exchanges served as a barometer of U.S.-Soviet relations. When relations between the two superpowers were good, exchanges flourished and expanded; when relations chilled, exchanges suffered. During the worst years of the Vietnam War, the Soviets cut back on several exchanges. And after the Soviet invasion of Afghanistan, the Carter administration suspended high-visibility exchanges such as exhibitions, performing arts, high-level delegations, and U.S. participation in the Moscow Olympics of 1980, as well as much of the cooperation in science and technology. Scholarly exchanges continued, however, despite the ups and downs in relations, although at reduced levels at times.

4 | SCHOLARLY EXCHANGES

Historians dealing with the collapse of Communism will want to devote more than one chapter to the extraordinary impact of East-West scholarly exchanges on the societies of Eastern Europe and the USSR. Even during the years when the rapid spread of Soviet influence to Europe, Asia, Africa and Latin America made Moscow look all but invincible, seeds of change that would later blossom into the democratic revolutions of 1989–90 were being sown by scholars from East and West.

—ALLEN H. KASSOF, "Scholarly Exchanges and the Collapse of Communism"

One chapter alone, as Allen Kassof rightly regrets, will not suffice to credit the role of scholarly exchanges in bringing about change in the Soviet Union, but I will attempt it here. As Kassof explains:

> Among the thousands of Soviet and East European academics and intellectuals who were exchange participants in the United States and Western Europe . . . many became members of what, in retrospect, turned out to be underground establishments. They were well-placed individuals, members of the political and academic elites, who began as loyalists but whose outside experiences sensitized them to the need for basic change. Together with the more radical political and cultural dissidents, towards whom they were ambivalent or hostile, they turned out to be agents of change who played a key part, sometimes unintentional, in the demise of European Communism.[1]

Kassof was executive director of the International Research and Exchanges Board (IREX), established in 1968 by the American Council of Learned Societies (ACLS) and Social Science Research Council (SSRC) to represent the U.S. academic and scholarly community in its exchanges with the Soviet Union and Eastern Europe. IREX was the successor to the Inter-University Committee on Travel Grants (IUCTG), which conducted the exchanges from 1956 to 1968 under the chairmanships of Schuyler C. Wallace, Columbia University, and Robert F. Byrnes,

---

1. Allen H. Kassof, "Scholarly Exchanges and the Collapse of Communism," in *The Soviet and Post-Soviet Review* 22, no. 3 (1995): 263–74.

Distinguished Professor of History at Indiana University.[2] Kassof, a sociologist and specialist on the Soviet Union, directed the IREX exchanges from July 1968 to May 1992. During those years, more than 110 U.S. colleges and universities were participating members of IREX.

Soviet Students and Scholars

The enormous impact of the exchanges on U.S. relations with the Soviet Union and Eastern Europe, and with the post-communist successor states that emerged from the collapse of 1989–91, has yet to be fully understood and appreciated.

—HERBERT J. ELLISON, "My 40 Years with IUCTG/IREX"

Among the many provisions of the cultural agreement was an exchange of graduate students, young faculty, and senior scholars. Eisenhower wanted to exchange as many as ten thousand students and had drafted a letter to Chairman Nikolai Bulganin, the Soviet head of state, offering to invite several thousand Soviet students to the United States, all expenses paid, and let the Soviet leaders decide whether they would invite an equal number of American students in exchange. Eisenhower even checked out his proposal with FBI Director J. Edgar Hoover, who told the president, "Though bringing ten thousand Soviet students into the United States would undoubtedly cause some additional problems, I'm all for the idea. It's an affirmative, dynamic proposal."[3]

Eisenhower's proposal was not made public because the State Department, at the time, was trying without success to get the Soviets to agree to exchange a hundred students, and it was thought that Eisenhower's bold proposal would only alarm them and delay the negotiations. The Soviets eventually agreed to exchange no more than twenty graduate students a year during the first two years of the agreement, and in subsequent years that figure rose to only fifty. Moreover, the "graduate students" that the Soviets would send were mostly in their thirties, well advanced in their careers, and had already earned their candidate degrees (roughly equivalent to a U.S. Ph.D.). The larger exchange that Eisenhower envisioned had to wait thirty years when free and unfettered exchanges became possible. Nevertheless, over the next thirty years, despite the ups and downs in U.S.-Soviet relations, thousands of Soviet students, scholars, and scientists would come to the United States, and an even larger number of Americans would go to the Soviet Union.

2. Schuyler C. Wallace, IUCTG founding chairman, served from 1956 to 1960 when he was succeeded by Byrnes, who served until 1968.

3. Eisenhower, *Waging Peace,* 411.

Prior to the signing of the Lacy-Zarubin Agreement in January 1958, a start had been made in scholarly exchanges between the two countries. In February 1956, IUCTG was established to represent the American academic community in scholarly exchanges with the Soviet Union. With funding from the Ford Foundation, IUCTG provided travel grants to enable American scholars to visit the Soviet Union for mostly thirty-day visits, but as tourists, the only way they could obtain visas in those years, and at a cost of $16 per day in the Soviet Union. Between 1956 and 1960, more than two hundred scholars representing fifteen academic disciplines from seventy-five U.S. academic institutions took advantage of that early opening in the Iron Curtain. With the signing of the Lacy-Zarubin Agreement in 1958, IUCTG was designated by the State Department to conduct the official academic exchanges under the agreement, and it performed those functions until July 1968, when it ceased to exist and its programs were transferred to the newly established IREX.[4]

Under the Lacy-Zarubin Agreement, IUCTG and IREX conducted three types of academic exchange with the Soviet Ministry of Higher and Specialized Secondary Education. The flagship program was the Graduate Student/Young Faculty Exchange, which in a typical year exchanged some forty to fifty Americans and an equal number of Soviets for one or two semesters of research. (As noted above, the graduate student exchange began with an agreed quota of twenty students in its first year and eventually reached fifty.)[5] For postdoctorates, the Senior Research Scholar program exchanged ten or more persons on each side for two to five months of research. A Summer Language Teacher program exchanged thirty (later thirty-five) American teachers of Russian and an equal number of Soviet teachers of English for nine weeks each summer.

IREX also administered, on behalf of ACLS and the Social Science Research Council, an exchange of postdoctoral scholars with the Soviet Academy of Sciences—up to sixty person-months a year on each side for some fifteen Americans and thirty Soviets (who came for shorter periods of time). In addition, IREX, from 1975, administered a program of collaborative research, conferences, and workshops between ACLS and the Soviet Academy under their bilateral Commission on the Humanities and Social Sciences. Under that program, some eighty Americans and eighty Soviets were exchanged each year for visits of about one

4. Much of the material on IUCTG has been drawn from Robert F. Byrnes, *Soviet-American Academic Exchanges, 1958–1975* (Bloomington: Indiana University Press, 1976). Byrnes (98–117) also discusses in detail the controversies within the American academic community over selection procedures for U.S. students and scholars, and the role of the U.S. government in scholarly exchanges.

5. In the first year, 1958–59, only seventeen students from each side were exchanged. The Soviets had nominated twenty but withdrew three, without explanation, prior to their scheduled arrival in the United States, and the number of American students was similarly reduced by the Soviets.

week. (For more on the commission's activities, see Chapter 6.) From 1958 to 1988, an estimated five thousand American and a similar number of Soviet graduate students, scholars, and teachers were exchanged through the IUCTG and IREX programs.

University lecturers were exchanged under the Fulbright Program, starting with the 1974 academic year, the earliest year in which the Soviets agreed to such an exchange, despite repeated proposals from the State Department. The exchange began with lecturers in American and Russian history, and grew gradually until it reached some fifteen or more lecturers on each side in various academic disciplines. Administering the program on the U.S. side was the Council for International Exchange of Scholars (CIES), and on the Soviet side, the Ministry of Higher Education. Funding on the U.S. side came from the State Department and the participating American universities.

In addition, there were several private one-way exchanges under which American students, mostly undergraduates, studied Russian in the Soviet Union, paying all costs in dollars, but with no Soviet students coming to the United States in exchange. The largest of these was conducted by the Council on International Educational Exchange (CIEE), which began to send students to Leningrad State University in 1966. Under the CIEE program, some two hundred Americans went to Leningrad each year for a summer session or one to two semesters of intensive Russian-language study. The CIEE program was affiliated with thirty-four U.S. colleges and universities but students from other institutions were also accepted. Between 1966 and 1986, more than four thousand Americans studied Russian at Leningrad under the CIEE program. Another two hundred or more American students studied Russian each year at Moscow's Pushkin Russian Language Institute under a program administered by the American Council of Teachers of Russian (ACTR). Both of those programs, as well as a few smaller ones, produced a growing pool of Russian-speaking Americans knowledgeable about the Soviet Union, many of whom went on to some kind of work or study related to Soviet affairs.

From the start, the administration of scholarly exchanges was beset with difficulties. There was criticism of the concept of quotas in student exchanges. As Robert F. Byrnes himself once put it, the Russians and Americans were exchanging students like so many sacks of grain. Moreover, the exchange agreement specified a maximum number of persons to be exchanged in each category, rather than a minimum number on which to build increases.

While there was exact numerical reciprocity in the numbers of persons exchanged each year, there were several disparities. Most of the Americans in the graduate student exchange were in their mid-twenties and doing research for their doctorates in the humanities and social sciences, mainly in Russian history, language, and literature. The Soviets, as noted above, were mostly in their thirties, already had their candidate degrees, and were predominantly in various fields of science and technology. Moreover, the Americans, in accordance with U.S. academic tradition, were selected by IUCTG and IREX in open competition, while on the Soviet side, fields of study were determined by an interagency governmental committee according to the needs of the Soviet economy, and there was no open competition. Universities and research centers were canvassed to find the best talent in each field, and Soviet participants were simply told, without prior consultation, that they were being sent to the United States on a *komandirovka,* the Russian term for an official trip.

In most years, a number of nominees were rejected by each side. Soviets were turned down by the Americans because they were in fields of high technology related to defense. Americans were turned down by the Soviets because they were in fields considered sensitive, usually history, sociology, or political science on contemporary (i.e., post-1917) topics. And because the exchange was numerically reciprocal, one turndown led to another until there was an equal number of exchangees accepted by the two sides in a given year. (The procedures for such turndowns will be discussed in Chapter 24.) The administrators of the exchanges faced three other problems for Americans in the Soviet Union—housing, access to archives, and travel.

Housing was a perennial problem, especially in Leningrad, where the Americans had to accept the substandard dormitory housing to which the Soviets assigned them, although in fairness it must be said that, by American standards, all student housing in Leningrad was substandard.

Working conditions for Americans in the Soviet Union were also less than satisfactory, and successful research required persistence and ingenuity. American researchers could experience delays of several months in obtaining access to archives necessary for their research. And because the Soviets would not allow research on the Soviet period, most of the U.S. scholars did work on the tsarist years, and security considerations therefore could not have played a role. The delays were believed to have been due as much to an overburdened Soviet bureaucracy as to the Russian penchant for secrecy. As a West German scholar has described it: "Among Western exchange persons it became proverbial to accept that they use one third of the time to satisfy Soviet bureaucracy, one third to queue up, and the rest to work."[6]

Such difficulties were experienced by all Westerners and were not limited to Americans, as London's Royal Society has reported:

6. Ingeborg Fleischhaur, "Some Practical Aspects of Academic Exchange" (paper presented at the conference "Russia and the West: Cultural Contacts and Influences," Schloss Leopoldskron, Salzburg, Austria, October 30–November 3, 1973).

Soviet scientists programmed to present papers at conferences do not turn up, or turn up too late. Correspondence about visits goes unanswered for long periods of time, the matter eventually being decided by expensive exchanges of telegrams. Complicated programs are arranged for visiting scientists whose visits are postponed or canceled at short notice. Visas to enable British scientists to enter the Soviet Union, even under the agreement, or after formal invitations from the Academy, are often received only after several visits to the [Soviet] Consulate, cables to and from Moscow, and generally disproportionate administrative effort. When visits finally do take place, the Soviet visitors or hosts, as the case may be, turn out to be largely blameless for and even unaware of the preceding bureaucratic difficulties.[7]

Arranging travel within the Soviet Union was another bureaucratic obstacle for Western students. Travel beyond the place of study was usually difficult for foreign students to arrange, which both disappointed and annoyed them. Like other foreigners in the Soviet Union, American exchange participants were limited to travel within forty kilometers of their place of study. Any travel beyond that limit had to be approved in advance by the Soviet authorities and was often denied. Students interested in learning more about the Soviet Union, its people, and their way of life usually wanted to travel during the semester recess and the weeks at the end of the academic year. But as one Soviet diplomat put it during a negotiation where the American side had complained about travel restrictions, "Your students have come to our country to study, and that is what they should be doing, not traveling." Repeated American efforts to lift such travel restrictions were unsuccessful, and the United States, in retaliation and with reluctance, eventually imposed similar travel restrictions on Soviet students and scholars in the United States.

The Soviets never objected to U.S. travel restrictions on their students because their own restrictions on Americans in the Soviet Union were much more severe. Some 20 percent of the Soviet Union was closed to travel by all foreigners, and travel plans had to be filed with the Soviet authorities in advance of the projected travel. Moreover, travel requests by Americans to open areas, whether for scholarly or touristic purposes were often denied. The United States offered several times to abolish or ease such travel restrictions on a mutual basis, but the Soviets showed no interest. In retaliation, the United States closed about 20 percent of its territory to travel by Soviet citizens. Those controls, however, did not apply to Soviet exchangees, who were free to travel for pleasure to any part of the United States.

7. John Deverill, "The Royal Society's Experience in Facilitating Scientific Interchanges with the Soviet Union" (paper presented at the conference "Russia and the West: Cultural Contacts and Influences," Schloss Leopoldskron, Salzburg, Austria, October 30–November 3, 1973).

In the early years of the exchanges, most of the Soviet graduate students and senior scholars were from Russia, Ukraine, or Byelorussia, with one or two each year from the Baltic, Caucasus, or Central Asian republics. In later years, however, as the quotas established under the cultural agreement increased, there was a corresponding increase of participants from the non-Slavic republics.

Aleksandr Yakovlev

It was Russian political elites that overthrew communism and disbanded the Soviet Union. It was not the United States or NATO.

—ALEKSEI ARBATOV, "America's Impact on Russia"

Aleksandr N. Yakovlev is best known as the godfather of glasnost, Mikhail Gorbachev's policy of promoting openness in Soviet society. "Without his influence," wrote Robert G. Kaiser of the *Washington Post*, "events at many key junctures would have developed differently": "From the outset he was Gorbachev's ambassador to the intellectuals, the new leader's first critical constituency. He was the architect of glasnost and the most important protector of the liberal editors who, beginning in the summer of 1986, began to give the Soviet Union its first critical and independent press."[8]

Yakovlev's rise from a small peasant village to the Politburo of the Communist Party and senior adviser to Gorbachev was not unprecedented for an ambitious and bright young Russian. But Yakovlev was different from run-of-the-mill Soviet apparatchiks. He read widely, had an open mind, studied American history at Yaroslavl State Pedagogical University, spent a year in the United States as a graduate student at Columbia University, and served ten years as Soviet ambassador to Canada. That lengthy exposure to the West, much longer than any previous member of the Politburo, differentiated him from other rising young Russians, whose backgrounds were more insular.

Yakovlev was one of four Soviet graduate students enrolled at Columbia University in New York City in autumn 1958 in the first year of student exchange under the Lacy-Zarubin Agreement, signed earlier that year by the two governments. At Columbia, Yakovlev studied modern American history and politics under Professors David Truman and Richard Hofstadter, in particular the foreign policy of Franklin D. Roosevelt. Professor Truman, Yakovlev has said, was an ideal mentor, who left him free to pursue his research as he wished but who gave good advice on which books and articles were worth reading and which could be ignored.[9]

8. Robert G. Kaiser, *Why Gorbachev Happened: His Triumph and His Failure* (New York: Simon and Schuster, 1991), 106.

9. Jack Matlock Jr., *Autopsy on an Empire: The American Ambassador's Account of the Collapse of the Soviet Union* (New York: Random House, 1995), 75.

A diligent student, Yakovlev spent much of his time in the Columbia library but he could not fail to note the differences between the United States and the Soviet Union: "I was enormously impressed by the difference in material well-being between the United States and my country. It was 1958 and our country continued to experience great economic difficulties. At the same time, I was terribly irritated by the primitive criticism of my country by the Americans. I took it very hard."[10]

At the end of the 1958/59 academic year, a tour of the United States took the Soviet students to Philadelphia, Chicago, parts of Wisconsin and Iowa, New Orleans, and Washington, D.C., where they stayed in American homes and observed firsthand the prosperity and overall development in the United States compared to what they knew in the Soviet Union.[11] Yakovlev was angered on behalf of his home country. "It was offensive, offensive. That here people were capable of constructing buildings, and we were not. We went from war to war to war."[12]

Also taken hard by Yakovlev was the intense FBI surveillance to which he was subjected. Of the four students assigned to Columbia that year, two were KGB, one was GRU (Soviet military intelligence), and the fourth, Yakovlev, was from the Central Committee of the Communist Party.[13] And because, at age thirty-three, Yakovlev was the oldest of the four and had worked for three years at the Central Committee, the FBI assumed that he was the *starosta* (senior) in charge of the group. Many years later, in a strange turn of events, Yakovlev was accused by Russian communist party chief Gennadi Zyuganov of being an "agent of influence, trained by American agents to rise high in the Soviet bureaucracy and undermine the state."[14] George Feifer, who would later be a U.S. exchange student at Moscow, reports that he interviewed Yakovlev and his fellow Soviet students at Columbia for an article he was writing for the *New York Times Magazine*. "It failed miserably," says Feifer. "Convinced that I was a CIA sleuth, they repeated the slogans as if they were taking exams in dialectical materialism; not a hint of how their experience was changing them. But it did, didn't it? Yakovlev himself was heavyweight proof of the pudding."[15]

10. Aleksandr Yakovlev, in Harry Kreisler, "Conversation with Alexander Yakovlev," November 21, 1996, Berkeley, Institute of International Studies, University of California (http://globetrotter/ berkeley.edu/Elberg/Yakovlev/yak-conO.html).

11. Costs of the academic year for the Soviet students were borne by the participating universities and the Ford Foundation. Costs of the U.S. tour were covered by a grant of $10,500 from the State Department, probably the best bang the Department ever got for its bucks.

12. Aleksandr Yakovlev, in Dianne Davenport and Eugene Shekhtman (trans.), "Architect of Perestroika Discusses Primakov and Market Reform in Russia," *Frontline* 3, no. 4 (winter 1998–99): 16.

13. Oleg Kalugin with Fen Montaigne, *The First Directorate: My 32 Years in Intelligence and Espionage Against the West* (New York: St. Martin's Press, 1994), 26.

14. David Remnick, *Resurrection: The Struggle for a New Russia* (New York: Vintage Books, 1998), 298.

15. George Feifer, in correspondence with author, March 13, 1998.

Yakovlev returned to Moscow still a convinced communist, and several books he wrote in the following years, in keeping with the tenor of the times, were stridently anti-American. Yet he was deeply influenced by his year at Columbia, which he later described as more meaningful to him than the ten years he later spent as Soviet ambassador to Canada.[16]

When asked many years later what had been most useful in his year at Columbia, Yakovlev said it was the books he had read there. "I read more than two hundred books," he explained, "including all the works of Hans Morgenthau and books of other American scholars of international affairs. These were books that I could not have read in the Soviet Union."[17]

Returning to Moscow in 1959, Yakovlev rose high in the Soviet bureaucracy, not as an "American agent of influence," as charged by Zyuganov, but as a man of his own mind, which eventually got him into trouble. In 1972, while acting director of the Central Committee's Ideology and Propaganda Department, Yakovlev wrote an article critical of nationalism, Great Russian chauvinism, and anti-Semitism within the Communist Party. A few months later he was banished by Brezhnev to Canada from his post in the Central Committee apparatus where he had served for twenty years.

In Canada, the peasant boy turned diplomat studied the workings of a Western democracy while hobnobbing with such Canadian leaders as Governor General (chief of state) Edward Schreyer and Prime Minister Pierre Trudeau. Yakovlev met often with Trudeau, and of those meetings he has written, "We sometimes had long private sessions without ever talking politics. We discussed philosophical issues, Dostoyevsky, and Pushkin."[18] But in Canada Yakovlev also continued his studies, although on a more practical level: "I just decided that I was going to look at everything through the eyes of a pragmatic politician. As a former peasant, needless to say, I was drawn by the way agriculture, the farmer's economy, was organized. And I would use the opportunity to live on a farm for three or four days to look closely at the way they really do things. I sent endless cables back to Moscow regarding agriculture. I never received any answers."[19]

Yakovlev's ousting to Ottawa took an auspicious turn in 1983 when Mikhail Gorbachev, then the young party secretary for agriculture as well as Politburo member, was given permission by Party General Secretary Yuri Andropov to accept Yakovlev's invitation to visit Canada. "I wanted very much," recalls Yakovlev, "for

16. Yakovlev, in conversation with Nina Bouis, reported by Bouis in personal communication with author.

17. Yakovlev, author's interview, Washington, D.C., September 14, 1998.

18. Yakovlev, cited in Dusko Doder and Louise Branson, *Gorbachev: Heretic in the Kremlin* (New York: Penguin Books, 1990), 48.

19. Yakovlev, in Kreisler, "Conversation with Alexander Yakovlev."

the man who was responsible for agriculture in Russia to visit Canada. . . . It was a very useful visit for Gorbachev. What struck me is the kind of detailed interest and care Gorbachev took in the farmer economy."[20]

The two traveled widely across Canada during their ten days together. At first, they "kind of sniffed around each other," as Yakovlev has put it, and their talks did not touch on serious issues. But, continues Yakovlev,

> as often happens, both of us suddenly were just kind of flooded and let go. I . . . threw caution to the wind and started telling him about what I considered to be utter stupidities in the area of foreign affairs. . . . We were completely frank. He frankly talked about the problems in the internal situation in Russia. He was saying that under these conditions, the conditions of dictatorship and absence of freedom, the country would simply perish. So it was at that time, during our three-hour conversation . . . that we poured it all out and . . . we actually came to agreement on all our main points."[21]

Two weeks later, Yakovlev was recalled to Moscow to head the Institute of International Relations and World Economy (IMEMO), a prestigious think tank of the Soviet Academy of Sciences, and from there it was straight to the top. One year later he was in charge of propaganda at the Central Committee; by 1986, a member of the Central Committee Secretariat; by 1987, a full member of the Politburo; and by 1988, chairman of the Central Committee's Commission on International Policy. In those posts, writes New York University professor Stephen F. Cohen, Yakovlev earned a reputation as "the most reliable and powerful protector of the liberal intelligentsia . . . and, as foreign policy adviser, Yakovlev was often at Gorbachev's side during the Soviet leader's five summit meetings with President Reagan."[22]

But it was as director of the prestigious IMEMO think tank that Yakovlev made perhaps his greatest contributions to the reform movement that had been building slowly within the ranks of the Communist Party. As U.S. political scientist Jeffrey T. Checkel relates:

> [Yakovlev] brought a more open atmosphere to IMEMO and encouraged serious, scholarly research. Indeed, within weeks after arriving at the institute, Yakovlev held a meeting of its scientific collective—the group comprising IMEMO's intellectual and administrative leadership—where he

---

20. Ibid.
21. Ibid.
22. Stephen F. Cohen and Katrina vanden Heuvel, *Voices of Glasnost: Interviews with Gorbachev's Reformers* (New York: W. W. Norton, 1984), 33.

urged researchers to be guided by "strictly scientific principles" and not by Marxist-Leninist dogma. These were bold instructions given the prevailing conservative political mood in Moscow.[23]

Yakovlev now had not only direct access to a rising political leader, Gorbachev, but also at his service a large, professional research organization to which he gave carte blanche to advocate radical changes in how the Soviet Union practiced its international politics.

Immediately after his arrival at IMEMO, Yakovlev formed a group of institute scholars to prepare foreign policy reports for Gorbachev, some of which were so sensitive that Yakovlev would deliver them personally.[24] Among the policies developed by IMEMO in those years, and which later showed up in Gorbachev's speeches and actions, were the interdependence of all countries, the downgrading of Soviet support for national liberation movements, and the nonviability of attempts to attain security unilaterally. These issues showed up in Gorbachev's speech to the Twenty-seventh Party Congress in February 1986 in which he signaled a clear shift in foreign policy that resulted in Soviet withdrawal from Afghanistan, rapprochement with the United States, and noninterference in Eastern Europe.

IMEMO became even bolder in its "new thinking," particularly on international security matters, under Yevgeni M. Primakov, who succeeded Yakovlev as director in late 1985. Primakov—journalist, scholar, Middle East expert, frequent visitor to the United States, future foreign intelligence chief, and Russian foreign minister and prime minister—had earlier served for seven years as an IMEMO deputy director and knew the ropes there. He also had close ties to Yakovlev and, through him, to Gorbachev and his advisers; indeed, in those years the two worked together as a team to reform Soviet foreign policy.[25] Thus Soviet policy was being influenced by pragmatists who had worked abroad and seen the world as it really was, and not by the dictates of communist dogma.

During autumn 1990, however, as opposition to reform built within the Communist Party, Yakovlev lost influence. His independent mind and "new thinking" did not sit well with Russian conservatives and extreme nationalists, and he was expelled from the Party only two days before the ill-fated coup of August 1991.

After the coup, Yakovlev left the government and joined the democratic opposition. Retiring from active political life, he chaired the board of directors of Russian Public Television as well as the Presidential Commission for Victims of Political Repressions, and became president of the Moscow-based International

23. Checkel, *Ideas and International Political Change*, 82.
24. Ibid., 99.
25. Ibid., 93.

Democracy Foundation, where he continued to support political openness and market reform. In his late seventies he was still busy working on a forty-volume *Secret Documents of the Soviet Regime* and a ten-volume history of twentieth-century Russia.

Long past retirement age, Yakovlev has one final mission, to compile a formal count of the number of victims of Soviet repression. By his estimate, as many as 35 million people were shot or died as a direct result of Soviet decisions. By March 2001, his commission had rehabilitated four million victims of Soviet prisons and purges, and still had 400,000 cases to examine.[26]

Oleg Kalugin

Exchanges were a Trojan Horse in the Soviet Union. They played a tremendous role in the erosion of the Soviet system. They opened up a closed society. They greatly influenced younger people who saw the world with more open eyes, and they kept infecting more and more people over the years.

—OLEG KALUGIN, author's interview, May 29, 1997

Another Russian student at Columbia in that first year of exchange was Oleg D. Kalugin, a young KGB officer who was later to make a brilliant career in Soviet intelligence, reaching the rank of major general and chief of counterintelligence before aligning himself with the Democratic Platform of the Communist Party and being elected to the Congress of People's Deputies, the Soviet parliament.

Kalugin, like Yakovlev, was very impressed by his first visit to the West, starting with his arrival in Copenhagen en route to New York: "As we walked through the airport, I was to experience a feeling I would have countless times on future trips abroad: the shock of leaving the gray, monochrome world of the Soviet Union and landing in a place virtually exploding with colors and sights. We spent a few hours in the Danish capital, overwhelmed by the almost clinical cleanliness, the beauti-ful shop windows, the sea of lights."[27]

New York was equally exciting for Kalugin, as it has been for many other visitors, but his instructions from the head of KGB Counterintelligence in New York were clear, he writes: "Stay out of trouble, act like an ordinary student, and don't try to recruit anyone. It was not a tough assignment, and I dove into it with enthusiasm."[28]

Acting like an inquisitive student in New York for the first time, Kalugin was determined to make the most of his year in the Big Apple. "For the first few weeks," he writes, "I walked ceaselessly around Manhattan, overwhelmed by its power and

26. Geoffrey York, in *The Globe and Mail* (Toronto), March 9, 2001.
27. Kalugin, *First Directorate*, 27–28.
28. Ibid., 29.

beauty and bustle."[29] "I visited scores of neighborhoods and all the major museums. I saw ball games and went to the Metropolitan Opera. I rode buses and subways for hours, and saw more than one hundred films. I went to a strip club in Greenwich Village, shelling out $40 for a drink with one of the dancers. I even won election to the Columbia University Student Council, undoubtedly the first KGB officer—and, I suppose, the last—to serve on that body."[30]

But like his colleague Yakovlev, Kalugin also read at Columbia, and when asked (in a 1997 interview) which books had impressed him most, he cited Max Lerner's *America as a Civilization* and Arthur Koestler's *Darkness at Noon,* the latter a devastating critique of Stalin's show trials of the 1930s.[31]

Like Yakovlev, however, Kalugin's faith in communism did not falter during his year in New York:

> My first year in New York actually strengthened my faith in Communism. . . . Although we were far far poorer than the United States, we at least tried to offer all our citizens a decent level of education, housing, and health care. Odd as it looks now, it seemed clear to me then that the United States didn't have the Soviet Union's vitality. Our achievements in science and the triumphs of our space program convinced me we would overcome our relative poverty and our Stalinist past and—by the end of the century—become a far better place to live than America.[32]

Of his three-week trip around the United States with his Columbia colleagues at the end of their studies, Kalugin writes:

> We were treated to an intimate view of the American heartland, which was then riding the boom years of the late 1950s. It was a land of Cadillacs and Chevrolets, of Zenith and Motorola TV consoles, of the latest refrigerators and dishwashers and toasters, of drive-ins and jukeboxes and countless miles of gorgeous roads. The supermarkets were packed with a dizzying description of goods, and everywhere people seemed friendly and guileless. I was a guest for several days on a farm in Iowa, where the hospitable but laconic owners woke me at 6:00 A.M., fed me a hearty breakfast, and spent the next twelve hours instructing me in the intricacies of driving a tractor and sowing corn.[33]

29. Ibid.
30. Ibid., 30–31.
31. Kalugin, author's interview, Washington, D.C., May 29, 1997.
32. Kalugin, *First Directorate*, 30.
33. Ibid., 31–32.

But that trip, he continues, and all of his time in America

> gave me a brief twinge of doubt about our Communist system. The free-
> dom I experienced to poke around America, to engage people in discus-
> sions on any topic—all of it contrasted sharply with the mood in my
> country, where such a friendly, open attitude often was met with a stiff
> rebuke or a door slammed in one's face. As the years went by and I would
> return to the USSR from operations abroad, I increasingly experienced
> the sense that I was slipping behind some gloomy Communist curtain.
> In 1958, I knew our life was grimmer, but just figured we had a longer way
> to go than the more fortunate people of America.[34]

Kalugin spent another ten years in the United States as a KGB officer in New York
and Washington, and returned to Moscow apparently unchanged in his views.
But, he wrote later, the decade in America, "had changed me irrevocably. I had
learned to speak my mind, and I had learned not to cringe. In the 1970s, as the
Soviet Union became more deeply mired in the stagnation of the Brezhnev era,
these were not highly prized qualities. Ultimately, my outspokenness, my reluctance to kowtow to superiors, would lead to my break with the KGB. And for that
I am grateful to America."[35]

Indeed, Kalugin's decade-long exposure to America and his increasing knowledge of its society showed results years later when he became a reformer and critic
of the Soviet system. After more than thirty years of KGB service, in which he
became Chief of Foreign Counterintelligence and the youngest general in KGB
history, Kalugin in 1980 had a run-in with the hierarchy, which suspected him of
being an agent of the CIA. His career curbed, he was transferred to a domestic job
as the number-two KGB man in Leningrad, where over a period of seven years, his
disillusionment with the system grew as he came face to face with the reality of
Soviet life and the KGB role in it. "I came to see," he writes, that

> we had created not only the most totalitarian state apparatus in history
> but also the most arcane . . . in the course of seven decades our Commu-
> nist leaders had managed to construct this absurd, stupendous ziggurat,
> this terrifyingly centralized machine, this *religion* that sought to control
> all aspects of life in our vast country. . . . I left Leningrad in 1987 utterly
> disgusted with the KGB and the Soviet system, and unconcerned how my
> increasingly rebellious stance would affect my future.[36]

34. Ibid., 32.
35. Ibid., 120.
36. Ibid., 288.

Kalugin's rebellion did indeed affect his future, and in February 1990, at age fifty-five, he was forcibly retired, one week after he had given an interview to Radio Liberty, the American radio broadcaster. Retirement papers in hand, he exited the KGB headquarters in Moscow's infamous Lubyanka prison, walked a few blocks to the Historical Archives Institute and asked to see its rector, Yuri N. Afanasyev, a leader of the Communist Party's fledgling democratic movement. Ushered into the rector's office, Kalugin showed Afanasyev his KGB identification papers and said, "I want to help the democratic movement. I am sure that my knowledge and experience will be useful. You can use me in any capacity. I'll be with you."[37]

He was indeed with them, and they did use him. On June 16, Kalugin addressed a public meeting of the Democratic Platform, a social democratic faction of the Communist Party, where he crossed the Rubicon and openly explained why the KGB had to be radically reformed and the number of its agents reduced drastically. "We cannot begin a serious restructuring of society," he began his talk, "until we rid ourselves of the restraints imposed by an organization which has penetrated every sphere of our lives, which interferes with all aspects of state life, political life, the economy, science, arts, religion, even sports . . . the hand of the KGB is everywhere. . . . In order to secure genuine changes in our country, this structure of violence and falsehood must be dismantled."[38]

Two weeks later, Gorbachev, under pressure from party conservatives, issued a decree that revoked Kalugin's rank as general, canceled his awards, and terminated his pension. Two months later, however, after campaigning on the reform platform, Kalugin was elected to fill a vacant seat in the Congress of Soviet Deputies, the Soviet parliament, and one year later, in August 1991, he rallied with other Russian reformers before the parliament's White House as they countered the coup attempted by party hard-liners.

Kalugin now lives in a suburb of Washington, D.C. Asked if he would ever return to Russia, he replied, "I'll live longer in America."[39]

Alfred J. Rieber, one of the U.S. exchange students in Moscow while Kalugin was at Columbia, and today a professor emeritus of history from the University of Pennsylvania and long-time student of Russia and the Soviet Union, has called Kalugin's memoirs "one of the most honest accounts by a former official to come out of the post-Soviet period. . . . His break with the KGB, like so much in the book, has the ring of truth. His enthusiasm for perestroika and his denunciation to Gorbachev of KGB abuses are matters of public record. Each one of these steps required courage that was all too rare among top Soviet officials."[40]

37. Ibid., 329.
38. Ibid., 332–33.
39. Kalugin, in *Sobesednik* (Moscow), January 1, 1999.
40. Alfred J. Rieber, in *Philadelphia Enquirer*, September 18, 1994.

Boris Yuzhin

Another young Russian whose faith in the Soviet system was shattered by a stay in the United States was Boris N. Yuzhin, a graduate student in journalism at the University of California in 1975–76. But Yuzhin was also a captain in the KGB when he arrived in Berkeley, where among his assignments he was to cultivate opinion makers, scholars, and scientists at the California campus. Yuzhin's impressions of the United States can be seen as representative of other Soviet students, although he can afford to be more candid than most, since he now lives in the United States.[41]

Prior to his departure for Berkeley, Yuzhin had undergone an intensive six-month KGB briefing on the United States, which included, among other topics, its history, geography, government, transportation, the work of the FBI and CIA, and the activities of U.S. anti-Soviet organizations. But the real basis of his attitude toward the United States, he says, were the KGB documents he was shown that portrayed the United States as the "main adversary" of the Soviet Union. Also influencing him were the Soviet mass media, which, even in the détente years, he notes, sought to create a one-sided view of the United States as a country grown rich by exploitation of its workers and Third World countries.

However, after his arrival in the United States, continues Yuzhin, he experienced a "feeling of freedom," and for the first time in his life he no longer had an "internal censor," as he calls it. In the Soviet Union, he explains, the majority of the people had to reconcile their deeds and thoughts with the official ideology of the Communist Party and its "armed vanguard," the KGB. Even among the closest of friends, he adds, one had to control oneself. In the United States, by contrast, he felt for the first time "completely liberated, and recognized how fine it felt."

When Yuzhin heard how Americans openly criticize their government and even their president, when he saw how Americans enter the Capitol building in Washington dressed casually, wearing shorts and sandals without socks, and with infants on their backs, he understood how they felt themselves to be the real masters of their country. "In my own country," he observes, "I could not imagine anything of the sort."

As for the American standard of living, Yuzhin says that he and his fellow Soviet students knew beforehand that there were no shortages of goods and food in American stores but what they saw here, in his words, "staggered our imagination. We went to stores where, even with our modest stipend of 260 dollars per month, we could acquire presentable items of clothing." Questions immediately

41. The information in this section was provided by Boris N. Yuzhin in a fax to the author on September 23, 1999, in response to questions posed by the author, and in subsequent e-mail exchanges.

arose. "Why are we, the builders of a society of abundance, even at the stage of developed socialism, so far from all this? Why are the triumphal reports of the successes of our enterprises not realized in goods on the shelves of our stores?"

When asked what books had influenced him most during his year at Berkeley, Yuzhin replied that they were books in the Russian language that he could not read in the Soviet Union but were readily available at the university library. Among the books that impressed him most and led to his disillusionment with the Soviet system were the collected works of Aleksandr Solzhenitsyn, including his *Gulag Archipelago;* Andrei Sakharov's seminal *samizdat* essay, "Thoughts on Progress, Peaceful Coexistence, and Intellectual Freedom"; Aleksandr Ginzburg's writings on the trials of Daniel and Sinyavsky; Svetlana Alliluyeva's *Twenty Letters to a Friend;* Boris Pasternak's *Doctor Zhivago;* and many other books, which, he notes, he had heard of in the Soviet Union but could not read there. Such books, he adds, helped him understand that all his ideological training, all his former knowledge, was based on lies. He was also moved by the poetry of Marina Tsvetayeva, Anna Akhmatova, and Boris Pasternak. As someone who had himself written poetry, Yuzhin could not understand why such authors were in the "half-forbidden" category.

Yuzhin's disillusionment with the Soviet system led him to cooperate with the FBI and become a double agent even before his year at Berkeley was up and he had to return to Moscow. Two years later, however, in 1978, he was back in San Francisco, this time as a correspondent for the Soviet news agency TASS but also as a KGB major, soon to be promoted to lieutenant colonel, but continuing his work as a double agent for the FBI and the KGB. Recalled to Moscow in 1982, he was given several routine assignments until 1986 when he was arrested, charged with high treason, and sentenced to fifteen years in the *gulag.*[42] After serving more than five years in prison and labor camps with "strict regime," Yuzhin was amnestied by President Yeltsin in 1992, presumably at the request of the U.S. government.

To the question of whether exchanges played a role in bringing change to the Soviet Union, Yuzhin has a complex response. As a rule, he notes, those who came to the United States on exchanges belonged to the elite of Soviet society and had no reason to be dissatisfied with their status in that society. The question therefore follows, were they interested in changes and reform, especially in domestic politics, of the system that had treated them so well?

Yuzhin's response is decidedly affirmative. Many of those who were exchanged, he claims, were convinced at least of the necessity for economic reform. He recalls hearing from Soviet scientists of the excellent laboratory equipment they saw at

---

42. Yuzhin is believed to have been betrayed by Aldrich Ames, who was reporting to the KGB while working at the CIA, and by Robert Hanssen, an FBI agent who was cooperating with the KGB.

U.S. scientific centers and the rapid transfer of scientific and technical discoveries to the production line, a process that took much longer in the Soviet Union. Soviet athletes, medical personnel, and cultural figures spoke of the high earnings of their American colleagues, and Soviet economists were impressed by the efficiency of the U.S. economy. Despite their favored positions in society, he concludes, those Soviet citizens, after visits to the United States, recognized the need for change and reform.

Yuzhin has no regrets about his past. His imprisonment, he notes, showed him a side of the Soviet system that he had not known in his privileged KGB position and confirmed his belief in the course he had chosen. "The more I thought, the more I realized I did the right thing," he adds, "because I got another taste of the system."[43]

Yuzhin now resides in California, where he works as a writer and archivist and is active with ARK, an organization investigating the fate of U.S. civilian and military personnel believed to have been imprisoned in the Soviet *gulag*.

Yuri Afanasyev

There is not and has never been in the world a people and a country with such a falsified history as ours.

—YURI AFANASYEV

If the Soviet reform movement needed a historian, it found one in Yuri N. Afanasyev, who was instrumental in disclosing Stalin's crimes against the Soviet people. Afanasyev condemned Soviet history as it was written from the end of the 1920s.

The son of a household repairman, Afanasyev was raised in Ulyanovsk, Lenin's home town; and like many of his contemporaries, he was a convinced and loyal communist in his early years. After graduation from Moscow State University, he worked as a Young Communist League (Komsomol) leader, instructor at the Komsomol higher school in Moscow, and editor at the party theoretical journal *Kommunist* in the late 1970s and early 1980s. But he had also made several exchange visits to France to study French history, and altogether spent some three-and-one-half years there. And it was in France that he first read the books by Soviet émigrés and dissidents that changed his political life. Afanasyev notes that he spent almost twenty-five years studying French history, and it was his study of Western historians that made him understand just how badly the Soviet historical profession had declined.[44]

43. *New York Times*, July 17, 1994.
44. Yuri Afanasyev, "The Agony of the Stalinist System," in Cohen and Heuvel, *Voices of Glasnost*, 99.

"The Soviet state," wrote Afanasyev, "needed historians for whom political expediency ranked ahead of historical accuracy. This criterion was reflected not only in professional historical training but also in character formation. A historian was a professional to the degree to which he defined himself as a 'party activist.' This condition frequently led to professional and moral deformities."[45]

Described by David Remnick as "the democratic movement's master of ceremonies,"[46] Afanasyev campaigned for a return of history and, in 1986, as rector of Moscow's Historical Archives Institute, used his position to organize the first public lectures criticizing Stalin. He called for the opening of secret archives of the Stalin years, and he initiated a project at his institute to record film interviews with victims of Stalinist oppression. Two years later, he edited what has been called "the most important book of the Gorbachev era," *Inogo ne dano* (*There Is No Other Way*), a collection of thirty-five essays by leading intellectuals of the "thaw" generation, men and women who had become the torchbearers of glasnost.[47] In 1989, he was elected cochair of the Memorial Society, a Russian organization dedicated to uncovering the crimes of Stalinism. Together with Andrei Sakharov, Boris Yeltsin, and Galina Starovoitova, Afanasyev was also one of the founders of the reform-minded Interregional Group in the Soviet parliament and *DemRossiya* (Democratic Russia), the political party it later became.

Afanasyev was committed to openness and reform but his brashness and outspoken attacks on Stalinism, and eventually on Gorbachev, aroused opposition from conservatives. In a meeting with Moscow editors on October 13, 1989, Gorbachev criticized Afanasyev and several other members of the Interregional Group and their program, which he said included "a multiparty system, the right to leave the USSR, a market economy, free press, and everyone doing whatever they please." Moreover, Gorbachev questioned whether Afanasyev, in light of his public statements, had a right to remain a member of the Communist Party.[48] Afanasyev did indeed quit the party the following year, one of the first reformers to do so, and became one of Gorbachev's strongest critics. In April 2000, together with several other Russians prominent in the democratic awakening of the late 1980s and early 1990s, Afanasyev called for a Russian government coalition based on civil liberties, rule of law, openness to international cooperation, liberal economics, anticommunism, and independence of the media.[49]

45. Yuri Afanasyev, "Reclaiming Russian History," *Perspective* 7, no. 1 (September–October 1996).

46. David Remnick, *Lenin's Tomb: The Last Days of the Soviet Empire* (New York: Random House, 1993), 113.

47. Yuri N. Afanasyev, *Inogo ne dano* (Moscow: Progress Publishers, 1988).

48. Anatoly S. Chernyaev, *My Six Years with Gorbachev*, eds. and trans. Robert E. English and Elizabeth Tucker (University Park: Pennsylvania State University Press, 2000), 241–42.

49. *Moscow Times*, April 5, 2000.

Now retired from political life, Afanasyev serves as rector of Moscow's Russian State University for the Humanities, where he continues to be a spokesman for humanism and liberalism.

Rem Khokhlov

Rem V. Khokhlov came to the United States in September 1959 for a year of study at Stanford University in the second year of the U.S.-Soviet Graduate Student/Young Faculty Exchange. As a senior lecturer in physics at Moscow State University (MSU), Khokhlov already had his candidate degree and was well along in his research on radio waves in nonlinear systems. At Stanford, where he did research under Hugh H. Heffner on problems of parametric influence on self-sustained oscillatory systems, Khokhlov spent most of his time in the laboratory and in visits to other U.S. scientific centers.[50]

Returning to Moscow in 1960, Khokhlov made his most important scientific discoveries during the years 1961–65, but that work was a logical continuation of his previous scientific research and does not appear to have been a result of his year at Stanford. Nevertheless, according to his son, Aleksei R. Khokhlov, his father's year at Stanford had a "profound but indirect influence" on his scientific research: "He was able to see the organization of research in American universities, get more acquainted with modern scientific literature and the 'hottest' scientific topics of the time, and develop multiple scientific contacts with American scientists in his field. This gave him a much wider overview and helped him a lot in his subsequent scientific research."[51] In addition to his scientific work in the United States, Rem Khokhlov became interested in the organization of study and research at Stanford and other U.S. universities he visited. In comparing what he saw in the United States with the Soviet educational system, he concluded that, in experimental physics, undergraduate education was at a higher level in the Soviet Union but the reverse was true at the graduate level.

Recognition came rapidly. In 1962, Khokhlov defended his doctoral dissertation.[52] In 1966, he was unanimously elected a corresponding member of the Soviet Academy of Sciences, and a full member in 1974. In 1970, he was awarded the prestigious Lenin

50. The author has drawn here from a letter of July 10, 1999, from Aleksei R. Khokhlov, Rem Khokhlov's son and himself a professor of physics at MSU. In consultation with his mother and Professor Vladimir I. Tropin, the then prorector (vice-president) for international relations at MSU, Aleksei R. Khokhlov has provided many details of his father's initiation of direct exchanges between Soviet and U.S. universities.

51. Ibid.

52. In the Soviet and Russian educational systems the doctorate follows the candidate degree and is the highest academic degree.

Prize for his joint research on nonlinear coherent interactions in optics. In 1974, he became a member of the Moscow City Council and the Supreme Soviet (the Soviet parliament), and in 1975, he was named vice president of the General Assembly of the International Association of Universities.

Khokhlov's year in the United States was to prove significant for U.S.-Soviet exchanges when, in 1973, he became rector (president) of MSU and began to look at possibilities for direct exchanges with American universities. At that time, MSU had direct exchange agreements only with universities of the capital cities of East European countries. Moreover, all exchanges with the West were conducted through the Ministry of Higher and Specialized Secondary Education.

Khokhlov's efforts to establish direct exchanges with U.S. universities came to fruition in autumn 1975 when he headed an MSU delegation on a coast-to-coast three-week tour of U.S. universities under the State Department's International Visitor Program. The itinerary included Stanford, Berkeley, Cal Tech, UCLA, the Universities of Illinois and Chicago, Harvard, MIT, and the State University of New York (SUNY). Khokhlov's instructions from the Ministry of Higher and Specialized Secondary Education were not to sign agreements but to bring back any proposals he received for review by the ministry.

Stanford, where Khokhlov had studied, was an obvious first choice; and when the president of Stanford visited Moscow in summer 1975, he told Khokhlov that he would like to establish a direct exchange with MSU. When the MSU delegation visited Stanford a few months later, it was received cordially and had a good visit, but the exchange proposal was not repeated, and Khokhlov, acting on his ministry's instructions, was also silent. The same was repeated at Berkeley and Cal Tech, the next two stops on the itinerary. According to Prorector (vice president) Vladimir I. Tropin, also a member of the delegation, he and Khokhlov discussed the situation during their flight to the University of Illinois at Urbana-Champaign, and Khokhlov decided that if his delegation did not take the initiative in proposing an agreement, their trip across the United States would be nothing more than academic tourism.

Accordingly, at Urbana, Tropin proposed an exchange of students and researchers, and Illinois accepted. However, the talks broke down on the payment modalities when MSU, which had no hard currency of its own, was unable to accept the Illinois proposal that each side pay the costs for its own students in the exchange. Similar talks came to nought at other stops on the tour, until Albany, New York.

At Albany, the last stop on the itinerary, agreement in principle on a direct exchange was easily reached in talks between Khokhlov and Ernest L. Boyer, the dynamic chancellor of the newly established SUNY, subsequently U.S. Commissioner of Education under President Carter, and president of the Carnegie Foundation for the Advancement of Teaching.[53] SUNY, one year earlier, had signed an agreement with the Ministry of Higher Education for a direct exchange of undergraduates in Russian and English language studies with the "Maurice Thorez" Moscow State Pedagogical Institute of Foreign Languages. The SUNY-Thorez exchange, the first involving Soviet undergraduates to the United States, was going well, and SUNY was interested in a more comprehensive exchange of graduate students and faculty.

With its sixty-four campuses and more than 350,000 students, SUNY was the largest university system in the United States but was not well known in international circles at the time, and even less well known in the Soviet Union. Moreover, the Soviets expected that MSU, as the "first" university of the Soviet Union, would sign agreements with the "first" universities of other countries, and for Soviet officialdom that meant Harvard. Khokhlov, therefore, had some selling to do before obtaining the approval of Soviet officials for the SUNY exchange.

By chance, a resolution of the Central Committee of the Communist Party came to the rescue. In early 1976, the Central Committee passed a resolution requiring Soviet universities to expand their education of specialists in American and Japanese studies. And so, although Khokhlov's main interest was in the natural sciences, for the sake of easier approval by Soviet officials, he came up with the idea of emphasizing American studies (politics, history, language, and culture) in the agreement with SUNY, and it was agreed that students sent from Moscow would be from the humanities departments of MSU, and research scholars from the natural sciences. The agreement with SUNY was signed on October 4, 1976, and the first graduate students and faculty were exchanged the following year. Other agreements between MSU and U.S. universities followed—with the Midwest University Consortium for International Affairs (which included Illinois) in 1977, and the University of Missouri at Kansas City and the University of Wisconsin in 1980.

The SUNY-MSU exchange, which began in 1977, has continued to the present. Between 1977 and 2000, SUNY hosted 279 Moscow participants, of whom 153 were faculty, 62 graduate students, and 64 undergraduates. During the same period, Moscow hosted 307 SUNY participants, of whom 138 were faculty, 152 graduate students, and 80 undergraduates. Numbers, however, do not tell the whole story.

In pushing the exchange through to completion, Khokhlov struck a blow for the independence of Soviet universities and their right to negotiate and conduct

---

53. The question of finances was finessed by agreeing that the sending university would deliver its students to the receiving country, where the receiving side would cover the in-country costs. This did not entail hard currency expenditures for MSU, since it could send its students to the United States via Aeroflot, the Soviet airline, and pay costs for the SUNY students in Moscow in rubles. A part of the dollar costs to SUNY were defrayed by an annual grant from the State Department.

exchanges directly with foreign universities. This did not please Soviet official-dom, which did not want to lose its control and was often at odds with the admin-istration of the SUNY exchange. One such quarrel between MSU and the Ministry of Higher Education actually occurred in my presence. At a reception in Moscow in 1976 at Spaso House, the U.S. ambassador's residence, a ministry official, stand-ing to my left, insisted that MSU had to deal with Albany through the ministry. Prorector Tropin, standing to my right, was equally insistent that MSU would deal directly with Albany, as it indeed did. Such challenges to Soviet central authority were rare in those days, but because of his stature as a member of the Supreme Soviet and Soviet Academy, Khokhlov prevailed.

Khokhlov, unfortunately, did not live to see the results of his efforts. An avid outdoorsman, jogger, and physical-culture enthusiast, he died in 1977 at the age of fifty-one, victim of an ill-fated mountain-climbing expedition in the Pamir Mountains of Tajikistan.

Regarding international cooperation in education, Khokhlov was a prophet and, for the Soviet Union, a man ahead of his time. As he predicted in a report on August 20, 1975, to the General Assembly of the International Congress of Univer-sities, meeting in Moscow:

> Our contacts with the higher educational institutions in the developed capitalist countries are on a steady increase. At present, especially after the Helsinki Final Act, the world has entered a new phase of international relations, which finds its expression in the strengthening of international ties and cooperation in the fields of economy, science, and culture. We think that this process cannot be reversed, that it is an example of the regularities in the historical development of the world.[54]

As testimony to Khokhlov's foresight, on September 1, 2000, MSU opened a Center on the United States and Russia at its Sparrow Hills campus in Moscow. In exchange, SUNY opened in Albany a Center on Russia and the United States.[55] And it all began in 1958 when a young Russian physicist came to study in the United States.

Nikolai Sivachev

In autumn 1961, the fourth year of the U.S.-Soviet graduate student exchange, a young historian from Moscow State University named Nikolai V. Sivachev arrived

---

54. Rem Khokhlov, in V. I. Grigoryev, *Rem Khokhlov,* trans. G. G. Egerov, revised from the 1981 Rus-sian edition in the series *Outstanding Soviet Scientists* (Moscow: Mir Publishers, 1985), 84.

55. By 2002, there were thirty-seven U.S.-Russian university partnerships.

in New York for a year of study at Columbia University. His main adviser was the renowned Richard Hofstadter, and the subject of his research was the U.S. presidential election of 1936. But Sivachev, in later years, confided to American friends that he had been sent to Columbia to learn why the United States, under Franklin D. Roosevelt, had had a New Deal and not a communist revolution. Sivachev learned why and, in doing so, became one of the Soviet Union's leading authorities on Roosevelt and Soviet-American relations.

In New York, Sivachev met Eleanor Roosevelt, who when she learned that he was studying the New Deal, provided a room for him at her home, Val-Kill, up the Hudson River, and had a car pick him up every morning and drive him to the nearby Roosevelt Library, where he did some of his research. Sivachev's interest in Roosevelt continued after his return to Moscow; and in 1982, when the Soviet Union marked the centennial of Roosevelt's birth with a TV special, Sivachev was the featured speaker.

Sivachev's greatest achievement, however, came in 1973 when he played a key role in establishing the Fulbright Lecturer Program in the Soviet Union. Sivachev had the support of his close friend, Rem Khokhlov. They had both studied in the United States, which made them more open to initiating the lecturer exchange and making it an annual affair. The Fulbright exchange will be discussed later in these pages.

In 1975, Sivachev established and chaired the Scholarly Coordinating Council on American Studies at MSU, which brought together the work of American studies in the various departments of the university. As a further impetus to American studies, he also established, in 1977, a Laboratory on the History of the U.S. Political System, whose first task was a study of the two-party system in the United States.

From Sivachev's earlier research came a book which he coauthored in 1980, *Russia and the United States,* a history of U.S.-Russian relations from the years before the American Revolution up to the 1970s.[56] The book resulted from an invitation to MSU from the University of Chicago Press to write a book in its series, "The United States and the World: Foreign Perspectives," an effort to examine American relations with other countries from a foreign viewpoint. There was some debate in Moscow over accepting the invitation from Chicago, but as Sivachev wrote in his preface to the book, "The decisive factor in dispelling our doubts was the desire to take what part we could in overcoming the negative heritage of the cold war."[57] A key role in dispelling those doubts appears to have been played by Rector Khokhlov. In his foreword to the book, Khokhlov reviewed MSU's scholarly exchanges with the United States and concluded that "the scholarly exchange has made a great contribution to the improvement of Soviet-American relations, to

56. Sivachev and Yakovlev, *Russia and the United States.*
57. Ibid., xiii.

widening the effectiveness of the principles of peaceful coexistence, and to improved cooperation between our peoples and nations."[58]

Sivachev's book, which is still in print, should be seen as a period piece in the context of its time. It includes the obligatory references to Lenin, is replete with communist clichés, and reads in part like a propaganda tract. At the same time, it displays many objective insights on how Russians have regarded their relations with the United States. As Sivachev pointed out in his preface, it was written from a Marxist-Leninist perspective, and "historical materialism requires that we point out both the major differences between the foreign policy of bourgeois and social-ist states, and at the same time *the objective inevitability of peaceful coexistence between countries with different socioeconomic systems.*"[59]

Elbert B. Smith, professor emeritus of American history from the University of Maryland and a three-time Fulbright Lecturer in the Soviet Union, describes the Sivachev book as "Marxist and pro-Soviet but not unfriendly to the United States."[60] In fact, says Smith, Sivachev liked the United States and was an amelio-rating influence on U.S.-Soviet relations. During the 1970s, Sivachev visited the United States five times on IREX grants, although his wife, to his great regret, was not permitted by the Soviet authorities to accompany him.[61] Other Americans who knew Sivachev well describe him as a paradoxical figure—a communist and loyal Soviet citizen but one who was open to the outside world. And in tribute, they add that he let his students do their own work, without ideological blinders.

Sivachev did not live to see the full results of his pioneering work on American studies in the Soviet Union; at age forty-nine, he succumbed to a brain tumor. In a eulogy, Donald Raleigh wrote:

> Regardless of how American historians regard Sivachev's conceptualiza-tion of "state-monopoly capitalism," it [the book], as well as the work of his students, represents a serious and scholarly effort to understand the complexities of American political life. In fact, when compared with Soviet writings on American history published before the late 1950s, recent Soviet scholarship in this area can be looked upon as a fine illus-tration of the elevation of history from an arm of Stalin's propaganda machine, into a respectable academic discipline. In this regard, Sivachev's impact on his students may ultimately prove to be his most important long-term contribution to scholarship.[62]

58. Ibid., xi.
59. Ibid., xiv; emphasis added.
60. E. B. Smith, author's interview, Dunkirk, Md., October 26, 1998.
61. Ibid.
62. Donald J. Raleigh, "In Memory of N. V. Sivachev," *Soviet Studies in History* 22 no. 4 (a journal of translations published by M. E. Sharpe) (spring 1984): 3.

Perhaps the greatest tribute to Sivachev was given by the renowned Russian historian, Pyotr A. Zayonchkovsky, professor of history at MSU. After a meeting with Sivachev, Zayonchkovsky remarked to one of his American graduate students, "He's an honest man."[63]

Boris Runov

Boris A. Runov already had his degree in agricultural sciences and was an assistant professor at Moscow's Institute of Agricultural Mechanization and Electrification when he came to Iowa State University in 1960 for a year of study in the third year of the Graduate Student/Young Faculty Exchange. After completing his studies at Iowa State, Runov (also spelled Rounov) asked to visit some American farms, and spent one week on each of six farms where he worked as a farmhand, an experience he later described as "university number one."[64]

Runov apparently enjoyed his stay at Iowa State, because two years later, as a member of a high-level Soviet delegation about to visit the United States, he asked permission to revisit his American alma mater, if only for a day, in response to an invitation he had received from the university's president. Soviet authorities, however, vetoed his request, and when Runov asked why, he was told that he had too many friends in Iowa and meetings with them were not desirable. Runov promptly told this to his Iowa State friends so they would understand that it was not he who had turned down their invitation.[65]

During 1965–68 Runov was posted to the Soviet Embassy in Ottawa as agricultural counselor; and after his return to Moscow, he took a temporary assignment in the Agricultural Department of the Communist Party central apparatus. With his fluency in English and firsthand knowledge of agriculture in the United States and Canada, two grain-producing nations like the Soviet Union, he was a logical candidate for his next position in 1970, deputy minister of agriculture with responsibility for international affairs.

Well known by then to U.S. officials, Runov in 1973 became cochair of the Joint U.S.-USSR Commission on Cooperation in Agriculture and was a mainstay of Soviet participation in the commission's work during its more than five years of existence. Americans who worked with him in those years believe that his experience in the United States led him to see the need to develop contacts in the U.S. agribusiness and agricultural-research communities, and to acquire the technology and business know-how that Soviet agriculture needed. He was not a

---

63. E. Willis Brooks, e-mail to author, January 13, 2000.

64. Boris A. Runov, *Vspominaya proshloye, dumayu o budushchem* (*While Remembering the Past, I Think of the Future*) (Moscow: MGF Znanie, 1996), 44.

65. Ibid., 48.

reformer in the sense of wanting to change the institutions of Soviet agriculture, but he saw the need for improved technology and expertise. Although a tough negotiator for Soviet interests, his experience as a student at Iowa State made him a strong supporter of improved relations with the United States.

In 1995, as the world food problem became a recurring item on the Dartmouth Conference agenda, Runov became a regular participant in the Dartmouth discussions. In the deliberations of Dartmouth and the Joint Commission, Runov ably represented the Soviet Union, but the United States was fortunate in having such a well-informed Russian seated at the table.

U.S. Students and Scholars

For forty years these programs have provided unique field experience and advanced training for leading American experts on the countries of Central and Eastern Europe and Eurasia. These specialists now make up the backbone of our nation's expertise on the area. They have also brought the overseas insights and experience they acquired to U.S. university research and teaching, corporate management and commerce, government policy-making and diplomacy, and the media. They are a powerful national asset.

—DANIEL C. MATUSZEWSKI, former president, IREX

While Yakovlev, Kalugin, Khokhlov, Sivachev, and their Soviet colleagues were studying in the United States and learning about that strange country, an equal number of American graduate students were studying in the Soviet Union, doing research in their academic disciplines and familiarizing themselves with that vast and mysterious land.

In the early years of the exchange, most of the Americans were students of history, language, or literature, fields which gave them the incentive and language skills to pursue graduate studies in the Soviet Union. In later years, as the Russians became more accustomed to the exchanges, IREX was able to also place students and scholars in political science, sociology, and other social sciences. And to fill the need for scholars with Soviet expertise in disciplines inadequately represented in American academia, IREX, in 1972, inaugurated a Preparatory Fellowship Program, which provided language and area training for Americans in sociology, economics, anthropology, and other disciplines, as well as the study of the Caucasus and Central Asia. After a year of language and area studies, IREX was able to place those American scholars in its Soviet exchange programs.

Thus, Americans going to the Soviet Union had the language skills that enabled them to converse with Soviet citizens and gain an understanding of the Soviet Union and its people that they could never have gotten from books alone. While their numbers were small in the early years of the exchange, over the next thirty years thousands of Americans students participated in the exchange and came to constitute the next generation of American teachers and scholars with "hands-on" experience in Russia and other republics of the Soviet Union. As the Cold War continued, and at times heated up, they became a national resource that helped to educate Americans about the realities of Russia and to separate fact from fiction about the Soviet Union.

Bernard Gwertzman, editor of the *New York Times on the Web*, and a former Moscow correspondent and later foreign editor of the *Times*, first visited the Soviet Union as a Harvard graduate student with an American youth group in summer 1959. The Americans stayed in university dormitories and at a youth camp in Crimea, but Gwertzman says that he learned more about life in the Soviet Union and Soviet society and its mores from that visit than he did years later as the *Times* correspondent in Moscow, where he could not have meaningful contacts with Soviet citizens.[66]

A similar sentiment was voiced by Alexander Dallin, the late Stanford professor of Russian history, who reported that the exchanges gave us "a feel for the scene . . . the instinct to judge the plausible from the ludicrous."[67] Such firsthand knowledge of the Soviet scene reduced the likelihood of misinterpreting Soviet behavior, especially in a country where there was often a dramatic gap between what people said and what they really meant. "It gave us reality," adds Robert Belknap, professor of literature at Columbia University, "We made contacts with people and learned how things were really done in Russia."[68]

Many of the American alumni of the student exchange went on to service in the U.S. government, including the Foreign Service, where they put their Soviet experiences to good use. The best known is James Collins, who studied history at Moscow State University in 1965–66 and was the American ambassador to Russia from 1997 to 2001. On his departure from Moscow, Collins, an expert on Russia and fluent in its language, was awarded an honorary doctorate by the Russian Academy of Sciences for his contributions to political science and international relations. In a message to IREX, Collins said: "My experience as an IREX exchange participant in Moscow in the early 1960s laid the foundation for a lifetime career devoted to promoting better relations and understanding between the United States and Russia. I hope that the young Americans studying in Russia and the other Newly Independent States today through IREX will follow in this tradition."[69]

In contrast to the analysts at CIA, who for security reasons were prohibited by their own agency from traveling to the Soviet Union, American scholars on the

---

66. Bernard Gwertzman, author's telephone interview, November 29, 1998.

67. Alexander Dallin, in Wray Herbert, "Eastern Bloc—U.S. Scholarly Exchanges: Assessing Two Decades," *Humanities Report* 1 (June 1979): 7.

68. Robert Belknap, author's recollection, at Slavic Conference, Boca Raton, September 26, 1998.

69. James F. Collins, in message of congratulation to the IREX Moscow office, June 4, 1999.

exchange got a view of the Soviet Union that they never could have had from the outside. Living in the Soviet Union and interacting with its people gave them a firsthand look at the economic and social fabric of the country that was denied to CIA analysts who were preparing top secret analyses of the Soviet Union for the U.S. government.

But life in the Soviet Union and interaction with its people was not without its hardships for American and other Western students and scholars, especially in the early years of the exchange. In addition to the difficulties with housing, research, and travel described above, to get anything done in the highly regimented and politically hostile Soviet Union required much patience and some ingenuity in coping with the bureaucracy. Standing in long lines for the most simple procedures of daily life was routine, and the response of bureaucrats to any request was usually *nyet*. Sharing a dormitory room with a Russian student was great for perfecting your Russian but not when you knew that much of what you said or did would be reported to the KGB. And students had to be constantly on the alert for attempts at entrapment by the KGB, which did occur in the early years of the exchange. That so many endured the hardships and even returned to the Soviet Union for further study and research is a tribute to their perseverence and dedication.

An entire book could be written about the experiences of American students in the Soviet Union but what follows here are sketches of a few of the early participants in the Graduate Student/Young Faculty Exchange conducted by IUCTG and IREX, and how they benefited from their study there.

Alfred Rieber

Scholarly exchanges served to considerably expand contacts between Americans and Russians, which had previously been limited largely to diplomats and newspaper correspondents. As Alfred J. Rieber, one of the American graduate students in Moscow during the first year of the exchange, 1958–59, has put it:

> The exchanges kept open an avenue of contact when others were closed, established a set of long-term relationships which proved of great importance after 1985. . . . Perestroika did not have to begin at ground zero; there were all kinds of contacts, personal and professional relationships that could be infused with fresh energies and aims once the official barriers to free exchange had been abolished. There were many people on both sides who could immediately pick up the strands of old ties and knit them into a strong life line between the two societies.[70]

70. Alfred J. Rieber, e-mail to author, March 8, 1999.

Rieber, who went on to become a professor of Russian history at the University of Pennsylvania, has described how the exchange affected him personally:

> I still feel the effects myself. Because of ties established in the '60s I have become a trustee of the history department at the European University in St. Petersburg and the Moscow School of Social and Economic Sciences as well as many other activities connected with the training of young historians from the former Soviet Union. I must attribute many of these opportunities to influence the future development of education in Russia to the long experience of participation in the exchanges and the reservoir of trust that has been built up over the years. . . . Many of the deepest influences [of the exchanges] are just emerging or are yet to come.[71]

Terence Emmons

Terence Emmons, professor of Russian history at Stanford who spent two years as a graduate student in the Soviet Union, 1962–64, has described the effect of the exchanges on Soviet historical scholarship:

> The exchanges had an enormous impact on Soviet historical scholarship, not so much through visits of Soviet scholars to the United States (most were not historians), although this aspect should not be discounted, as through the visits by the very numerous American historians and history graduate students to the Soviet Union, as exchangees attached to Soviet scholars, as lecturers, and so on. As a result, the last generation of historians (at least in St. Petersburg and Moscow, and many of the professorate in the provinces, took their degrees in one or the other capital), the generation that is today approaching retirement age, if not retirement, was infinitely more aware of foreign scholarship on Russia, could read English widely, and so on, more than had been the case before. This all worked in various ways, not least of all by the dissemination of western books among Soviet advisers and colleagues, who showed them to their students, many of whom . . . could read English.[72]

All this, adds Emmons, is only part of the story, no doubt a fairly small part, "of the evolution of the views and values of Soviet educated society that in the end

---

71. Ibid.
72. Terence Emmons, letter to author, March 5, 1999.

was, I believe, a fundamental aspect of the collapse of the Soviet Union. Stalin and his epigones were right; intercourse with the West was a dangerous thing and, whatever the play of circumstances and intention that led to it, had the buffer zone of the 'peoples' democracies' not been created after the war, the collapse would have come much sooner."[73]

Michael Cole

There is no doubt in my mind about the value of my experiences [abroad]. They have fundamentally changed the way I think about the world, the way I teach, and the way I conduct my research. All aspects of my professional life have been made much more enjoyable than I can imagine them being otherwise.

—MICHAEL COLE

There were also many benefits to Americans who studied in the Soviet Union. As Michael Cole, professor of psychology, University of California, San Diego, who was a postdoctoral student at Moscow State University in 1962–63, writes: "Hundreds of young doctorate holders from many fields studied in the Soviet Union, absorbing to varying degrees the life of the people with whom they worked. Their writing has been crucial to enriching America's knowledge of its most prominent international competitor. . . . Personally, my professional work has gained enormously."[74]

Cole cites another important result of his many years of contact with Soviet science that began with his study at Moscow State University twenty-three years earlier. Due to his dogged determination, he was able to introduce open-access e-mail to the Soviet Academy of Sciences, a process that facilitated direct two-way communication between Soviet and American scholars and scientists and played a part in the gradual disintegration of seventy years of controlled communication routes between the Soviet Union and the rest of the world. As Cole describes his e-mail overture:

> On October 31, 1985, two psychologists, one from the University of California at San Diego [i.e. Cole], the other from the Institute of Psychology in Moscow, sent an electronic mail message from the Institute of Automated Systems in Central Moscow to San Diego. Technically there was nothing remarkable about this event. The equipment they used was readily available in the United States and Western Europe. The message traveled through a leased line to Helsinki where it was automatically uploaded

73. Ibid.
74. Michael Cole, "The World Beyond Our Borders: What Might Our Students Need to Know About It?" *American Psychologist* 39, no. 9 (1984): 1001.

onto a facility called the Source on Telenet, a satellite-based communications facility with a downlink in Virginia. From there it was forwarded to San Diego, where it was read by researchers at the Laboratory of Comparative Human Cognition at the University of California. Nor was the content of the message remarkable. It simply announced that the connection had been made, and that everyone in Moscow was doing fine.[75]

But that was not a routine event, continues Cole: "There was an armed soldier standing at the door [to the Institute]. Inside, visitors had to present a document from the Vice President of the Academy of Sciences requesting that they be allowed to send a message. They had to be given special passes in order to proceed beyond the foyer. . . . The Institute representative who greeted the visitors was polite but tense."[76] All went smoothly, however, and a precedent had been set. It became possible for an American and a Soviet researcher to use the internet as a medium for organizing joint research. Another dent had been made in the tightly controlled international communications of the Soviet Union.

Herbert Ellison

My study in Leningrad reaffirmed much of what I had read in the West but it gave me a fuller sense of how the system operated, and its vulnerabilities. . . . I met and talked with many Russians within and outside academia, and I got a real feel for Russia. I also got a full exposure to Russia, so to speak, when there was no hot water in our dormitory and I had to go to the *banya* (public bath) where we saw another side of Russia.

—HERBERT J. ELLISON, telephonic interview, June 8, 1999

Herbert J. Ellison has seen many sides of Russia since 1964 when he was a history student at Leningrad State University. Since then, his many visits to Russian foreign policy institutes—Institute for U.S. and Canadian Studies (ISKAN), IMEMO, Institute of Far Eastern Studies, Institute of Oriental Studies—as well as the many Soviet scholars he has received at the University of Washington where he is a professor of history—have given him a sense of the influence of the exchange experience. Ellison is convinced that

exchanges had an enormous impact on Soviet exchange participants, modifying their views of their own country and the United States in ways

75. Michael Cole, *An Experiment in Computer-Mediated Cooperation Between Nations in Conflict: The Velikhov-Hamburg Project, 1985–94* (La Jolla, Calif.: The Laboratory of Comparative Human Cognition, University of California, San Diego, n.d.), 1.
76. Ibid.

which one can measure from direct conversations and from the changing character of articles in the publications of the various institutes. The accumulated effect of these experiences and attitude changes had its greatest impact once Gorbachev came to power, bringing some of the key people onto the Central Committee and soliciting opinions from many others through the institute leaders. . . . Many of us who read the USA Institute [ISKAN] journal regularly noted the amazing change in the tone and content of its articles on contemporary American life; and when visiting the China-oriented institutes, I noted how the discussions of many of their scholars with American specialists (and American journals) were changing their view of the changes in China as well as other areas of the world.[77]

Ellison believes that the impact of the exchanges began to accelerate rapidly among the younger generation of Soviet scholars during the 1970s and early 1980s. In his view, "the exchanges influenced powerfully key members of the community that provided the Soviet view of the outside world on both questions of international relations and the understanding of developments within the major foreign societies that the Soviet Union was concerned with."[78]

George Demko

Exchanges were a very, very significant leakage pipeline of "truth" or Western values and information that diffused through a large swath of the intellectual community in the Soviet Union. In the long run . . . they prepared a large portion of the elite community for the changes that culminated in Gorbachev's administration.

—GEORGE J. DEMKO

George Demko was a graduate student in geography at Pennsylvania State University in 1962 when he was awarded an IUCTG grant for a year of study at Moscow State University. His research topic, "The Pre-revolutionary Migration of People from European Russia to the Governor-Generalship of the Steppes of Present-day Kazakhstan," was rejected by the Soviets, who found it politically too sensitive. However, in the tit-for-tat of numerical reciprocity in exchanges, a deal was arranged. The U.S. side would accept a Soviet student it had previously rejected if he would change his research topic. The Soviets, in turn, would accept Demko if he would change his topic.

77. Herbert J. Ellison, e-mail to author, January 11, 1998.
78. Ibid.

And so Demko went to Moscow, ostensibly to study "Trends and Techniques of Soviet Population and Settlement Geography." However, his faculty adviser at Moscow State University, after several long discussions with Demko and a display of academic independence, allowed him to work on his original topic despite objections from the Ministry of Higher Education.

Demko completed his research in Moscow and wrote a thesis on the Russian colonization of Kazakhstan; and although not required to do so, at the request of his Russian advisers he defended his thesis for two hours in a lecture hall overflowing with students and faculty. His defense touched on some very sensitive issues, such as Russian colonization and the displacement of native peoples, and many Soviet students told him afterwards that they were surprised that such issues had been openly discussed in the session. The following year, Demko formally defended his thesis at Penn State and was awarded his doctorate.[79]

As a student at Moscow State, Demko had an advantage over most other Americans. His parents had been born of peasant stock in the Transcarpathian region of present-day Slovakia, and many Soviets saw him as a true son of the proletariat and were impressed by his rise to the status of scholar and intellectual. He was elected cochair of the MSU Foreign Student Council; and in an unusual example of Cold War cooperation, he shared his leadership role on the Council with a North Vietnamese student. When Demko was in the chair, he followed *Robert's Rules of Order,* invoking procedures which surprised his Soviet colleagues because they were far more fair and reasonable than Soviet operating rules. The use of *Robert's Rules* also prevented the Council's faculty adviser from forcing several resolutions on the Council without any discussion. This may have been the first instance of *Robert's Rules* being used in the Soviet Union, but they did not prevent Demko from being relieved of his post in midyear when the adviser arbitrarily ruled that his term of office was for only one semester.

During his year in the Soviet Union, Demko traveled extensively—to Kiev, Tbilisi, Irkutsk, and Tallinn, among other cities—thanks again to his faculty adviser, Yulian Glebovich Saushkin, head of the geography department, a war hero and a scholar, who took an interest in Demko's studies and referred to him as "my academic grandson." Saushkin argued successfully with Soviet officials that, as a geographer, Demko's travels were necessary to his studies. Traveling always by train, Demko met hundreds of people—scholars, political leaders, and just plain ordinary folks—and with his good command of Russian, would engage them in long discussions about the United States and the Soviet Union.

79. When Demko's thesis was published in 1969, he sent a copy to the Geography Department at Moscow State, which found it to be anti-Soviet and banned it from the university library. But in a happy ending to the story, in 1999 Demko's book was published in Almaty, Kazakhstan, in both Kazakh- and Russian-language editions.

After receiving his doctorate, Demko taught at Indiana University and Ohio State before becoming head of the Geography and Regional Science Division at the National Science Foundation. From 1982 to 1989 he was Geographer at the State Department, and in 1989, became director of the Rockefeller Center for the Social Sciences at Dartmouth College where he is today professor emeritus of geography.

When the ACLS and the Soviet Academy of Sciences in 1975 established the U.S.-USSR Commission on the Social Sciences and Humanities, Demko was appointed a member and served as U.S. chair of its Subcommission on Geography from 1975 to 1990. The subcommission held seminars for geographers of the two countries and conducted joint research that led to the publication of several books and numerous scholarly articles.

As cochair, Demko insisted that the commission's seminars and other scholarly events have a representative set of scholars from the entire Soviet Union, and he succeeded in bringing into the commission's work scholars representing regions of the Soviet Union beyond Russia. "I am certain," says Demko, that "I and the Commission members over the years had a very large impact in opening minds, inserting accurate information about the United States and the West, and generally provoking our Soviet colleagues to examine their own system."[80]

This successful interaction between U.S. and Soviet geographers, explains Demko, was due in large part to his earlier study at Moscow State and the long-term friendships he has maintained in the Soviet geographic community.[81]

Peter B. Maggs

Had he not gone to Leningrad for a year of study under the IUCTG program in 1961–62, says Peter B. Maggs, professor of law at the University of Illinois at Urbana-Champaign, he probably would have become another big city corporate lawyer. Instead, in Leningrad he greatly improved his knowledge of the Russian language, Russian culture, and the Soviet system, and today he is a leading authority on Soviet and Russian law and the civil codes of the former Soviet states, the author of more than one hundred articles, and the author, editor, or translator of some two dozen books.[82]

More important, Maggs had the good fortune to study with Professor O. S. Ioffe, the leading civil law expert of the Soviet Union, with whom he collaborated on two books after Ioffe was forced, for political reasons, to emigrate to the United States. Because he studied with Ioffe, Maggs is accepted today as an equal by the

80. George Demko, e-mail to author, December 30, 1999.
81. Demko, e-mail to author, December 29, 1999.
82. Peter Maggs, e-mail to author, June 26, 2000.

current generation of senior Russian experts, many of whom also worked or studied with Ioffe, in the ongoing process of drafting new civil codes in the former Soviet Union.

At a 1995 meeting in Bishkek where Maggs was working with experts from Kyrgyzstan, Kazahkstan, and Russia on a draft civil code for Kyrgyzstan, he offered a toast to Professor Ioffe and other Soviet-era professors of civil law who, during the years of Soviet power, had kept alive the idea of a civil code protecting property rights and freedom of contract. Maggs compared them to the monks who, during the barbarian invasions, had preserved national cultures in their monasteries. His toast was enthusiastically received by the assembled company.

Maggs is on the list of arbitrators of the International Arbitration Court at the Russian Federation's Chamber of Commerce and Industry, and has advised on legal reform in Armenia, Belarus, Kazakhstan, Kyrgyzstan, Moldova, Russia, and Ukraine. He has also consulted on litigation involving Russia, Ukraine, and several countries of Central Asia in cases involving war crimes, black marketeering, libel, international finance, purloined oil and oilfields, offshore oil platforms and ships that do not pay their debts, pirated music, news, trade secrets, vodka trademarks, and spontaneously combusting tobacco.

And it all began at Leningrad State University some forty years earlier.

Robert Sharlet

There is also a view among some American scholars that the many years of exchanges affected the United States more than they did the Soviet Union. That view is supported by Robert Sharlet, currently professor of political science at Union College, who studied in Moscow in 1963–64: "Absent the exchanges and given the closed nature of the Soviet system, U.S. perceptions, scholarship, and public policy would probably have depicted the USSR as a far more harsh, hostile, and largely immutable system than it actually was. Inferentially, I would guess that such a situation would have significantly ratcheted up Cold War tensions, or, conversely, not allowed them to gradually wind down as they did."[83]

Responding to the question, "What did the American exchange scholars observe, learn, and write about that shaped our views of the Soviet Union," Sharlet cites three things: "(1) The limits of power in a putatively absolutist system; (2) the view of the system 'from below' and from outside the Kremlin walls; and (3) the exceptional inefficiencies of the economic system—the Soviets were not ten feet tall."[84]

In his own field, state and law, where his contacts in Moscow were almost exclusively with law professors, Sharlet believes that the exchanges that brought Soviet

83. Robert Sharlet, e-mail to author, June 21, 1999.
84. Ibid.

Americanists to the United States had a positive impact on them as individual scholars, deepening and broadening their understanding of our system of separation of powers and judicial review. Sharlet also points out that many of the ideas for reform in law, politics, and economics had been "in the air" or, more specifically, in circulation in Soviet elite journals far removed from the public eye. "Did these ideas," asks Sharlet, "such as presumption of innocence, judicial review of administrative conduct, et cetera, originate from readings of foreign literature, from contact with visiting foreign scholars, from visits to Europe or America, or all of the above?"[85]

Irwin Weil

Irwin Weil had his Harvard doctorate and was a professor of Russian and comparative literature at Brandeis University when he went to the Soviet Union in 1960 and began a relationship with Russia that would last a lifetime.[86] During a second visit, in 1962–63 under the IUCTG exchange, he did research at Moscow State University on the Russian writer Maxim Gorky. One result of that research was a book, *Gorky: His Literary Development and Influence on Soviet Life,* published in 1966.

In Moscow, Weil also developed a close relationship with the noted children's writer and literary critic Kornei I. Chukovsky and was a frequent visitor at his home in Peredelkino, the community outside Moscow where many writers resided, rested, and wrote. There he met many members of the older generation of the Russian intelligentsia, who considered themselves Russian rather than Soviet *intelligenty.* Those conversations, which continued episodically over the next nine years until Chukovsky's death in 1969, laid the basis for much of Weil's later lectures and scholarly work.

Wherever Weil went in the Soviet Union during his year in Moscow and his many subsequent visits, he made it a point to talk to as many Russians as possible, ordinary people as well as intellectuals—people in parks, workers in factories, chambermaids in hotels. During his year on the exchange, he estimates that he spoke with hundreds of people, most of whom had a very positive attitude toward the United States and wanted to learn more about it. No matter what he said about the United States to those Russians, Weil recalls, they would relate it to how their own lives could be improved and how they might be able to do things in the United States that they could not do in the Soviet Union.

Weil believes that he introduced J. D. Salinger's *Catcher in the Rye* to the Soviet Union in 1960. An official at the Soviet Writers Union, who was also a publisher's representative, had asked Weil if he had any new books for him, and Weil lent him

85. Ibid.
86. Erwin Weil, author's interview, Skokie, Ill., July 17, 2000.

a copy of *Catcher,* which had just become a favorite of American youth. The following year it was published in Moscow, in Russian, where it also became a hit.

Russian studies in the United States have declined since the end of the Cold War but are still strong at Northwestern University, where Weil has been teaching for thirty-five years and is known as "Mr. Russia." His course on Dostoyevsky attracts more than a hundred students each year. Even more popular is his "Introduction to the USSR and its Successor States," a study of Soviet and post-Soviet cultural and political history which uses history texts, literature, film, and Weil's own experiences in the Soviet Union and Russia to draw more than 550 undergraduates, most of them non-Russian majors who want to learn about the new Russia and its roots in the old Russia.

Weil also lectures to scores of American organizations across the country that want to learn more about Russia. Audiences sense his deep feelings for the best aspects of the Russian language and tradition, to which they react strongly, as have his students over his fifty years in academia.

Promoting the study of Russian in the United States has been another of Weil's causes. He is a founder of the American branch of the International Association of Teachers of Russian Language and Literature (MAPRIAL) and a cofounder of the American Council of Teachers of Russian (ACTR).

Weil is also active in today's Russia. Under the auspices of the Committee for Russian-American Cultural Relations, he lectures in Moscow and St. Petersburg on Russian cultural influences on America—in music, dance, film, literature, and science. He is also associated with two new Russian universities that promote the study of the humanities, Moscow's Russian State Humanities University and St. Petersburg's Nevsky Institute.

James Muller

A crucial task for the future of the human race is to identify the factors that led to the end of the Cold War, and the termination of a dangerous nuclear confrontation and wasteful arms race. While it is commonly stated that the Reagan military build-up brought the Soviet Union to its knees, I believe it likely that cultural and scientific exchanges, and the resulting cooperative contacts between the USSR and the USA, played a more important role than increasing nuclear over-kill.

—JAMES E. MULLER, M.D.

Another American student in Moscow in the early years of U.S.-Soviet exchanges was James E Muller, a future founder of International Physicians for the Prevention of Nuclear War (IPPNW). Muller first came to Moscow in 1967 on the IUCTG exchange as a medical student from Johns Hopkins University, and it was in Moscow where I first met him when he was riding with the *Skoraya pomoshch,* Russian paramedics.

Muller had studied Russian as an undergraduate at Notre Dame and wanted to spend a semester at a Soviet medical school. But he had also been influenced by Senator William J. Fulbright's book, *The Arrogance of Power,* in which Fulbright, speaking of U.S.-Soviet relations, argued that nations would get along with each other only after they had developed habits of cooperation through work in fields of common interest. That search for U.S.-Soviet cooperation would become a passion for Muller over the next twenty years.[87]

Muller first tried to establish a continuing medical exchange between the two countries and was encouraged in this effort by Johns Hopkins and Moscow's First Medical School where Muller had studied. But the year was 1967, and the proposal had to await the improvement in U.S.-Soviet relations which came with détente in the early 1970s.

While serving as an officer in the U.S. Public Health Service in 1970, Muller was assigned as interpreter to a U.S. delegation headed by Dr. Roger O. Egeberg, Assistant Secretary of the Department of Health, Education, and Welfare, which was going to the Soviet Union to study its health system. On that trip, however, Muller was more than an interpreter. He helped Egeberg establish a good working relationship with Dr. Boris Petrovsky, the Soviet minister of health, and won Egeberg's support for a health agreement between the two governments. Talk about such an agreement continued later that year when Muller was assigned to travel with a return visit to the United States by a delegation of Soviet physicians headed by Dr. Yevgeny Chazov. Another Muller visit to Moscow followed as the two sides continued their discussions for the Agreement on Cooperation in Medical Science and Public Health, which was signed by Richard Nixon and Leonid Brezhnev at their 1972 Moscow Summit.

After completing his residency at Johns Hopkins and taking a position at Harvard Medical School, Muller had an opportunity to implement the U.S.-Soviet agreement when he went to Moscow for three months in 1975 to administer an experimental drug to patients who had just suffered heart attacks. His research project was supervised by Chazov, who by then had become a deputy minister of public health and was later to play a key role in the founding of the IPPNW.

In 1978, Muller proposed to Dr. Bernard Lown, a senior colleague at Harvard Medical School, an annual conference of U.S., Soviet, and Japanese physicians to

---

87. Much of the information on Muller is from the author's conversations with him and from Irwin Abrams, "Origins of International Physicians for the Prevention of Nuclear War: The Dr. James E. Muller Diaries" (paper presented to the Peace History Commission, Fifteenth General Conference of International Peace Research Association, in Malta, November 1994). Copies are available at http://college.antioch.edu/%7Eiabrams/mullerdiaries.html.

discuss the dangers of the nuclear-arms race. Lown broached the subject to Chazov in a letter later that year; and after a preparatory meeting with the Soviets in Geneva, in which Muller played a major role, the Soviet Union in 1980 gave its approval for such a conference. As an indication of the high level of Soviet interest in the conference, the approval came in the form of a letter from Brezhnev to Lown delivered in person by the Soviet ambassador in Washington, Anatoly Dobrynin.

The IPPNW had its first meeting in the United States in 1981 with more than 70 delegates from eleven countries in attendance. At the fifth annual meeting, held in Budapest in 1985, more than 840 delegates and observers came from fifty-four countries, and by the end of that year there were 145,000 members in forty-one national affiliates. At the Budapest meeting, congratulatory messages were received from Presidents Ronald Reagan and Mikhail Gorbachev, UN Secretary-General Perez de Cuellar, and Pope John Paul II. The organization had clearly become a major player in the international debate over nuclear arms control.

Muller played a leading role in the IPPNW as secretary, but his major job was to use his fluent Russian to smooth over differences with the Soviets, who were inclined to raise political issues at the annual meetings. He also drafted the organization's constitution; and in 1982, in a nationwide TV address seen by an estimated 100 million Soviet viewers, he addressed the audience, in Russian, on the dangers of nuclear war.[88]

The IPPNW was awarded the Nobel Peace Prize in 1985, and the award was highlighted by a "live" example of U.S.-Soviet medical cooperation. At a press conference in Oslo following the award, a Soviet radio and television correspondent, Lev Novikov, suffered a sudden cardiac arrest. American and Soviet cardiologists at the press conference immediately joined in attending the stricken man, but it was Muller who took charge and administered CPR (cardiopulmonary resuscitation), which probably saved Novikov's life. Moreover, Muller accompanied Novikov to the hospital in an ambulance and remained with him until he was stabilized.

As Irwin Abrams, a Quaker peace activist, has written, "The young medical student who went to Moscow with the hope of promoting international understanding stayed the course and went on to make a difference in the world."[89]

Fulbright Lecturers

Down in the trenches of exchanges . . . an enormous amount of spade work was done, by individuals as well as groups, which helped inspire and prod the Soviet Union forward in a

88. *New York Times,* June 27, 1982.
89. Abrams, "Origins of International Physicians."

process of self-examination, one that began haltingly and then burst into the open and prospered spectacularly under the aegis of perestroika. Indeed . . . without this spade work, without the influence of Americans visiting the USSR and of American programs bringing increasing numbers of Soviet citizens to the U.S. (and back, usually), the implementation of perestroika would have been both much more difficult and . . . considerably delayed.

—MARK TEETER, Middlebury College

It was not until the end of the nineteenth century that American history began to be taught as a subject at Moscow University, at about the same time that Archibald Coolidge introduced the first course in Russian history at Harvard in 1894. It was an early recognition that the two great countries needed to know more about each other.

That need did not diminish over the coming decades—in fact it grew—but it was not until the signing of the Lacy-Zarubin Agreement in 1958 that it became possible for Soviet and American scholars to work in the archives and libraries of each other's country on a regular basis. And it was not until 1973 that the Soviet Union agreed to exchange university lecturers with the United States. Although by that time there had been fifteen years of scholarly exchanges, Soviet authorities had repeatedly rejected U.S. overtures to establish a lecturer exchange at the university level. Americans and Soviets had given occasional lectures at institutions in the other country, but the Soviets were not prepared to accept U.S. lecturers for a full semester or academic year. That changed in 1973 when they agreed to include in the cultural agreement a provision for a reciprocal exchange of university lecturers. The exchange began at MSU in 1974 and was extended in subsequent years to other universities across the Soviet Union. In addition to lecturing, the Americans also had individual and group consultations with their students, and examined and graded them.

Instrumental in establishing the lecturer exchange, as noted earlier, was Nikolai V. Sivachev, the MSU professor of American history who had studied in the United States and was interested in having American historians lecture to his students. As a result of a "five-year plan" that Sivachev worked out with Donald J. Raleigh, then with the Fulbright Program in Washington, MSU in successive years had a Fulbright lecturer for successive periods of American history, and Soviet students could therefore hear five different Americans during their five-year course of study.[90]

Sivachev was in the United States when E. David Cronon, the first Fulbright lecturer for Moscow, was appointed in autumn 1973. Cronon was a distinguished

90. Donald J. Raleigh is today a professor of Russian history at the University of North Carolina, Chapel Hill.

professor of American history at the University of Wisconsin, and Sivachev made it a point to visit him in Madison and assess his suitability for the position. Invited to stay with the Cronons at their home, they discussed what Cronon would teach at Moscow, and settled on twentieth-century American reform movements, from Progressivism through the New Deal. Later, in 1974, when Cronon was lecturing in Moscow, Sivachev asked whether he planned to discuss the role of the American Communist Party and was visibly relieved when Cronon replied that he did not plan to do so because it was insignificant. Sivachev said that he and Cronon knew that was true, but that was not how they taught it at MSU, and it would be best not to mention it because, otherwise, he and his colleagues might have to say something about his "bourgeois" view. To this Cronon comments: "That was the only hint of censorship during my four months. I never felt I was being manipulated or told what I could or should say. I always suspected that the eighteen students taking my course for History credit (fifty to ninety others from around the University usually attended my lectures) got a corrective Marxist-Leninist interpretation from my three Soviet faculty colleagues who attended all my lectures."[91]

Other Fulbright lecturers report that there were no "off-limit" subjects, and no one ever suggested what they could, or could not, say in their lectures or consultations with students.

When Cronon, during his stay in Moscow, gave a lecture on American history at ISKAN, his remarks were sharply attacked by several younger scholars there who deplored his failure to understand and be guided by Marxist-Leninist principles and insights. At that point, Sivachev rose and said that what was wrong with so much of Soviet historical scholarship was its reliance on "principles" and historical inevitability rather than undertaking archival research to try to understand why the long-heralded collapse of American capitalism had not yet taken place. "It was a rather gutsy thing to do," says Cronon, "and it suggested that he felt secure in his position as a rising star in the history department and the university."[92] Cronon considers his experience in Moscow to be "one of the defining periods of my life, primarily by expanding my intellectual horizons and my knowledge and interest in a previously unfamiliar part of the world."[93]

Other Americans who followed Cronon as Fulbright Lecturers at the MSU History Department report that under Sivachev's nominal supervision neither politics nor ideology limited what they could say in their lectures, which were delivered in English. Communication in English was a problem for some students in the early years of the exchange, but with time, more students came to their American history studies better prepared in English.

91. E. David Cronon, e-mail to author, September 29, 1999.
92. Ibid.
93. Ibid.

According to Elbert B. Smith, the University of Maryland historian who was three times a Fulbright Lecturer in the Soviet Union, Sivachev was eager to have the Americans teach things that the Soviets did not teach, and he advised them, "Say anything you want but stick to your period." Sivachev also maintained that Soviet history students needed someone to argue with, but he counseled Smith, "Don't send us Marxist professors, we can teach that ourselves; and don't send New Leftists either; they will only cause trouble for both our countries." Sivachev often said to Smith after a lecture, "I know you're right, but we don't teach it that way here."[94]

Smith's experiences at MSU were similar to those of Cronon and other American lecturers. Fifteen or so students took his U.S. history course for examination and credit but his lectures usually attracted another fifteen or more students as auditors, several professors of American history, and other faculty members.

What was the result of having a Fulbright lecturer in American history at Moscow State University every year without interruption from 1974 to the present? According to a report prepared in 1997 by former MSU Prorector Tropin, some forty Moscow graduates who heard the Fulbright lecturers were working at various institutes of the Russian Academy of Sciences, in the press, and in television where they were able to reach people who had influence in the government and society at large. In addition, many graduates were teaching American history at Russian universities in Samara, Vladimir, Kaluga, Penza, Saransk, and Ufa, as well as in Ukraine, Latvia, Georgia, Kazakhstan, and Tajikistan.[95] The American lecturers also brought books which they left with MSU, which now has one of best American history libraries in Russia.

As Smith adds: "We created a generation of highly educated people, with friendly attitudes toward the United States, a generation of bright young historians who had had a good American experience, either here in the United States or at our lectures at MSU. And they, in turn, impacted on Gorbachev and his allies in reform."[96]

Who were the students of American history at MSU? As explained by John Milton Cooper Jr., a University of Wisconsin historian who lectured at MSU in 1987, they were all well-connected young people. All twelve of his students were from Moscow, as contrasted with less than 30 percent of the entire university student body. Moreover, all of his students were sons and daughters of professors in institutes, journalists

94. E. B. Smith, author's interview, Dunkirk, Md., October 26, 1998. Smith was a Fulbright lecturer at MSU in 1976 and 1982, and at Leningrad State University in 1981.

95. From a paper received by the author, "On the Fulbright Lecturer Program at the History Faculty of Moscow State University named after M. B. Lomonosov"; author and date of publication unknown but presumed to have been written at Moscow in 1997.

96. E. B. Smith, author's interview, Dunkirk, Md., October 26, 1998.

stationed abroad, army officers, theater producers, and other privileged professions of the Soviet elite.[97] One of their best students, say several former American lecturers, was Vyacheslav A. Nikonov, a grandson of Molotov, who is today a prominent Russian democrat and head of Moscow's Politika Foundation.

In assessing the value of the Fulbright lecturer exchange, Cooper noted, in 1987, that every significant Soviet who studies and interprets the United States has passed through the American History program at MSU. "Their views of America inform and to some extent influence Soviet policy toward the United States. A little bit of influence on these students and faculty, a small seed of doubt or reconsideration, a slight willingness to think longer and harder and gather more information before rushing to judgment—these can go a long way toward affecting the most important international relationship in the world."[98]

Another assessment of the Fulbright Program in the Soviet Union is given by Eugene P. Trani, who lectured in American history at MSU in 1981 and is today president of Virginia Commonwealth University. Trani describes his Moscow experience as one of the highlights of his academic career: "The Fulbright program was a major factor in the gradual opening up of Soviet societies via its universities and, thus, part of the foundation for the eventual demise of the old Soviet system. . . . Academic exchanges are crucial to, if not one of the best means of influencing Russia's future, notwithstanding how distressing things are there at present."[99]

97. John Milton Cooper Jr., "My Mission to Moscow: An American Historian in the Soviet Union," *Wisconsin Magazine of History* 72, no. 1 (autumn 1988): 45.

98. Ibid., 50.

99. Eugene P. Trani, letter to author, November 11, 1998.

5 | SCIENCE AND TECHNOLOGY

Science and technology have acted powerfully as moderating influences, as forces pulling
Russia towards the West, as factors reducing the differences between Russia and the West.

—LOREN R. GRAHAM, *What Have We Learned About
Science and Technology from the Russian Experience?*

Science, and scientific exchange, can be a universal solvent in dissolving animosities and
securing normal relations. No country can do without science. The scientists of the world
are fully prepared to talk to one another even when their statesmen will not.

—JEREMY J. STONE, *Every Man Should Try*

"The scientific and academic communities traditionally have been the most pro-
Western segments of Russian society," writes Loren Graham, professor emeritus of
the history of science from MIT, who studied at Moscow State University in
1960–61 under the Graduate Student/Young Faculty Exchange program.
"Throughout the Soviet period," continues Graham, "the most prominent calls for
democracy and human rights came from their ranks—Andrei Sakharov, the noted
physicist and father of the Soviet hydrogen bomb, is only the best known of a
number of leaders in the human rights movement during the Soviet period."[1]

Indeed, many of the leading Soviet dissidents and human rights advocates were
scientists. A former U.S. science attaché in Moscow, John M. Joyce, has written
that in the basically conservative Soviet society, "the most outward-looking people, the people most susceptible to external influence, are the scientists." Joyce
added that they are also more likely to be advocates of change; and as examples, he
noted that many of the most influential Soviet dissidents—Andrei Sakharov,
Aleksandr Lerner, and Yuri Orlov—were scientists, as were five of the ten members of the [Moscow] Helsinki Watch Committee, established to monitor the
implementation of the Helsinki accords on human rights.[2]

Science and technology, however, were also the most controversial of U.S.-
Soviet exchanges. "They are stealing us blind," cried critics of the exchanges,

1. Loren Graham and Andrew Kuchins, in *Washington Post*, November 19, 1998.
2. John M. Joyce, "U.S.-Soviet Science Exchanges: A Foot in the Soviet Door," paper no. 11 in *Soviet
Science and Technology: Eyewitness Accounts* (Cambridge: Russian Research Center, Harvard University, 1981).

"going around the United States like vacuum cleaners sucking up all kinds of scientific information and technical know-how."

True, the Soviet Union did use exchanges to learn from the West, as Russia had often done in the past. Roald Z. Sagdeev, the former Soviet physicist and space scientist now at the University of Maryland, recalls the advice given him in 1958 before his departure for Geneva as a member of the Soviet delegation to the first international conference on the peaceful use of nuclear energy. "The main focus of your activity at the conference," warned a deputy minister in his final briefing to the delegation, "should be to learn a dollar's worth of science and show a *kopeck*'s worth in return."[3]

The balance in dollars and kopecks of that conference is not known, but we do know that Sagdeev and his fellow Soviet scientists were shocked on their visit to Geneva, their first to the West, by the lack of fear on the faces of people they saw on the streets, and by the prosperity and high standard of living in Switzerland. The Soviet scientists asked each other, "Where is the oppressed working class? Where are the proletarians? . . . When at last would Russia catch up? When would Russia have enough wealth to move people from communal apartments to decent housing?"[4] "Trips abroad," adds Sagdeev, "were windows to the outside world. They provided the reference points we needed to judge our own society."[5]

Scientists the world over need to travel and gain reference points by exchanging views with other scientists working in the same or related fields. Like world-class athletes, they need the stimulus of international competition. When the great Soviet physicist Pyotr Kapitsa was told by Soviet authorities in 1935 that he would no longer be allowed to work abroad, he wrote to his mentor, the British nuclear physicist Ernest Rutherford, "I still feel like a half-prisoner because I have no chance to travel abroad, to see the world, to visit labs. It is a great loss. Undoubtedly, it will lead in the final account to the narrowing of my expertise and ability."[6] And, Kapitsa added, "There are no socialist laws of physics, and no capitalist laws of physics."[7] Kapitsa was not permitted to travel outside the Soviet bloc until 1966 when he came to England for four weeks at the invitation of the Royal Society.

One major impediment to foreign travel was Soviet government control of travel abroad by its citizens, even for a few days to attend an international conference. Another impediment was the Russian practice of giving travel priority based on seniority. As Sagdeev explains: "The directors of the scientific institutes tried to

3. Roald Z. Sagdeev and Susan Eisenhower, ed., *The Making of a Soviet Scientist: My Adventures in Nuclear Fusion and Space From Stalin to Star Wars* (New York: John Wiley and Sons, 1994), 70.
4. Ibid., 71.
5. Sagdeev, author's interview, College Park, Md., December 11, 1998.
6. Sagdeev, *Making of a Soviet Scientist*, 87.
7. Ibid.

monopolize all the foreign travel, and the younger scientists, who were doing the actual research, consequently had much fewer opportunities to travel. For scientists, power was in the hands of octogenarians in the Politburo and septuagenarians in the Academy of Sciences."[8] The aging of the Academy eventually became a source of concern to the Soviet government. By the mid-1980s, 40 percent of Academy members were reported to be over the age of seventy-five, and there was talk of enforcing mandatory retirement at sixty-five.[9]

Foreign travel was controlled by the KGB, which had officers placed in the foreign departments of various ministries and institutes of the Academy. One such officer was Stepan G. Korneyev, who headed the Academy's foreign department and reportedly held the rank of KGB general. When I once asked Korneyev why the Soviet Union did not send scientists to the United States in their younger, most creative years, he replied flatly, "They are too young to represent their country abroad."

Soviet scientists had been isolated since the mid-1930s, but after Stalin's death in 1953 they sought to reestablish links with the international scientific community. A continuing impediment, however, was control of foreign travel. "Exit permission to take foreign trips," says Sagdeev, "was almost a ticket to outer space."[10] But, in contrast to the dissidents who directly challenged the system, Sagdeev says that he and other like-minded moderates

> were in favor of acting within the system, avoiding the alienation of the government and authorities. Maybe subconsciously we simply were not ready to sacrifice the privileges given to us by the system—the chance to do science and enjoy certain well-controlled dosages of foreign trips. We thought that the expression of our concern in letters or in speeches at academy gatherings would, in the final account, be able to produce the net effect. The authorities played against our moderate internal opposition with the carrot and the stick—and they knew that we didn't much like the latter.[11]

The Soviet Union had the largest number of scientists and engineers in the world, and they were a privileged class. From Lenin to Brezhnev, Soviet leaders saw science and technology as the key to transforming the Soviet Union from a

8. Sagdeev, author's interview, College Park, Md., December 11, 1998.

9. Arthur E. Pardee Jr., testimony before the House Subcommittee on International Scientific Cooperation of the Committee on Science, Space, and Technology, *Hearings to Examine U.S.-Soviet Science and Technology Exchanges,* 100th Cong., 1st sess. [no. 26], June 23, 1987, 108.

10. Sagdeev, *Making of a Soviet Scientist,* 137.

11. Ibid., 142–43.

backward agricultural state to an industrialized great power that would rival, and even surpass, its main adversary, the United States.

Accordingly, in the cultural agreements they signed with Western countries, and with the United States in particular, the Soviets gave high priority to activities that would provide opportunities for their scientists and engineers to study, travel, and attend scientific conferences abroad and thus acquire technological information useful to Soviet development. Such efforts were supported by Soviet scientists, who saw them as a means to reestablish scientific links with the West, and especially with the United States.

The Lacy-Zarubin Agreement had five components for science and technology. The exchange of graduate students and young faculty between the U.S. Inter-University Committee on Travel Grants (IUCTG, superseded by IREX in 1968) and the Soviet Ministry of Higher Education provided opportunities for research visits of one or two semesters in all scholarly disciplines, although the Soviets chose to nominate most of their exchangees in the basic and engineering sciences.[12] An agreement between the ACLS and the Soviet Academy provided for a similar exchange of senior scholars but was reserved exclusively for scholars in the humanities and social sciences, and did not include scientists. The cultural agreement also provided for exchanges of delegations in industry, agriculture, and medicine, usually for two-week periods.[13] In 1959, the U.S. National Academy of Sciences and the Soviet Academy of Sciences signed an agreement for the exchange of scientists. That agreement, annexed to the cultural agreement in 1962, provided for short-term exchanges of scientists to deliver lectures, conduct seminars, and gain familiarization with scientific research, as well as longer-term exchanges for scientific research and advanced study.

There was some reluctance within the U.S. National Academy to conduct exchanges with the Soviet Union. The National Academy was an honorific and advisory institution with no institutes, laboratories, or researchers of its own, while the Soviet Academy exercised central control over institutes conducting virtually all basic scientific research in the Soviet Union. Nevertheless, the National Academy decided to go ahead with an agreement in order to establish individual and institutional contact with the Soviet scientific community, learn what it was doing, and contribute toward improved U.S.-Soviet relations.

12. Under the IUCTG/IREX–Ministry of Higher Education exchange, the Soviets chose to send mostly scientists, while the Americans were mostly in the humanities and social sciences.

13. These exchanges of delegations were reciprocal, that is to say, U.S. and Soviet delegations were exchanged in the same fields, and their itineraries were the subject of lengthy negotiations to ensure mutual benefit. Although they were largely familiarization tours, they provided the U.S. scientific and technology communities much of the basic information used to design the U.S.-Soviet cooperative programs of the 1970s.

Finally, a Memorandum of Cooperation between the U.S. Atomic Energy Commission and the USSR State Committee on the Peaceful Uses of Atomic Energy was signed in 1959, and was also annexed to the cultural agreement.

Those science and technology (S&T) exchanges were not large in numbers, and from 1959 to 1972 no more than fifty persons from each side were exchanged annually. But despite the small numbers, they served to establish the first postwar linkages between American and Soviet scientists, helped to increase American knowledge of Soviet science, and prepared the way for an expansion of S&T exchanges during the détente years.

During the 1970s S&T exchanges expanded dramatically with the signing of eleven agreements for cooperation between agencies of the two governments in various fields of science and technology, an element in the Nixon/Kissinger grand strategy of engagement with the Soviet Union. Under the cooperative agreements, more than one thousand Soviet scientists visited the United States each year during the mid- and late-1970s, and most of them were true scientists, members of the Soviet scientific elite, and not so closely screened by the KGB.

The cooperative agreements, in the order signed, were in Science and Technology, Environmental Protection, Medical Science and Public Health, Space, Agriculture, World Ocean Studies, Transportation, Atomic Energy, Artificial Heart Research and Development, Energy, and Housing and Other Construction.

The U.S. motivation was primarily political—to develop, within the framework of détente, patterns of cooperation and interdependence that would lead to shared interests and more moderate behavior on the part of the Soviet Union. But there were other objectives as well—to use the exchanges to help solve practical problems in U.S. science and technology, and gain increased access to the Soviet science community and learn what it was doing. The cooperative agreements also represented a new phase in U.S.-Soviet exchanges. Instead of individual scientists pursuing their own research interests in the other country, American and Soviet scientists would be working together on problems of common interest.

Much of the Soviet motivation, as in the past, was to gain access to U.S. technology that would be useful to Soviet development. Not to be dismissed, however, was the psychological factor—the prestige the Soviets always saw in being recognized as equal to the Americans.

On the U.S. side, the cooperative agreements were a joint effort of the U.S. government and the scientific community. For each agreement, a U.S.-Soviet commission was established, cochaired by cabinet- or subcabinet-level officials of the two countries, which met annually to review ongoing work under the agreement and plan future activities. Working groups of American and Soviet specialists were formed for cooperation on specific projects of interest to the two sides.

Some 240 working groups were established under the eleven agreements, and after an initial startup period, some one thousand Americans and about the same number of Soviet specialists were exchanged annually for one- to two-week periods each year to discuss work being performed in each country under the agreements.[14] Initially, work under the agreements consisted of an exchange of information, but as the two sides became more comfortable with the idea of cooperation, joint research projects became more common, with longer stays abroad.

The number of projects and persons exchanged grew from year to year until the Soviet Union invaded Afghanistan in December 1979. That event, followed by the imposition of martial law in Poland in 1981 and the shooting down of Korean Airlines Flight 007 by the Soviets in 1981, caused a steady deterioration in U.S.-Soviet relations and cooperation between the two countries. Four of the cooperative agreements were suspended—Space, Energy, Science and Technology, and Transportation—and by 1983 the level of activity under the remaining agreements had fallen to about 20 percent of the 1979 level. The cultural agreement was allowed to lapse, although scholarly exchanges continued.

It was not until June 1984 that President Ronald Reagan, in an effort to improve relations, called for renegotiation of the cultural agreement and the revival of four of the noncontroversial agreements still in effect—Environmental Protection, Housing and Other Construction, Public Health and Medical Science, and Agriculture. A further boost to cooperation came with the Geneva Summit of 1985, when a new cultural agreement was signed and several other cooperative agreements were renewed or initiated. In the following year, a new agreement for cooperation in space was also signed.

How were Soviet and American scientists affected by the exchanges? One answer is given by Murray Feshbach, professor emeritus of demography from Georgetown University and a long-time visitor to the Soviet Union and Russia, with fifty-one working visits between 1969 and 1998.

During the 1970s and 1980s, Feshbach was a member of five working groups under the S&T agreement, and he recalls how the Soviet demographers he worked with changed during those years. Initially, says Feshbach, the Soviets were rarely forthcoming in responding to questions by visiting Americans. Unsure of what they could discuss with foreigners, they would play games with words and answer questions without really saying anything. But gradually, as time went on, adds Feshbach, and as the Soviets began to understand the Americans' questioning, they became more forthcoming. Their reporting also became more sophisticated, more in line with what was being written in the West, although it was still more descriptive and analytical than critical. Moreover, visits to the United States by

14. See Richmond, *U.S.-Soviet Cultural Exchanges,* 76.

Soviet demographers broadened their perspectives, enabling them to see that demography is not just the collection of statistics but may also involve ethnic, economic, geographic, education, and fertility issues.[15]

As for the American scientists who participated in the joint working groups under the S&T agreement, many of them resigned, says Feshbach, disillusioned by Soviet secrecy and failure to provide meaningful information. However, adds Feshbach, "those who stuck it out learned much. They were exposed to the Russian 'psyche,' how Russians thought, and how they approached problems."[16]

Talent in the Soviet era was attracted to science and technology, where opportunities were many and political risks few. Indeed, in the Soviet Union, young men and women who might have become humanists or social scientists in an earlier generation, became natural or physical scientists, "safe" occupations in communist countries where independent thought in the humanities and social sciences was severely circumscribed. Yet those young scientists came to their new professions with a degree of skepticism and an ability to recognize the truth when they encountered it.

Scientists everywhere are trained to examine the evidence and seek the truth, and Soviet scientists were no exception. Those who came to the United States, after examining the evidence could only have come to the conclusion that what the official Soviet media had been telling them about the United States and their own country was far from the truth.

As Thorstein Veblen wrote many years ago: "The first requisite for constructive work in modern science, and indeed for any work or inquiry that shall bring enduring results, is a skeptical frame of mind. The enterprising skeptic alone can be counted on to further the increase of knowledge in any substantial fashion. This will be found true both in the modern sciences and in any field of scholarship at large."[17]

Leszek Kołakowski, the Polish philosopher who now lives in England, wrote, as early as 1972, about those "skeptical" Soviet scientists and their support of intellectual freedom:

> Scholars who are members of the Soviet Academy of Sciences, whose institutes correspond to the more prestigious research-oriented graduate schools in the United States, are much more likely to exhibit anti-establishment thought and behavior than those who teach in the relatively low

15. Murray Feshbach, author's interview, Washington, D.C., October 9, 1998.

16. Ibid.

17. Thorstein Veblen, in Seymour Martin Lipset and Richard B. Dobson, "The Intellectual as Critic and Rebel: With Special Reference to the United States and the Soviet Union," *Daedalus* 101, no. 3 (summer 1972): 164.

status, non-research-oriented Soviet universities and the specialized technical institutions of higher education. The Soviet authorities have had more difficulty with their best scholars and scientists, and with intellectuals generally, than with those who distribute intellectual products as teachers. Soviet science institutes and "science cities" tend to be centers of opposition; they are among the principal supporters of free intellectual life and the "underground press."[18]

Moreover, added Kołakowski, scientists led the movement for human rights in the Soviet Union: "Political dissidence and critical activity are more pronounced among students and faculty in the natural sciences than in the social sciences and the humanities. Significantly, it is not scholars in the humanities and social sciences, but Andrei Sakharov, Andrei Tverdokhlebov, and Valery Chalidze, three prominent physicists, who founded the Committee for Human Rights, an organization devoted to the strengthening of legal norms and basic human rights."[19]

Scientists indeed played a leading role, in both the Soviet Union and the United States, in helping to effect the policy changes that led to the end of the Cold War. As Metta Spencer, a Canadian political scientist, notes: "It was Gorbachev who took the lead in ending the Cold War. And it is clear that to some degree, Gorbachev was influenced by the international community of scientists—Millionshchikov, Artsimovich, Velikhov, von Hippel, Rotblat, Stone, Sagdeev, Sakharov, and hundreds of others."[20]

A broader assessment of the value of expanded contacts between the two superpowers during the détente years has been made by Robert M. Gates, longtime CIA Soviet analyst and CIA director in the first Bush administration: "Détente's greatest achievement was the opening of consistent contact between the United States and the USSR in the early 1970s—a gradually intensifying engagement on many levels and in many areas that, as it grew over the years, would slowly but widely open the Soviet Union to information, contacts, and ideas from the West and would facilitate an ongoing East-West dialogue that would influence the thinking of many Soviet officials and citizens."[21]

18. Leszek Kołakowski, "Intellectuals Against Intellect," *Daedalus* 101, no. 3 (summer 1972): 164.

19. Ibid., 166–67.

20. Metta Spencer, "'Political' Scientists," *Bulletin of the Atomic Scientists* 51, no. 5 (July/August 1995): 68.

21. Robert M. Gates, *From the Shadows: The Ultimate Insider's Story of Five Presidents and How They Won the Cold War* (New York: Simon and Schuster, 1996), 49. Although Gates had devoted his entire adult life to the study of the Soviet Union, because the CIA prohibited its high-level officials from traveling there, he did not make his first visit until May 1989 as a member of a delegation headed by Secretary of State James Baker. See Jeremy J. Stone, *Every Man Should Try: Adventures of a Public Interest Activist* (New York: Public Affairs, 1999), 241–48. As evidence of what that misguided travel policy led to, George Shultz,

How a highly placed Soviet scientist was influenced by a visit to the United States in the early 1980s has been described by an IREX official. He had invited the Soviet visitor to breakfast and had brought along his laptop computer, new at the time. In explaining what it could do, he noted that it could produce data on scientists such as the Russian himself. When the scientist asked if the computer had a file on him, the IREX official brought it up on the screen. The scientist read it, paused for a full minute, and said to the American in a very serious voice, "We are finished, aren't we," meaning that the Soviet system was at a dead end and, with its closed information system, could never compete with the West.[22]

And what did Soviet scientists write about their visits to the United States? With the opening of formerly closed Soviet archives, we are now able to read the reports they submitted to their ministries and agencies after their return home. For scientists and scholars in universities and technical institutes, the reports were submitted to the head of the Ministry of Higher and Specialized Secondary Education or one of his deputies, and they may be seen today in the State Archive of the Russian Federation (GARF).[23] While writers of the reports had to be circumspect about what they could say about the United States, several common threads run through their reports.

Most of the reports were written by scientists and scholars with candidate degrees and the rank of docent or professor who were in the United States for a semester or more of study and research or to attend a scientific or scholarly conference. While their reports, for the most part, are nonpolitical and focus on the scientific or scholarly aspects of their visit, they nevertheless reveal that the authors were most impressed by the material resources available to their American colleagues and their freedom to pursue research. In report after report, the Soviet visitors speak of the latest equipment available to Americans working in fields similar to their own, the ease with which they make copies of papers to be distributed to their students, the wide range of journals and other publications from all over the world available in libraries, the ease with which Americans communicate and interact with their colleagues at home and abroad, and the frequency with which they travel abroad to do research or attend conferences. No direct comparisons are made with corresponding conditions in the Soviet Union, but the message to the ministry was clear—Americans work under much more open conditions, and open communication greatly facilitates their research.

---

in his memoirs, writes that "back in Washington, and especially from the CIA and its lead Soviet expert, Bob Gates, I heard that the Soviets wouldn't change and couldn't change, that Gorbachev was simply putting a new face on the same old Soviet approach to the world and to their own people." See George P. Shultz, *Turmoil and Triumph: My Years as Secretary of State* (New York: Charles Scribner's Sons, 1993), 703.

22. Related by Daniel Matuszewski, in e-mail to author, December 10, 2001.

23. Gosudarstvennyi Arkhiv Rossiiskoi Federatsii (GARF), fond 96, opis' 1.

With regard to the oft-stated charge that Soviet scientists were traveling around the United States sucking up scientific and technical data like vacuum cleaners, they appear indeed to have been under instructions to do exactly that. Many of the reports cite the number of copies of papers collected at various scientific conferences. Such papers, of course, were unclassified, in the public domain, and intended for distribution to conference participants.

Soviet exchange participants also appear to have been under instructions to disseminate widely the results of their travel and study abroad. Many of the reports list the number of lectures given after returning home, the titles of papers or articles prepared for publication, and the nature of research acquired abroad which was used in Soviet dissertations. It is not known how much of the lectures was devoted to strictly scientific and technical subjects, and how much to life in the United States, but it can be safely assumed that the lecturers must have told their educated and perceptive audiences much about the world beyond Soviet borders.

Illustrative is a report by Yu. D. Dyadkin, Professor of Thermal Physics, Leningrad Mining Institute, who visited the United States for six weeks during October-November 1972 (under which agreement or program is not clear).[24] In his lengthy report to the Ministry of Higher and Specialized Secondary Education, Dyadkin described in detail his visits to the Universities of Pennsylvania, Minnesota, and California (Berkeley), the Bureau of Mines Research Center in Minneapolis, the Geological Survey in Menlo Park, and the Colorado School of Mines.

During his visit, Dyadkin gave six lectures on the results of research at his institute; held many discussions with American scientists working in his field—the use of geothermal sources for power generation; arranged to have one of his research papers published in the United States; prepared for publication several research papers coauthored with American colleagues; and received a proposal for publishing an English-language edition of his book, *Principles of Thermal Physics in Mining*. Dyadkin also reported receiving a proposal from the University of Minnesota for an agreement with the Leningrad Mining Institute on research cooperation which he presented to the Soviet Embassy in Washington and his ministry in Moscow. (The ministry took no action on the proposal, and it was not for another four years that it would agree to direct exchanges between U.S. and Soviet universities.)

Dyadkin also reported that American pure research in his field was comparable to that of the Soviet Union but the level of applied research was not as high. Nevertheless, he described the scope and organization of American laboratory research as "first class," which he attributed to the effectiveness of the dollar as an

24. Yu. D. Dyadkin, "Report of a Scientific Mission to the United States of America, October 11 to November 26, 1972," GARF, fond 9606, opis' 1, delo 5253 (author's translation).

incentive for high performance. And in the next sentence he concluded with an indictment of Soviet science: "In my opinion, the output of scientists in the United States at the present time is higher than in our country."[25]

How did the exchanges affect Soviet science overall? One conclusion is given by Robert G. Kaiser of the *Washington Post,* a former Moscow correspondent and the author of several books on the Soviet Union. "The modernization of the Soviet Union," wrote Kaiser, "and the breakdown of its isolation actually began in the early 1970s, in the time of the Nixon-Brezhnev détente, when

> thousands of Soviet citizens first saw the West and realized how far their country lagged behind. Stalinism required isolation; only in ignorance would successive generations continue to accept the myths that propped it up. In the seventies Soviet young people discovered and joined the international youth culture; large numbers of Western tourists began to visit the U.S.S.R.; Soviet scientists caught on to the computer revolution and what it might mean, though because of the country's inability to produce the hardware, they could not easily take part in it.[26]

A more tangible example of the benefits of scientific exchange is the case of Zhores I. Alferov, the Nobel laureate in physics in 2000. Alferov first came to the United States in 1970–71 for six months of research on semiconductor lasers at the University of Illinois under the exchange between the U.S. National Academy of Sciences and the Soviet Academy of Sciences. His host at Illinois was Nick Holonyak Jr., now Professor of Electrical and Computer Engineering and Physics, whom he had met in 1967 when he hosted Holonyak's visit, also under the inter-academy exchange, to the Ioffe Physico-Technical Institute in Leningrad where Alferov worked. That was the start, says Holonyak, of thirty-three years of collaboration between them, in visits, exchanges of letters, phone calls, seminars, and the writing of scientific papers. Moreover, during Alferov's six months at Illinois, Holonyak also gave him "a shock-treatment exposure" to English: "I got him an unexpurgated English-language dictionary, and taught him exactly the English that Americans taught poor Eastern European immigrants in the coal fields of Southern Illinois. Why not—why should his English competence, in form, be different than mine?"[27] After the 1960 breakthrough of U.S. semiconductor lasers, Alferov did groundbreaking work that later earned him the Nobel prize. He was one of the first to introduce and demonstrate the concepts that led to the development of

---

25. Ibid., 17.
26. Kaiser, *Why Gorbachev Happened,* 403–4.
27. Letter, Nick Holonyak Jr. to Ralph T. Fisher, University of Illinois, December 4, 2000.

small, efficient lasers. Also partly dependent on his work are present-day laser devices found in fiber optics, CD players, and supermarket checkout counters.

Among Alferov's other awards are the Franklin Institute's Ballantyne Medal in 1971, the Lenin Prize in 1972, and the Nick Holonyak Jr. Award in 2000. He is also a Life Fellow of the Franklin Institute, a Foreign Associate of the U.S. National Academy of Engineering and the U.S. National Academy of Sciences, and a member of the Optical Society of America.

6 | HUMANITIES AND SOCIAL SCIENCES

For Soviet scholars, communication meant liberation.
—NORMAN NAIMARK

Another important but less well known element of U.S.-Soviet exchanges was the work of the U.S.-USSR Commissions of ACLS. Established in the mid-1970s, the commissions facilitated direct contact in the humanities and social sciences between scholars of the two countries through joint conferences and cooperative research.[1]

Prior to establishment of the commissions, there was virtually no cooperation between the two countries in the humanities and social sciences. Individual scholars were exchanged through IUCTG and IREX to pursue their own research, but the centralized and hierarchical nature of Soviet research made it difficult for American scholars to collaborate with their Soviet colleagues, either individually or in groups, without the permission of the responsible Soviet authorities. And those authorities were unlikely to give permission without the authorization of a formal agreement.

In the early 1970s, however, the détente years when the political climate was right and the United States and the Soviet Union had signed eleven cooperative agreements in various fields of science and technology, there was a precedent for similar cooperation in other disciplines. IREX, with the assistance of the ACLS, established with the Soviet Academy of Sciences a committee to create an agenda for cooperative projects that would be most useful to scholars of the two countries. That committee evolved into an ACLS–Soviet Academy Commission on the Humanities and Social Sciences, which had its first meeting in 1975. Subsequent meetings were held every two years through the early 1990s, and subcommissions were established for various scholarly disciplines, including, among others, international relations, economics, sociology, psychology, political science, geography, and philosophy. The commission was chaired originally on the U.S. side by ACLS President Frederick Burkhardt, and on the Soviet side by Academician Nikolai Inozemtsev, and after his death, by Georgi Arbatov. Participants on the U.S. side included such luminaries as sinologist John Fairbank, sociologist Talcott Parsons, and economist Wasily Leontief.

1. This section is based on the author's own recollections and his interview with Wesley A. Fisher, Washington, D.C., February 24, 2000. Fisher, a sociologist, served as secretary to the commission.

The original ACLS intent was only to establish an agenda for cooperation in the humanities and social sciences. The Soviet Academy, however, with its penchant for centralization and control, sought to conduct the actual cooperative projects together with the ACLS. That created a problem for the Americans, who were not accustomed to conducting cooperative research on a national basis, but they went along with the Soviet proposal to establish an agenda, and then fund and run the projects with help from IREX.

The first collaborative efforts took the form of conferences and symposia, with papers contributed by the two sides. Over time, however, the commission's work was broadened to include joint field work, training for younger scholars, exhibitions, survey research, exchanges of data and archival materials, and joint publications. Funding on the U.S. side came from grants to IREX from the Carnegie Corporation of New York, Ford Foundation, W. Alton Jones Foundation, John D. and Catherine T. MacArthur Foundation, National Endowment for the Humanities, Rockefeller Foundation, Trust for Mutual Understanding, U.S. Department of State, and USIA.

Because the ACLS partner was the Soviet Academy, that necessarily defined the disciplines for which collaborative projects were initially possible. Excluded were disciplines under the Soviet Ministry of Culture, such as art history, musicology, and theater, as well as disciplines under other ministries. Eventually, however, other commissions were established with other Soviet agencies in archival administration, art, cinematography, education, libraries, music, and theater and dance.

The commission's most visible work was the first jointly researched and curated U.S.-Soviet scholarly exhibition, "Crossroads of Continents: The Cultures of Siberia and Alaska," which opened at the Smithsonian Institution in Washington, D.C., on September 23, 1988, and was subsequently shown in other cities of the United States, Canada, and the Soviet Union. Ten years in the making and the result of collaboration between Soviet and American anthropologists, the exhibition brought together the great early Siberian and Alaskan collections of the two countries in a panorama of remote regions and peoples unknown to the outside world until the eighteenth century.

Other activities of the commissions included exchanges of sociological data, the first joint archeological digs, and the first applications of Soviet students directly to U.S. universities. The first e-mail connection between U.S. and Soviet scholars, described earlier in these pages, was also made under the auspices of the commission. Several of its Soviet members later became advisers to Gorbachev or members of subsequent governments, including, among others, Yevgeni Primakov, Abel Aganbegyan, and Tatyana Zaslavskaya. The commission also exposed scholars of both countries to new ideas in various intellectual fields. American philosophers, for example, were surprised to learn that not all Soviet philosophers were writing about Marxism-Leninism, and that some of them had made major contributions in such fields as logic and the philosophy of science. And in the first attempt to get Soviet economists to understand the workings of a market economy, the commission took a group of visiting economists to New York City's Brighton Beach, home to a large community of Russian émigrés, to show what Russians could do in a free market.

Geography provides another example of what was done under the commissions. The Subcommission on Geography, consisting of some fifty to sixty Soviet and a similar number of American geographers, identified themes of common interest and held seminars in each country on those themes at which papers were delivered and were later published as books. For each book, extensive field excursions were conducted in the two countries. George Demko, U.S. cochair of the subcommission, was successful in ensuring that the seminars and other events were attended by a representative set of Soviet geographers, including non-Russians and Siberians. Demko believes that, over the years, the subcommission had a major impact in opening Soviet geography to the outer world, ensuring accurate information about the United States and the West, and provoking Soviet geographers to examine their own system more closely.[2]

Unlike the National Academy exchanges, which were suspended for a time because of Soviet human rights violations, the commission activities continued despite difficult times in U.S.-Soviet relations. The U.S. side pushed for direct relations with scholars in the various Soviet republics, but not always with success. It was not until the Gorbachev years, in the mid-1980s, when a new era in cooperative research opened, that the U.S. side was able to establish direct relations with, for example, the Ukrainian Academy of Science.

The first applications by Soviet students for U.S. degree programs were arranged through the commission. Tatyana Zaslavskaya, a leading Soviet sociologist, had wanted to train people in the growing field of public-opinion polling. When American sociologists pointed out to her that she needed to put people into Ph.D. programs, she went to the Party Central Committee in 1986 and got permission, for the first time, to interview applicants and administer the Graduate Record and TOEFL exams. Eventually seventeen Soviet students of sociology were enrolled at U.S. universities in 1988, and a like number in the following two years. A similar start was made with students in political science and economics. Since Russian public-opinion polling today uses Western methods and analysis, it has to be assumed that much of the polling is based on the work of students who came to the United States in the late 1980s and early 1990s.

The U.S. side also pushed hard to get Soviet cooperation in Asian and African studies. By 1988 there was contact with the Soviets in every field of the humanities

---

2. Demko, e-mail to author, December 30, 1999.

and social sciences. But by that time the Soviet Union was evolving, and there was criticism in the U.S. scholarly community that the commissions were monopolizing scholarly cooperation. On the Soviet side, Arbatov's institute began making its own arrangements with U.S. institutions, although American institutions could not do the same in the Soviet Union. As a result, the work of the commission was gradually phased out in early 1990s.

Over a period of more than fifteen years, however, the commission had served to provide much needed balance in U.S.-Soviet exchanges between those in the humanities and social sciences, and those in science and technology.

7 | MOSCOW THINK TANKS

Inside the research institutes and among the party intelligentsia a remarkably important evolution of political views occurred, and one simply cannot begin to understand the changes of the second half of the 1980s without taking account of it.

—ARCHIE BROWN

Until the mid-1950s the Soviet Union had no official body devoted to the study of foreign policy or international economic and political affairs. During the Stalin years, such issues were decided by the *Vozhd'*, the "Great Leader" himself, without the advice of experts, and at a time when there were few such experts in the Soviet Union. In a wartime interview, Maksim Litvinov, former Soviet ambassador to Washington, said that the Soviet Foreign Ministry was headed by three people, none of whom understood America. "The same has been true, a fortiori, to this day," commented Walter Laqueur in 1986, "with regard to the Politburo."[1]

Soviet ignorance about the rest of the world persisted through the Stalin years. Of the last years of Stalin's rule, Georgi Arbatov, the Soviet Union's preeminent Americanologist, has written: "Extremely primitive notions [were] cultivated in these years about the rest of the world and the world economy, about capitalism and international relations. For a long time we did not want to abandon these notions. They were drummed into the heads of a whole generation of our experts, and became sacrosanct dogma."[2]

After Stalin's demise, however, there was growing criticism in Moscow of the failure of the social science institutes of the Soviet Academy to analyze capitalist societies, and in 1956 the Academy established an Institute for World Economy and International Relations, commonly known by its Russian acronym IMEMO, which Georgi Arbatov has described as "an oasis of creative thought in the late 1950s and early 1960s."[3] The institute, explains Arbatov, "tried to concentrate the leadership's attention on reality, and on the problems that demanded radical change in the economy and domestic and foreign policy."[4] Led by Nikolai

1. See Walter Laqueur, "Julian Semyonov and the Soviet Political Novel," *Transactions-Society* 23 (July/August 1986): 72.
2. Georgi Arbatov, *The System: An Insider's Life in Soviet Politics,* trans. John Glad and Oleg Volkonsky, with an introduction by Strobe Talbott (New York: Time Books, 1992), 73.
3. Ibid., 211.
4. Ibid., 240.

Inozemtsev, its brilliant and sophisticated director, IMEMO became the model for similar institutes on Africa, Latin America, and the United States and Canada.

The Institute for U.S. Studies was established in December 1967 with Arbatov as director. It was renamed the Institute for U.S. and Canadian Studies (or ISKAN) in 1974. In his memoirs, Arbatov claims that Brezhnev, in his "catch up with America syndrome," agreed to establish the institute after it was pointed out to him that the United States had many scholars studying the Soviet Union while the Soviet Union had none who were studying America.[5] In the following years, the Soviet Academy would establish a number of similar institutes dealing with other parts of the world until, by the late 1980s, more than 7,400 specialists were working in twelve Moscow institutes in data collection and assessment essential to foreign policy formulations.[6]

Arbatov, a doctor of sciences in history, had worked as an editor in the party press during the 1950s, at IMEMO in 1962, and in the Central Committee apparatus from 1964 to 1967, where he became an adviser to Brezhnev. His proximity to Brezhnev was most important in the 1960s when, because of the indifference of other Politburo members, Soviet policy toward the United States was made largely by Brezhnev and Foreign Minister Andrei Gromyko. As a protégé of Brezhnev and Yuri Andropov, Arbatov in 1976 became a candidate member of the Party's prestigious Central Committee, and a full member in 1981.

Arbatov is a typical example of the Russian maxim, "It's not what you know but whom you know." Arbatov had never been to the United States but he was a fast learner, and quick with a quip. When I first met him in 1967 and asked how he had come to be appointed director of ISKAN, he replied with one of the one-liners for which he was to become known in the West. "Since I have never been to the United States," he said with a knowing smile, "I am considered neutral on the subject."

The new institute focused on various aspects of the United States—economics, foreign trade, domestic politics, social issues, foreign policy, the military, disarmament, and agriculture. And to provide advice on such a broad range of subjects, Arbatov assembled a staff of economists, political scientists, historians, sociologists, and military specialists, many of them iconoclastic scholars, in order, as he put it, to "tell the leadership frankly (and write in the press) what experts who followed events in the United States already knew but were somewhat afraid to say. We were bold enough to discard ideological blinders and base our conclusions on the practical interests of the Soviet Union."[7] Indeed, as Arbatov himself has

5. Arbatov, *The System*, 296.

6. Daniel Matuszewski, "Soviet International Relations Research," in John Stremlau, ed., *International Relations Research: Emerging Trends Outside the United States, 1981–1982*, a special report of the Rockefeller Foundation, November 1983.

7. Arbatov, *The System*, 173–74.

pointed out, it was at ISKAN and other institutes that young civilians rather than military officers began to analyze security and military issues.[8] For many years, the average age of ISKAN's researchers was no more than thirty.[9]

To assist in its research, Arbatov's staff had access to Western books and journals, and his institute's library earned a reputation as the best on the United States in the Soviet Union. Its well-informed researchers also served as consultants to other Soviet government agencies. They traveled often to the United States, benefiting from the many grants they were awarded by IREX and other American exchange and scholarly institutions. Indeed, among the institutes of the Soviet Academy, Arbatov's institute soon came to have "most-favored-institute" status, and its researchers, especially during and after détente, became regulars on U.S. scholarly exchange circuits.[10] ISKAN's presence in the United States grew even more when Arbatov had a position in the Soviet Embassy in Washington reserved for one of his staffers, as well as four internships in Washington and New York.

Because of his personality and persuasiveness, as well as his position and connections, Arbatov soon made the acquaintance of many prominent American political figures, one of the first of whom was former Michigan governor George Romney, who visited Moscow in 1967 during his campaign for the Republican presidential nomination.[11] And at a Pugwash meeting in Moscow in December 1967, Arbatov met Henry Kissinger, a Harvard professor at the time, with whom he would have many more meetings.

Arbatov became a fixture at the Dartmouth Conference for which his institute became a Soviet cosponsor in the 1970s together with the Soviet Peace Committee. From 1969 through Dartmouth's last full meeting in 1991, he served as Soviet cochair of the Conference, and his institute's staffers came to dominate many of the Soviet delegations to its meetings. As one American scholar has put it, they "provided the intellectual heart of the Soviet delegations although the contributions of other Soviet institutions, like the Institute for Oriental Studies and IMEMO, and individuals such as [Yevgeni] Primakov, were often significant."[12]

8. Cohen and vanden Heuvel, *Voices of Glasnost*, 311.

9. Arbatov, *The System*, 315.

10. The most frequent beneficiary of IREX grants was Andrei A. Kokoshin, an ISKAN national-security analyst who was a prominent advocate of "reasonable sufficient defense," eventually rising to ISKAN deputy director. Between 1976 and 1988, Kokoshin received nine IREX grants for studies in the United States on U.S. domestic and foreign policy, arms control, and international security. In the late 1980s, under the presidency of Boris Yeltsin, Kokoshin served as First Deputy Minister of Defense with primary responsibility for reform of the military-industrial complex, and Secretary of the Russian Security Council. As of this writing, he was a member of the State Duma and Director of the National Security Studies Center, Moscow State University.

11. For an account of Arbatov's meeting with Romney, see Yale Richmond, "A Tale of Two Georges," *Foreign Service Journal* 69 (October 1992): 38–40.

12. Voorhees, *Dialogue Sustained*, 69.

Given the Soviet obsession with secrecy, much of ISKAN's work was classified, but its researchers, nevertheless, had carte blanche for things Western. They were allowed to read things others could not. They were the first in the Soviet Union to have Xerox machines. They could call long distance when others had to book overseas calls twenty-four hours in advance. ISKAN also became known as the place in Moscow where visiting Americans could lecture and get a sounding on Soviet policy, present and future. By the late 1970s, its staff had grown to about four hundred, and IMEMO's to about eight hundred, and their doors were always open to visitors from the United States.[13]

Among the prominent Americans who visited ISKAN were Richard Nixon, Walter Mondale, Henry Kissinger, Brent Scowcroft, Zbigniew Brzezinski, Edward Kennedy, John Tower, John Kenneth Galbraith, Felix Rohatyn, and Madeleine Albright (as a Georgetown University professor). As Jerrold L. Schecter has critically written, "Their views were sampled and recorded for the benefit of the KGB and the Politburo," and "the institute . . . became the choke point for American access to the Soviet leadership."[14]

Visits to ISKAN by prominent and well-informed Americans, however, served to give its researchers an American perspective on many issues in U.S.-Soviet relations. As Raymond Garthoff has written:

> American academic and other visitors were not disciplined or instructed to carry an official "American line," but the variance in American viewpoints helped to create a more healthy awareness by Soviet "Americanists" of pluralism in American life, and in the long run a more accurate picture of America in Moscow was in our interest. Moreover, while Arbatov (who had ties to the KGB) and his institute served Soviet propaganda interests, through their publications as well as their contacts, they also gave increasingly realistic internal assessments of U.S. policy to the Soviet leadership as a result of their own growing sophistication. It was by no means a one-way street, and I believe on balance it was in the interests of better understanding and relations between the two countries.[15]

On his visits to the United States, Arbatov served as an active advocate of Soviet policies. As Henry Kissinger has described him:

> Arbatov was a faithful expounder of the Kremlin line, whom I had met at various international conferences on arms control when I was still a

---

13. English, *Russia and the Idea of the West*, 300 n. 195.
14. Jerrold L. Schecter, "Andropov's American Connection," in *Esquire*, May 1983, 106.
15. Raymond L. Garthoff, *A Journey Through the Cold War: A Memoir of Containment and Coexistence* (Washington, D.C.: Brookings Institution, 2001), 344.

professor. He knew much about America and was skillful in adjusting his arguments to the prevailing fashions. He was especially subtle in playing to the inexhaustible masochism of American intellectuals who took it as an article of faith that every difficulty in U.S.-Soviet relations had to be caused by American stupidity or intransigence. He was endlessly ingenious in demonstrating how American rebuffs were frustrating the peaceful, sensitive leaders in the Kremlin, who were being driven reluctantly by our inflexibility into conflicts that offended their inherently gentle natures.[16]

But Arbatov also had his critics within the Soviet system. Zbigniew Brzezinski, says that Soviet Ambassador Anatoly Dobrynin never lost his cool in discussions,

> . . . except—and invariably—whenever I suggested that Georgy Arbatov . . . was an influential Soviet figure. Dobrynin would become red in the face and vehemently inform me that Arbatov was a man of no standing and little influence—a creation of the American media.[17]

Much of Arbatov's effectiveness as a propagandist stemmed from his natural charm. As Robert Lundeen, an American participant in the Dartmouth Conference, has put it: "In a non-negotiating environment, when he didn't have to make a point, he charmed the socks off you. . . . We were having drinks before dinner and kind of talking about some of the issues which in presenting himself he was much more relaxed and thoughtful, not confrontational because he didn't have to impress anyone."[18]

Arbatov and his institute staffers also had their defenders in the United States, who cited long-range benefits from their meetings with Western experts. As Strobe Talbott explains, "They ended up absorbing a good deal about Western political institutions and values which they later put to use once perestroika was under way."[19] Arbatov also made the case, adds Talbott, that reform-minded academicians were preparing the way for eventual reform: "The level of thought developed in these 'oases' improved, enlivened, and modernized the intellectual atmosphere of our society and—this is the main thing—sowed seeds that sprouted many years later in the form of glasnost, perestroika, democratization, and new political thinking."[20] Indeed, after 1991, many of the ISKAN staffers came

---

16. Henry Kissinger, *The White House Years* (Boston: Little, Brown, 1979), 112.
17. Zbigniew Brzezinski, *Power and Principle: Memoirs of the National Security Adviser, 1977–1981* (New York: Farrar, Straus & Giroux, 1985), 153.
18. Robert Lundeen, quoted in Voorhees, *Dialogue Sustained*, 71.
19. Talbott, in Arbatov, *The System*, xv.
20. Arbatov, in *The System*, xii–xiii.

into the new Russian government, where their firsthand knowledge of the West gave them an advantage over others.

Arbatov eventually became a target of the Soviet military for his attacks on defense spending. In a speech to the Congress of People's Deputies in December 1989, he accused the Soviet military of being the main cause of the country's economic crisis, the stimulus for the Western military buildup, and the main impediment to perestroika.[21] "During discussion of prime minister Ryzhkov's budget," wrote Roald Sagdeev, "he [Arbatov] had attacked the military appropriations—and after the two-week session was over, he wrote scathing articles about the Soviet military-industrial complex and its insatiable appetite for money and resources."[22]

Much of Arbatov's attack on military spending was based on the research of scholars under his direction at ISKAN, and under Yakovlev's at IMEMO. Denied access to official Soviet military thinking and data, the scholars used their detailed knowledge of U.S. and NATO military affairs to develop practical proposals for a revised mission of Soviet military forces, including nuclear, and their downsizing under Gorbachev's "new thinking" and perestroika. At ISKAN, younger scholars, such as Andrei Kokoshin and Aleksei Vasiliev, were prominent in proposing new strategic concepts for the Soviet military. At IMEMO, Aleksei Arbatov (son of Georgi) introduced into Soviet military thinking Western concepts that, as William E. Odom has described them, "had been consistently rejected by the Soviet side during nearly two decades of arms control negotiations. Applying them to Soviet nuclear forces, Arbatov insisted that a 40–50 percent reduction in nuclear forces would leave an entirely adequate arsenal . . . and he called for a reconsideration of the ABM system around Moscow, permitted under the 1972 treaty, suggesting that it might be scrapped to save money."[23]

At IMEMO, Georgi Kunadze challenged the Soviet military by audaciously claiming that very few Soviet interests abroad, including the entire Third World, deserved to be defended by military means, and Soviet involvements there had created heavy economic burdens without any gains. If ideological objectives abroad were dropped, he added, the Soviet navy could be radically reduced in size. Kunadze's colleague at IMEMO, Sergei Blagovolin, agreed and charged that party leaders, once parity had been reached with the West, had continued needlessly to increase production of military hardware. Blagovolin also noted that territorial expansion did not necessarily increase state power, which now came from economic development based on trade and the introduction of new technologies.

21. The paragraphs here on rethinking Soviet military strategy are drawn from chapter 8 of William E. Odom, *The Collapse of the Soviet Military* (New Haven: Yale University Press, 1998).

22. Susan Eisenhower, *Breaking Free: A Memoir of Love and Revolution* (New York: Farrar, Straus & Giroux, 1995), 250.

23. Odom, *Collapse of the Soviet Military*, 182.

As Odom points out, the civilian analysts who proposed such major reductions in Soviet military forces did not appreciate the chaos that such reductions would bring to the military establishment.[24] Their proposals, however, demonstrate the extent to which institute scholars had been influenced by their exchanges and contacts with the West.[25]

Was ISKAN an adjunct of diplomatic and intelligence services as well as a research institute, as some have charged? While some Western observers acknowledge the professionalism of the staffers and their ability to influence the Soviet foreign policy establishment, others stress their propagandistic role. Morton Schwartz, a State Department analyst, has called the institute "a research adjunct of the Soviet foreign-policy apparatus."[26] Fritz Ermarth, a former CIA analyst who served on the National Security Council under Presidents Carter and Reagan, has called Arbatov an "old warhorse of Soviet propaganda."[27] Other Americans who dealt with Arbatov over the years say that after listening to him they could always tell which way the wind was blowing in the Kremlin.

A more positive view of the institute and other Soviet think tanks was held by Columbia University's Seweryn Bialer: "The role of these institutes in foreign policy-making is a subject of contention in the American academic and political community. They are not simply propaganda outlets to the West. They perform an important staff function for the leadership. They contribute to the Central Committee's evaluations of international events and trends. At the same time they provide an unofficial channel of communication to foreign political and scholarly communities."[28]

Such unofficial channels of communication were opened by Georgi Arbatov on his first visit to the United States in January 1969, a visit delayed by six months when the State Department had suggested that a visit so soon after the Soviet invasion of Czechoslovakia would not be appropriate.[29] On that maiden voyage, Arbatov made a courtesy call at the State Department and visited Harvard, MIT, Columbia, Berkeley, Stanford, the Rand Corporation, the Hoover Institution, and other U.S. centers of Soviet studies. He also met Averell and Pamela Harriman, with whom he was to maintain good relations for many years. In later visits, he

24. Ibid., 169–70.

25. For more on the role of the research institutes in defense reform, see Evangelista, *Unarmed Forces*, chap. 14.

26. Morton Schwartz, *Soviet Perceptions of the United States* (Berkeley and Los Angeles: University of California Press, 1978), 161.

27. Fritz W. Ermarth, "A Scandal, and then a Charade," *New York Times*, September 12, 1999.

28. Seweryn Bialer, *The Soviet Paradox: External Expansion, Internal Decline* (New York: Alfred A. Knopf, 1986), 294.

29. It fell to me, as Counselor for Press and Culture at the American Embassy, to inform Arbatov, in autumn 1968, that he would not receive a U.S. visa at that time.

met many prominent members of Congress, as well as political and business leaders, including Robert McNamara, David Packard, John McCloy, Cyrus Vance, David Rockefeller, Norton Simon, Charles "Tex" Thornton, and other public figures to whom he would have entrée over the following years. By 1990, he had made twenty-five visits to the United States.[30]

Was ISKAN infiltrated by the KGB as many Americans suspected? Citing U.S. intelligence sources, Jerrold Schecter has written that "about 15 percent [of ISKAN's personnel] have or have had an intelligence affiliation."[31] A long-time deputy director under Arbatov was Radomir G. Bogdanov, a KGB colonel and former KGB resident (station chief) in India. In his memoirs Arbatov acknowledges that "several of their [KGB] people worked at our institute" but adds that today [1991] "to my knowledge no one from the KGB is on the staff of the institute."[32]

Nevertheless, according to Christopher Andrew and Vasili Mitrokhin:

> The KGB's most successful strategy for cultivating American policy-makers was to use the prestigious academic cover of the Moscow Institute of the United States and Canada. The secret 1968 statute of the institute kept at the Centre authorized the KGB to task it to research aspects of the Main Adversary [the United States] which were of interest to it, to provide KGB officers with cover positions, to invite prominent American policy-makers and academics to Moscow and to undertake intelligence-related missions to the United States. Among the KGB's cover positions at the institute was that of deputy director, occupied by Colonel Radimir [sic] Bogdanov (codenamed VLADIMIROV), sometimes described behind his back as "the scholar in epaulets."[33]

The Reagan administration was ambivalent about Arbatov. In 1982, he was issued a visa to visit the United States, but the State Department shortened his stay to prevent his appearance on the Bill Moyers Show, and in 1983 he was given a visa with the condition that he have no contact with the media.[34] Moreover, as an indication of his disfavor with the administration, on one of Ronald Reagan's visits to Moscow, Arbatov was not invited to the American Embassy's reception for the president.[35]

Arbatov, however, claims that his institute was regarded as pro-American by many in the Soviet Communist Party, the military, and the government. And some Soviet

30. Alexander Rahr, A Biographical Directory of 100 Leading Soviet Officials (Boulder, Colo.: Westview Press, 1990), 17.

31. Schecter, "Andropov's American Connection," 107.

32. Arbatov, The System, 318.

33. Christopher Andrew and Vasili Mitrokhin, The Sword and the Shield: The Mitrokhin Archive and the Secret History of the KGB (New York: Basic Books, 1999), 211.

34. Ibid., 314.

35. Ibid., 321.

conservatives charged his institute with "Zionism," an indirect swipe at the ethnic origins of Arbatov and several of his researchers. In his memoirs, written after the collapse of communism, Arbatov says that he was a "rational believer" in the system: "I confess without hesitation that I was not a secret 'progressive' and 'reformer,' hiding my views in a closet and masquerading as a loyal Communist in front of others."[36]

Like many other institutes of the Soviet Academy, ISKAN was also a degree-granting institution, and many of its students were the sons of high Soviet officials, who upon graduation, went on to careers in the government, party, or diplomatic service. One such graduate was Igor Andropov, son of Yuri Andropov, the former KGB head and General Secretary of the Communist Party, and a patron of Arbatov. The Institute also developed a younger generation of specialists on the United States and provided them with opportunities for foreign travel and study. Many of them later went on to bigger jobs.

Vladimir Lukin, a young Soviet journalist in Prague who had protested the Soviet invasion of Czechoslovakia, found shelter in ISKAN for nearly two decades before becoming a prominent figure in the reform movement. Lukin also served as Russian ambassador to the United States from 1992 to 1995 and then as a deputy in the Duma, the lower house of parliament of the Russian Federation, and chair of its Committee on International Affairs. In April 1996, he was elected vice president of the Parliamentary Assembly of the Council of Europe and in February 2000, a deputy speaker of the Duma.

Another alumnus of Arbatov's Institute, and one of many who benefited from exchange visits to the United States, was Igor Ye. Malashenko, whom David Remnick has described as "a man of his time, skilled in the art of bureaucratic battles, interested in making money and a name for himself but, at the same time, linked to what remained of the liberal political forces.[37]

Malashenko was a researcher at ISKAN in the 1980s, and it was during those years that he came to the United States twice on ACLS grants to study the psychological aspects of nuclear deterrence doctrine and the relationship between American public opinion and U.S. military policy. In 1989, Malashenko moved up to the International Department of the Communist Party's Central Committee, where he worked for Aleksandr Yakovlev and served as deputy spokesman for Gorbachev. In 1991, he held several high positions in state television, where he became identified with liberal political forces, and in 1993 he became the director general of NTV (Independent Television), founded by oligarch Vladimir Gusinsky. Malashenko was also media adviser to Yeltsin in his 1996 election campaign.

ISKAN began as a Cold War institution and operated in that environment for many years. But while much of its work involved propaganda and reports prepared

36. Arbatov, *The System*, 37.
37. Remnick, *Resurrection*, 242.

for the state and party leadership, there was another, less noticeable, side of its work. According to Konstantine Tioussov, a research fellow at Samara State University who has written a critical study of the institute:

> Even though scholars were collected in the Institute for the purposes defined by the Party, the unique access to information, and extended research opportunities as compared to other Soviet scholarly institutions has made the Institute an important center of new ideas and concepts. These concepts were not necessarily propagated by the Institute's publications but still the scholarly community of the Institute became a medium in which a new generation of thinkers has been brought up.[38]

The institute, adds Tioussov, "played a very important role in establishing dialogue between the two superpowers on the peak of the Cold War. It also helped a great deal in educating the Soviet leadership about the West that helped mutual peaceful coexistence. The Institute played a crucial role in organization of summits and preparation of treaties on the arms reduction and disarmament."[39] That view is shared by U.S. political scientist Sarah E. Mendelson. When Gorbachev came to power, she writes, the researchers of the Soviet foreign policy institutes played a key role in helping shape the "new thinking" that emerged. They

> helped change the intellectual and political climate in which policy decisions were made. This change in climate only became dramatic once the specialists gained some access, whether direct or indirect, to members of the leadership favoring reform; the ideas espoused by specialists in the 1970s and early 1980s were used by the leadership to legitimize and guide controversial policy decisions of the mid and late 1980s. Without access to or salience for the leadership, the ideas would have existed only on the pages of journals and in the halls of the institutes.[40]

Scholars working in the institutes, writes Janice Stein, also had access to Western academics and their articles that critically analyzed both Soviet and American concepts of security: "From the late 1960s, academic specialists and journalists had come to know specialists in the Western European and U.S. arms control community, both through their work and personally. They met at Pugwash meetings, at

38. Konstantine Tioussov, "The Institute of the United States of America of the Russian Academy of Sciences" (master's thesis, Central European University, Budapest, 1997), 46–47.

39. Ibid., 47.

40. Sarah E. Mendelson, *Changing Course: Ideas, Politics, and the Soviet Withdrawal from Afghanistan* (Princeton: Princeton University Press, 1998), 89.

seminars organized by the American Academy of Arts and Sciences with the Soviet Academy of Sciences, at international scientific conferences, and through exchange programs."[41]

Whatever the role of ISKAN during the Cold War, its staffers, through their visits to the United States and their talks in Moscow with visiting Americans, developed a fondness for America and its people. As Pavel Palazchenko, Gorbachev's interpreter and foreign policy aide, has pointed out: "Most experts on the United States, regardless of differences of view on particular issues, seemed genuinely to like America and the Americans."[42]

That view is supported by Allen Kassof:

> We know in retrospect that many of the Soviet Americanists who came to do research on the United States as adversaries developed a very complex symbiotic relationship with their subjects. Beginning as analysts of American life, they gradually became supporters: the internal messengers of new conceptions of Soviet-American relations and, ultimately, spokesmen for alternatives. On the personal level, they developed significant friendships not only with their counterparts in the American sovietological community, who were their most readily accessible colleagues, but with a representative spectrum of American elites.[43]

Because of their travels and studies abroad, a generation of young scholars at the various institutes of the Soviet Academy—the *institutchiki,* as they were called—changed their views of the West. As Viktor Kremenyuk, a deputy director of ISKAN, has put it: "By the 1960s we had come a long way, but there was still far to go. We still didn't know the world. I remember my first trip to the U.S., and how quickly I realized that 90, maybe 99 percent of all that I had written was wrong. I'd read everything, we had facts and information, but we didn't yet *understand.*"[44]

Andrei Melville, another former scholar at ISKAN, confirms that he and his colleagues benefited enormously from their IREX grants:

> Actually, this was, at that time, practically the only way to get the opportunity to work in libraries, get books, information and—maybe even

---

41. Janice Gross Stein, "Political Learning by Doing," in Richard Ned Lebow and Thomas Risse-Kappen, eds., *International Relations Theory and the End of the Cold War* (New York: Columbia University Press, 1995), 241.

42. Pavel Palazchenko, *My Years with Gorbachev and Shevardnadze: The Memoir of a Soviet Interpreter* (University Park: Pennsylvania State University Press, 1997), 95.

43. Kassof, "Scholarly Exchanges," 270.

44. Viktor Kremenyuk, quoted in English, *Russia and the Idea of the West,* 75; emphasis in original.

more important—to meet peers, colleagues and "classics" in the field. A conference or a seminar could not have provided such opportunity. Another quite important aspect was to stay in U.S. universities alone (taking the conditions of the 1970s and 1980s)—i.e., without Big Brother's oversight. The educational, cultural, emotional, academic, etc. impact was enormous and I remain grateful to IREX.[45]

Arbatov retired in 1995 and was named honorary director of the institute he had led for twenty-eight years and which played a prominent role in U.S.-Soviet relations. He served as the Kremlin's eyes and ears for America, and his institute helped give the Soviet leadership a more realistic assessment of their "main adversary." From his many meetings with private Americans, he received information he could cross-check with what he was getting from administration sources. In return, for Americans, he was a good barometer of the atmosphere in the Kremlin. Many Americans who worked with Arbatov believe that he was a factor in improving relations with the United States. He tempered the views of the more ideological Soviets who had no experience in the West, and he often gave good advice to Americans on what to expect from the Soviet Union.

Something similar can be said of Yevgeni Primakov, whose resumé reads like a success story and belies the belief that a person of Jewish origin cannot rise to the top in Russia. Primakov began his career as an Arabist at Moscow's Institute of Oriental studies, and after graduation he went on to become, in succession, a radio and television journalist, *Pravda* correspondent in the Middle East, deputy director of IMEMO, director of the Moscow Institute of Oriental Studies, foreign policy adviser to Brezhnev, member of the Central Committee of the Communist Party and the Politburo under Gorbachev, special envoy to the Persian Gulf for Gorbachev, director of IMEMO, head of the Foreign Intelligence Service under Yeltsin, and foreign minister and prime minister of Russia, also under Yeltsin. Clearly a survivor, Primakov is known as an incorruptible loyalist, prepared to serve a succession of masters in the service of his country.

Although he eventually became head of foreign intelligence, Primakov made his career in journalism, academia, and the diplomatic service. He is believed, however, to have had a relationship with the KGB throughout the years, but who did not in the days when Soviet citizens who were authorized to deal with the world beyond Soviet borders also had to deal with the KGB? In fact, the future prime minister had to delay a visit to the United States in the 1970s while several U.S. government agencies deliberated over whether a U.S. visa for him should be authorized.

---

45. Andrei Melville, e-mail to author, January 13, 2001.

Americans who knew Primakov in his early years say that he was very partisan but not propagandistic, not as well liked by Americans as Arbatov, and less trusted by some. Primakov's frequent anti-American barbs gave an impression of disliking the United States but others who knew him well describe him as analytical, nonpolemical, and a fair defender of Russian interests. As a supporter of Russian national interests, Primakov believed that Russia served a positive and civilizing role in the Caucasus and Central Asia. He recognized that Russia had to change but he seemed to regard that change as a distasteful accommodation to reality. A pragmatist, his main interest appeared to be in maintaining Russia's status as a great power.

Since the Brezhnev years, Primakov has been close to the seats of Soviet power. As director of IMEMO he was a key adviser to Gorbachev and accompanied him to five U.S.-Soviet summits. Although not known as an Americanist, he made many visits to the United States under several of the exchange programs described in these pages. Starting in 1974, he was a Russian regular at the Dartmouth Conference for more than six years, and from 1982 to 1989, he cochaired its Regional Conflicts Task Force.

At Dartmouth meetings, Primakov was seen as a loyal member of the nomenklatura, but a long-time U.S. interpreter at Dartmouth notes that Primakov always gave a realistic analysis of the situation in the Soviet Union. As an intelligent and sophisticated observer of the international scene, he also brought home to Moscow from his U.S. visits his impressions of American strength and the urgent need for change in the Soviet Union. In trying to sell the Soviet leadership on the importance of improved relations with the United States, his intention was to strengthen the Soviet system, modernize and modify it in positive ways, liberalize its political and economic life, and make it more competitive with the United States. Like Gorbachev, he sought to reform the Soviet system, but also like Gorbachev, he was committed to it.

Primakov's reputation as a political outsider and incorruptible technocrat gained him popularity at home, which eventually led to his becoming prime minister. That popularity, despite his reputed KGB connections, even reached the United States. As a former American diplomat explains: "As Russian prime minister, Primakov was seen as something of a straight shooter. He held a weak hand but played it well, and seemed honest and straight-forward in his dealings with senior U.S. government counterparts, many of whom—sometimes to their surprise—ended up liking him."

In meetings with Americans, Primakov did not follow a strict party line but appeared to have a deep suspicion of the United States. With his access to KGB intelligence, he seemed, as one American has put it, "to see an American hiding behind every bush." Because his view of the United States was formed through the prism of Middle East politics, he also had a deep and abiding suspicion of the Arab-Israeli peace process, which he saw as threatening Russian interests.

There should be no illusions that Primakov was changed by his many visits to the United States. Nevertheless, to his meetings with Americans he brought many serious Soviet scholars to discuss serious issues, and he protected them if they got into trouble, which they did if they said or wrote something that Soviet higher-ups did not like.

As one American participant in a U.S.-Soviet forum has put it, "Arbatov would look for opportunities for cooperation, Primakov for opportunities where he could screw us." Both, however, were useful in keeping channels open, when U.S.-Soviet relations were bad as well as when they were good. Moreover, with both Arbatov and Primakov, Americans could be confident that what they said would get to Soviet policymakers.

8 | FORUMS ACROSS OCEANS

Arms control was, really, a coalition of doves in both camps against hawks. But only when they were in touch with one another could their full effectiveness be felt.

—JEREMY J. STONE, *Every Man Should Try*

Soviet think-tank staffers and scientists participated in several forums that provided an opportunity to meet and exchange views with American scholars, scientists, and public figures. There were a number of these, which have come to be called "transnational forums," four of which will be discussed here—Pugwash, the Dartmouth Conference, the U.S. United Nations Association (UNA-USA), and the meetings of the American Friends (Quakers).

The Soviets were regular participants in the Pugwash meetings, which as Arbatov notes, were particularly important in the 1960s and 1970s. Pugwash, writes Arbatov, "was our first course in Western thinking of security and disarmament."[1] Also useful, adds Arbatov, was the Dartmouth Conference, the U.S.-Soviet meetings begun by Norman Cousins and named after the site of the first conference: "The [Dartmouth] meetings were held even in the most difficult periods of Soviet-American relations, and they played a useful role. They seriously helped my institute, and me personally, to become familiar with various American points of view on extremely important questions of foreign, military, and economic policy, and they became valuable sources of our education in these areas."[2]

A similar series of meetings of the U.S. and Soviet United Nations Associations presented opportunities for additional contacts with a wider circle of American participants. Such meetings were especially useful to Soviet officials who worked on arms control. As Arbatov writes:

> People who worked in the Defense Ministry and the military-industrial complex (as well as the majority of Foreign Ministry officials and even academic experts) were intellectually unprepared for a dialogue with the Americans and for serious talks going beyond the bounds of political declarations. At first they could not properly grasp American concepts and terminology concerning strategic and disarmament issues. . . . Due

1. Arbatov, *The System*, 310.
2. Ibid.

to the [USA] institute's pioneering efforts, a new type of expert was created—the civilian expert on strategic-military, political-strategic, and
arms-control issues.[3]

Arbatov's recognition that Soviet disarmament experts were unprepared for a
dialogue with their American counterparts needs some explanation here. Not only
were the Soviets unprepared for serious and substantive talks with Americans, but
the two sides also spoke different languages with different vocabularies, and we
are not speaking here about differences between English and Russian. U.S. arms-
control experts had developed a new vocabulary to describe the situations they
faced in the nuclear age, and it was not until the Soviets had mastered that termi-
nology and become familiar with its usage, that the two sides could hold serious
talks. In this respect, the transnational forums discussed here, as well as many of
the exchanges conducted by IREX with various Soviet think tanks, helped prepare
the way for the U.S.-Soviet arms control agreements that followed, in which many
of those same Soviet experts played key roles.

If, as many claim, much of the U.S.-Soviet discord can be attributed to mis-
read signals and misinterpretations of intent, the transnational forums discussed
below played a major role in improving mutual understanding between the
superpowers.

Pugwash

Pugwash is an international movement, started in 1957, involving some of the most
famous men of learning and aiming to ensure that mankind will not destroy itself.
                              —JOSEPH ROTBLAT, *Scientists in the Quest for Peace*

The Pugwash Conferences on Science and World Security, one of the earliest and
longest-running forums involving citizens of the United States, the Soviet Union,
and several other countries, brought together prominent scientists and public figures concerned with reducing the danger of armed conflict and seeking cooperative solutions for global problems. Meeting as individuals rather than as
representatives of their governments or institutions, Pugwash participants
exchanged views and explored alternative approaches to arms control and tension
reduction with a candor, continuity, and flexibility seldom attained in East-West
discussions and negotiations. Yet, because of the stature of the participants in their
own countries—as science and arms control advisers to governments, key figures
in science and academia, and former and future holders of high government

3. Ibid., 174.

office—-their insights from the discussions penetrated quickly to high levels of official policymaking.[4]

The unique value of Pugwash was in providing a forum for informal talks at which proposals for negotiations between governments could be developed. As German scholar Bernd W. Kubbig describes it, Pugwash "offered an enduring and open organizational framework, even at a time when the dialogue between eastern and western governments was restricted to the exchange of mutual suspicions and propaganda. . . . Pugwash conferences kept open channels of communication at a time when the Soviet leadership was pursuing a policy of blocking official contacts during the Vietnam War."[5]

Pugwash had its origins in the Russell-Einstein Manifesto issued in 1955 by Bertrand Russell, the British mathematician-philosopher, and Albert Einstein, the American physicist, and cosigned by nine other prominent scientists, most of them Nobel laureates. The Manifesto called on scientists of all political persuasions to appraise the perils faced by humanity because of the H-bomb and proposed an agreement between East and West renouncing nuclear weapons. Two years later, the first meeting was held in Pugwash, a small Nova Scotian fishing village, the birthplace and summer home of Cleveland industrialist Cyrus Eaton, who funded the conferences in their early years. In attendance at Pugwash in 1957—only four years after the death of Stalin and in the same year that Soviet youth were meeting foreign youth in Moscow—were twenty-two eminent scientists—seven from the United States, three each from the Soviet Union and Japan, two each from the United Kingdom and Canada, and one each from Australia, Austria, China, France, and Poland. From its inception, the organizer, driving force, and secretary-general of Pugwash was Joseph Rotblat, a Polish-born British physicist who had worked on the U.S. Manhattan Project, which created the first atomic bomb.

That modest beginning was the start of a continuing series of meetings with a growing number and diversity of participants at locations in various parts of the world. By the summer of 1988 there had been 155 Pugwash conferences, symposia, and workshops, with a total attendance of some 10,000, including more than 300 Americans and 250 Soviets. The conferences, held annually, were usually attended by 100 to 250 people, and the more frequent workshops and symposia by 30 to 50.

The list of American participants reads like a Who's Who in science and public affairs, and includes, among others, Jerome Wiesner (later science adviser to

4. Data here on the Pugwash conferences have been drawn largely from two sources: (1) the Pugwash website (<http://www/pugwash.org>); and (2) author's interview with George Rathjens, Pugwash Secretary-General, Cambridge, Mass., May 4, 1999.

5. Bernd W. Kubbig, "Communicators in the Cold War: The Pugwash Conferences, the U.S.-Soviet Study Group and the ABM Treaty," PRIF Report No. 44, translated from the German by Gerard Holden (Frankfurt am Main: Peace Research Institute, 1996), 8.

President Kennedy), Bernard Feld, Jack Ruina, and George Rathjens of MIT; Paul Doty and Henry Kissinger of Harvard; Harrison Brown of the National Academy of Sciences; Eugene Rabinowitch of Illinois (also editor of the prestigious *Bulletin of the Atomic Scientists*); and Jeremy Stone of the Federation of American Scientists. As of this writing, the Pugwash meetings continue to be held.

The name Pugwash, however, as well as its funder Cyrus Eaton, created controversy. Eaton's political activities and pro-Soviet public statements—he received the Lenin Peace Prize in 1960—embroiled the conferences in controversy from the start, but efforts by U.S. scientists to change the name foundered on Soviet support for Eaton and the Pugwash name. The 1959 conference was the last held in Nova Scotia, and three years later, in London, the conferees decided to give the growing movement a formal name, the Pugwash Conferences on Science and World Affairs.

The conferences focused initially on the dangers posed by nuclear weapons; but as the movement grew, it took on such issues as disarmament, a nuclear test ban and freeze, international conflicts, European security measures, international scientific cooperation, and the banning of chemical and biological weapons. Funding in recent years has come from the MacArthur Foundation and Scandinavian governments.

Of prime importance was an adjunct of Pugwash, the Soviet-American Disarmament Study Group (SADS), which focused on arms control and nuclear-related issues, and served as a forum for informal discussions between leading U.S. and Soviet scientists and public figures. That bilateral forum held its first meeting in June 1964, with funding from the Ford Foundation, and met more than once a year from 1964 to 1975. It was administered on the U.S. side by the Cambridge-based American Academy of Arts and Sciences but was handled as a Pugwash activity on the Soviet side. Between Pugwash and SADS there was much overlap in participants and issues, and SADS came to be seen as an offshoot of the Pugwash movement.

SADS started small, with eight participants on each side, and grew to about twelve. The U.S. delegation, organized and chaired by Harvard biochemist Paul Doty, included, among others, Henry Kissinger of Harvard, Marshall Shulman of Columbia, Richard Garwin of IBM, Wolfgang Panofsky of Stanford, and Jack Ruina and George Rathjens of MIT. The Soviet delegation included several prominent nuclear physicists and other scientists, including, among others, Mikhail D. Million-shchikov, a vice president of the Soviet Academy of Sciences; Lev A. Artsimovich, who headed Soviet fusion research; Pyotr L. Kapitsa; and Aleksandr P. Vinogradov. The ubiquitous Georgi Arbatov later also became an active participant.

While the American participants represented only themselves, they kept the U.S. government fully informed of the talks, and although they did not seek instructions from Washington, they would meet with the secretaries of state and defense and the national security adviser before and after each meeting. The Soviet participants, by contrast, were government-appointed and had to follow a strict party line.

The question might therefore be asked, why did Western scientists agree to participate when they knew that their Soviet counterparts were "bound hand and foot by official instructions," as Soviet Pugwash interpreter A. D. Shveitser has put it in his memoirs? "The Western partners," answers Shveitser, "knew that their new ideas and new proposals would be reported to the Soviet government. It was particularly important during the Cold War when the official channels were sometimes blocked."[6]

Many of the nonofficial discussions between Americans and Soviets at Pugwash meetings led to talks and negotiations between the two governments. Pugwash initiatives, for example, helped lay the groundwork for the Limited Test Ban Treaty of 1963, the Non-Proliferation Treaty of 1968, the Anti-Ballistic Missile (ABM) Treaty of 1972, the Biological Weapons Convention of 1972, and the Chemical Weapons Convention of 1993. Pugwash workshops and study groups also served to bring together key analysts and policy advisers for in-depth discussions on such issues as chemical and biological weaponry, space weapons, conventional force reductions and restructuring, crisis control in the Third World, and problems of development and the environment.

The greatest successes of SADS were on strategic arms limitations and ABM systems. Through SADS, says Paul Doty, contacts between U.S. and Soviet scientists on technical matters laid the intellectual and political foundations for the policies that were codified by the United States and the USSR in the 1972 SALT I and ABM treaties.[7]

On strategic arms limitations and ABM, adds George Rathjens, "the Soviet position flipped 180 degrees" at a December 28–30, 1967, SADS meeting in Moscow, when for the first time, they signaled interest in limiting ABM defenses.[8] The importance of that meeting in influencing the still evolving Soviet government position on ABM was confirmed a few weeks later by Yuli Vorontsov of the Soviet Embassy in Washington in a conversation with Raymond Garthoff of the State Department.[9] The Soviet position was indeed evolving, and the Non-Proliferation Treaty was signed in July of the following year. Although further negotiations on strategic arms limitations and ABM defenses were delayed by the Soviet

6. A. D. Shveitser, *Glazami Perevodchika* (Moscow: Stella, 1996).

7. Paul Doty, in conversation with Loren G. Graham, in Graham, *What Have We Learned About Science and Technology from the Russian Experience?* (Stanford: Stanford University Press, 1998), 38.

8. George Rathjens, author's interview, Cambridge, Mass., May 4, 1999.

9. See Garthoff, *Journey Through the Cold War,* 218.

invasion of Czechoslovakia in August 1968, they were resumed with the election of Richard Nixon and the initiation of the policy of détente.

Actually, the December 1967 SADS meeting in Moscow was one in a series that took place over several years. Rathjens believes that the December 1967 meeting was particularly significant because it was at that meeting that the American participants got the distinct impression that their Soviet counterparts, namely Millionshchikov and Artsimovich, had come around to accepting the American view that the key to limiting the U.S.-Soviet arms race in strategic weaponry was in constraining the development and deployment of anti-ballistic missile defenses. Moreover, at that meeting, Millionshchikov informed Doty that they had gotten through with that viewpoint to the Soviet political leadership.[10] A reading of the minutes of that meeting shows how direct and uninhibited, as well as productive, the talks had become by that time.[11]

The Pugwash meetings also served as a forum for presenting to Soviet scientists U.S. concerns over human rights violations in the Soviet Union. At a 1968 meeting in Nice, France, for example, U.S. scientists presented to Soviet participants copies of Andrei Sakharov's essay, "Thoughts on Progress, Peaceful Coexistence, and Intellectual Freedom," which had been smuggled to the West and published in the *New York Times*.

As the agenda of Pugwash broadened, so did its cast of characters. Scientists predominated in the early years, but as security and other issues came to be discussed, social scientists and other public figures were invited to participate. On the U.S. side, Henry Kissinger, as a Harvard professor, attended six sessions, the first in 1967. A frequent Soviet participant, as noted above, was Georgi Arbatov, ISKAN director and adviser to five general secretaries from Brezhnev to Gorbachev. Yevgeni Primakov, a future Russian foreign minister and prime minister, was a Pugwash participant from 1974 to 1989 and served as cochair of its Regional Conflicts Task Force from 1982 to 1989.

What effect did Pugwash have on its Soviet participants? One answer has been given by Vitaly Goldansky, who attended several meetings: "I first went to the meeting in Munich in 1977, then Bulgaria in 1978 and Mexico in 1979. It was highly impressive . . . the foreign participants had such command of the scientific and political issues. I learned about non-proliferation, testing, and other matters. . . . It broadened my horizons in every way."[12] A broader Soviet view of Pugwash was provided by Mikhail Millionshchikov, chair of the Soviet Pugwash delegation. In a report to the ruling presidium of the Soviet Academy of Sciences in 1972 on the

10. George Rathjens, e-mail to author, July 5, 2001.

11. I am indebted here to Paul Doty for providing a copy of the minutes of the December 28–30, 1967, SADS meeting.

12. Viktor Goldansky, quoted in English, *Russia and the Idea of the West*, 151.

fifteenth anniversary of the Pugwash movement, Millionshchikov wrote: "In fifteen years the participants of this movement have examined many important proposals having substantial significance for the resolution of problems of disarmament and the achievement of a reduction in international tensions. Several of these proposals later became subject of examination at the government level and were used in working out international agreements and treaties."[13] Among the agreements listed by Millionshchikov were the nuclear nonproliferation treaty, the limited test ban treaty, international agreements banning the deployment of weapons of mass destruction on the ocean floor, the biological-weapons convention, the ABM Treaty, and SALT I. "Even accounting for hyperbole," comments Matthew Evangelista, "Millionshchikov's list of what he considers Pugwash's accomplishments is impressive."[14]

There was no hyperbole, however, in the award of the 1995 Nobel Peace Prize in two equal parts to British physicist Josef Rotblat, president and long-time secretary-general of the Pugwash Continuing Committee, and the Pugwash Conferences on Science and World Affairs. The award, said the Norwegian Nobel Committee, was made "for their efforts to diminish the part played by nuclear arms in international politics and in the longer run to eliminate such arms. . . . They have brought together scientists and decision-makers to collaborate across political divides on constructive proposals for reducing the nuclear threat."[15]

The Dartmouth Conference

Dartmouth was a conversation among leaders, people respected and trusted by their peers and by ministers, secretaries, presidents, and general secretaries. This respect and trust was the source of their influence—and the influence of Dartmouth—in both Washington and Moscow. . . . For the greater part of its existence, the people who came to the conferences could be characterized as influential, experienced, informed, and not involved in the day-to-day activities of formulating and implementing foreign policy.

—JAMES VOORHEES, *Dialogue Sustained*

The Dartmouth Conference, like Pugwash, had its origins in the Cold War. Contacts between the United States and the Soviet Union had been, at best, limited and sporadic. Suspicion ran high on both sides, fueled by the communist takeover in Eastern Europe, a standoff in Berlin, the Korean War, the Hungarian Revolution, the U-2 incident, and the resulting arms race. Into the breach came Dartmouth, an unofficial and continuing dialogue between Soviet and American

13. Mikhail Millionshchikov, quoted in Evangelista, *Unarmed Forces,* 146.
14. Ibid.
15. Norwegian Nobel Committee communiqué, October 13, 1995.

citizens in an effort to avert a nuclear holocaust. Seventeen plenary conferences were held, the first in 1960, the last in 1990, as well as scores of meetings of smaller task forces beginning in the mid-1970s. Funding came initially from the Ford Foundation and, beginning with the fifth conference, from the Johnson and Kettering Foundations.[16]

Norman Cousins, editor of the *Saturday Review of Literature*, had gone to the Soviet Union in 1959 under the cultural exchange agreement to lecture on American literature. After his return, Cousins met with President Eisenhower, who proposed a series of citizen meetings between the two countries. Eisenhower believed that private citizens who had the confidence of their governments could informally explore possibilities for reconciliation without committing the governments and leave the negotiation of formal agreements to the diplomats. The proposal was broached by Cousins to the Soviets, who responded favorably, and the first conference was held in 1960 at Dartmouth College, from which the series took its name.[17]

Cousins's objectives were to strengthen international organizations and law, and reduce the sovereignty of the nation state in order to foster cooperation and thereby minimize or end interstate conflict, all in the interest of a humanity threatened by nuclear holocaust. Our role, he wrote, is "to raise questions and seek answers that do not ordinarily come up in the official exchanges. We can speak and think in a larger context. We are not obligated to defend every action or decision that occurs on the official level. We can afford to think in terms of historical principle. We need not shrink from the moral issues that underlay the political problems of confrontation."[18]

The stated objective may have been to hold a candid discussion and establish a personal relationship among the participants, but Dartmouth was also used by the two governments to send signals and informally broach new proposals. The conferences, therefore, took place with the encouragement and cooperation of the U.S. and Soviet governments, and on the U.S. side with the express approval of the State Department. Such approval helped to ensure that the deliberations would be taken seriously by both governments.

As Harold H. Saunders, a former Assistant Secretary of State and long-time participant in the Dartmouth Conference, has described it: "The Dartmouth Conference . . . is formally understood on both sides as a dialogue among private citizens,

16. For this discussion of Dartmouth, the author has drawn from Voorhees, *Dialogue Sustained*, and James Voorhees, "The Dartmouth Conference: The Influence of a Transnational Community on U.S.-Soviet Relations, 1960–1991" (paper presented at the thirty-ninth annual convention of the International Studies Association, Minneapolis, March 17–21, 1998).

17. For details of Eisenhower's proposal, see Norman Cousins, *The Pathology of Power* (New York: W. W. Norton, 1987), 74–75.

18. Norman Cousins, quoted in Voorhees, *Dialogue Sustained*, 185.

although individuals in both groups are known to have greater or lesser contact with their own governments. During the talks, a precise informal effort is made on both sides to understand as fully as possible who has what contact and influence with his or her government, and conference leaders report fully to their governments."[19] Before each conference, U.S. delegations were briefed by the State Department on the current state of U.S.-Soviet relations, and after the meetings U.S. delegates briefed the Department. Through this procedure, the deliberations of the Conferences could be used to send signals of U.S. intentions to the highest levels of the Soviet government and Communist Party. In turn, the reactions of the Soviet participants at Dartmouth often indicated official Soviet reaction to the American trial balloons.[20]

As James Voorhees, a historian of the Dartmouth Conference describes it:

> The Dartmouth Conference was also a conduit for information from one state to the other. This was, in fact, an important function of the conference, recognized by the American and Soviet governments. They used participants in the conference as a way of transmitting information about their positions to the other state's policy-makers, either as a way of making those statements deniable or as a way of increasing their credibility by sending the transmission through a trusted source.[21]

Subjects discussed in the early conferences included, among others, U.S.-Soviet relations, arms control and disarmament, the United Nations, cultural and scientific exchanges, cooperative projects, and U.S.-Soviet trade. Subjects added in later conferences included Vietnam, the Middle East, European security, the environment, Africa, Afghanistan, regional conflicts, human rights, China, and Latin America.

Semantics was one of the first stumbling blocks for the conferees, as it was in many other early U.S.-Soviet encounters. As explained by Alice Bobrysheva, a Soviet interpreter at the first and several subsequent conferences, "Words such as freedom, revolution, the people, intervention, imperialism, and peace had different and sometimes even opposite meanings when spoken by Russians and Americans."[22] Human relations, however, overcame semantics, continued Bobrysheva:

19. Harold H. Saunders, "When Citizens Talk: A Look at Nonofficial Dialogue in Relations Between Nations," *Kettering Review* 2 (summer 1984): 50.

20. As a Soviet diplomat once advised the author, new proposals should always be floated in advance with Russian diplomats, officials, or public figures; if a proposal is presented without adequate preparation, Moscow will have to study it in depth, and that will only delay the negotiation.

21. Voorhees, "The Dartmouth Conference," 6.

22. Alice Bobrysheva, "Thanks for the Memories: My Years with the Dartmouth Conference" (an unpublished paper prepared for the Kettering Foundation, 1993).

After a few sessions, the participants on both sides, much to their surprise, began discovering human beings sitting across the table in what previously they regarded mostly as stereotypes. This process of coming together was greatly enhanced by having the conference, not in Washington or New York, but in a small town, actually, a college campus, away from the everyday responsibilities and commitments for the American participants, and big city distractions and opportunity to consult official Soviet representatives on your every step, for the Soviet group. . . . Most vivid in my memory are the hours after dinner we spent together in a cozy sitting room with a fire burning hospitably in the fireplace, Americans and Soviets sitting together in small groups in old-fashioned armchairs and couches talking comfortably with each other. Somebody would be playing the piano. Mostly it would be Norman Cousins, who played like a professional musician.[23]

In such settings, the Soviets were more forthcoming in their conversations, both at the conference table and in the informal conversations which followed. Ambassador George F. Kennan remarked that not until he came to the Dartmouth campus for the first conference in 1960 was he able to have the kind of full and direct exchange of intellectual substance with Russians that he had tried in vain to achieve in a quarter of a century of work on Soviet affairs.[24]

The meetings were successful, explained Cousins, "not in terms of agreements actually reached but in terms of the ability to clarify opposing positions, to submit to rules of order in debate, to subject facts to cross-examination, and to develop personal relationships that could be fruitful beyond the conference table."[25]

Another explanation for Dartmouth's success, particularly in later years, lies in the continuity of its membership, both American and Soviet. Knowing each other and being familiar with their views made it easier for participants to dispense with polemics and get to work. This was especially true for the Russians, who feel more comfortable in the company of familiar faces.

With few exceptions, the American participants at the Dartmouth Conference were not from the executive branch of government, the Soviet participants were not from the Foreign Ministry. This also made it easier to discuss issues of contention between the two governments.

Americans at Dartmouth represented a broad spectrum of U.S. public life, including academics, scientists, business people, and foundation officials, as well as persons who had formerly served in government or soon would. Some attended

23. Ibid.
24. Norman Cousins, "Experiment at Andover," *Saturday Review of Literature*, November 10, 1962, 24.
25. Ibid.

one or two sessions but others became mainstays of the conferences. Among the principal American participants over the years were David Rockefeller, Paul Doty, Arthur Larson, Philip Mosely, Norman Cousins, Marshall Shulman, John Kenneth Galbraith, Charles W. Yost, Landrum Bolling, Zbigniew Brzezinski, Seweryn Bialer, Antonia H. Chayes, Brent Scowcroft, Thomas E. Gouttierre, John Neumann, Susan Purcell, Arnold Horelick, Harold Saunders, John Stremlau, Helen Kitchen, David Mathews, and Philip Stewart, as well as a number of senators and congressional representatives. Other luminaries who attended some of the sessions include Henry Kissinger, Madeleine Albright, and Richard Holbrooke.

The Soviet participants came from a much narrower segment of society—the academic think tanks, various government agencies, the Communist Party, and journalism. Regulars included Georgi Arbatov, Andrei A. Kokoshin, Andrei V. Kortunov, Mikhail A. Milstein, Nikolai Mostovets, Boris Polevoi, Yevgeni Primakov, Roald Z. Sagdeev, Yuri Zhukov, and Vitaly Zhurkin. Many of the Soviet participants had access to the highest levels of Soviet power, and several of them attended the Reagan-Gorbachev summit at Reykjavik, which came close to reaching an agreement on eliminating all nuclear weapons.

In contrast to Pugwash, Dartmouth sought no publicity, and its deliberations were confidential and off-the-record, two factors which facilitated a more frank and open discussion. When transcripts of the sessions were made, names were not attached to individual statements, and participants were identified only as "Soviet Speaker A" or "American Speaker B." Moreover, many of the participants on both sides attended successive conferences that discussed the same or related subjects, a factor of great importance to Russians, who, as noted above, are more comfortable with people they know and trust from previous meetings. Continuity and frequency of participation were important factors in Dartmouth's success, as confirmed by Aleksandr Kislov, a Middle East expert from ISKAN: "The more we meet, the more easy it is to discuss the most difficult and delicate issues. If we meet only once in two or three years, we, in effect, have really very little contact and, therefore, have difficulty in maintaining the personal confidence needed for frank discussions."[26] As an example on the U.S. side, David Rockefeller attended the third conference in 1962 and all others but the last, held in Leningrad in 1990.

A crucial test for the Dartmouth Conference came at the third meeting, held at Philips Academy in Andover, Massachusetts, October 21–27, 1962. The meeting took place at the time of the Cuban Missile Crisis, and both delegations watched President Kennedy's TV broadcast in which he announced a blockade of Cuba to force the withdrawal of the Soviet missiles being installed there and prevent the arrival of additional missiles, which were already on their way. The Soviet delegation was

---

26. Aleksandr Kislov, quoted in Voorhees, *Dialogue Sustained,* 141.

split on whether to continue the conference, and they telephoned Ambassador Dobrynin in Washington for instructions. The ambassador advised them to continue the conference unless the Americans chose to end it, which they did not. A sharp debate followed, with each delegation defending its government's actions, but in that debate, wrote Cousins, rapport among the participants grew, and a new spirit of Dartmouth was forged: "There was no awkwardness in or strain in raising any question, however severe, or in venturing any response, however pointed. It was possible to be forthright without being caustic, impassioned without being abusive, severe without being cutting. You could disagree and still retain your respect for the person you were disagreeing with."[27]

While no agreements were reached, some of the ideas and proposals discussed at the conferences were accepted later by the Soviets. In 1982, at a Dartmouth task force on regional conflicts, Vitaly Zhurkin admitted that what happened in the Third World—in Angola, Afghanistan, and elsewhere—influenced the U.S.-Soviet relationship. As Harold Saunders, a key Dartmouth participant in the 1980s has described it, "In more than ten years of dialogue, no Soviet had openly made such an admission, in spite of both the evidence and endless American attempts to establish that such a relationship exists as a matter of fact, not rhetoric."[28]

Dartmouth also played a role in the signing of the Limited Test Ban Treaty, the first major U.S.-Soviet arms control agreement that banned nuclear tests in the atmosphere, underwater, and in outer space. Because of the trust that Cousins had built with Soviet participants at Dartmouth, he was used as an intermediary in April 1963 between President Kennedy and Premier Khrushchev on two important issues related to the treaty—he was able to reconfirm U.S. interest in having such a treaty, and he cleared up a major misunderstanding on the number of on-site inspections required by the United States. Those clarifications cleared the way for negotiation of the treaty, which was signed on August 5, 1963.[29]

Dartmouth also served an educational function for the Soviets, as Voorhees explains: "Until the 1980s almost all of the arms control experts in the Soviet Union remained in the military. . . . The ignorance of even basic technical information among the civilians had been clear to those involved in negotiations over SALT I."[30] The Soviets at Dartmouth had read the American literature on arms control but were poorly informed on Soviet programs and weapons. That changed as contacts in transnational forums and exchanges expanded and a new

27. Cousins, "Experiment at Andover," 25.

28. Harold Saunders, quoted by Voorhees, *Dialogue Sustained*, 151.

29. For Cousins's role in the Limited Test Ban Treaty, see Norman Cousins, *The Improbable Triumvirate: John F. Kennedy, Pope John, Nikita Khrushchev* (New York: W. W. Norton, 1972), 111–13; Evangelista, *Unarmed Forces*, 80, 84–85; Voorhees, *Dialogue Sustained*, 61–65; and Voorhees, "The Dartmouth Conference," 21–22.

30. Voorhees, *Dialogue Sustained*, 116.

generation of younger analysts came on the scene, among them Aleksei Arbatov, Andrei Kokoshin, and Andrei Kortunov. Much time was also spent on explaining U.S. society, the role of public opinion, civic and voluntary organizations, and the press, all of which was new to the Soviets.

A further example of how Dartmouth helped to change Soviet views over the years is given by Voorhees. In a January 1989 task force on arms control and political relations, a representative of the Soviet Foreign Ministry made a remarkable statement: "The fundamental question at this point in history is whether humanity can survive." As Voorhees observes, such a statement could have come from Norman Cousins at the first Dartmouth conference in 1960.[31]

The United Nations Association

A similar series of bilateral meetings with the Soviet Union was conducted by the United Nations Association of the United States of America (UNA-USA) from 1960 to 1993. While Dartmouth focused mainly on bilateral issues, UNA-USA's agenda had a more global orientation and emphasized international issues, including, among others, the environment, nonproliferation of nuclear weapons, European security, conventional-arms transfers, and the United Nations. Funding on the U.S. side came from the Carnegie, Ford, MacArthur, and Rockefeller foundations.

The nominal Soviet partner was the Soviet UNA but since that organization was under the Soviet Peace Committee, the Committee became the real partner. That proved to be an advantage, since the Peace Committee could bring to the meetings people from other Soviet institutions, thus avoiding the jurisdictional disputes that plagued so many U.S.-Soviet exchanges. The Committee thereby served as an umbrella for a broader exchange by bringing in experts from government ministries and agencies as well as the Soviet General Staff, who were difficult for Americans to contact in those years. And after the formal meetings, the Committee would arrange for the visiting Americans to meet with people in government ministries and the Party Central Committee.

There was often an overlap between American participants at the UNA-USA and Dartmouth meetings. The UNA-USA participants included such prominent persons as Elliot Richardson, John Tower, Brent Scowcroft, Cyrus Vance, Marshall Shulman, Frank Carlucci, Madeleine Albright, Hodding Carter III, Helmut Sonnenfeldt, Leon Furth, and James Rubin, some of whom also attended the Dartmouth conferences. As that stellar list indicates, a strong effort was made for balance in the delegations between Republicans and Democrats; Republican William Scranton, for example, headed several delegations. And, like Dartmouth,

31. Ibid., 235.

UNA-USA delegations received briefings in Washington, often at the cabinet level, before they met with the Soviets, and were debriefed by the administration after their meetings.

On the Soviet side were people of comparable stature. Some were the so-called American handlers, Russians who were authorized to deal with Americans and who showed up repeatedly at various U.S.-Soviet forums. Others, however, had never before met an American, and as the seminars progressed, new and younger faces began to appear. Among the more prominent Soviet participants and their future positions were Aleksandr N. Yakovlev (Politburo member), Andrei Kozyrev (foreign minister), Vladimir Lukin (ambassador to the United States), Sergei Lavrov (ambassador to the United Nations), Vladimir Petrovsky (deputy foreign minister), Vladimir Rakhmanin (Foreign Ministry spokesman), Roald Sagdeev (space scientist), and Igor Malashenko (ISKAN and Central Committee staffer). Yevgeni Primakov and Georgi Arbatov usually headed the Soviet delegations, accompanied at times by Arbatov's deputy, Vitaly Zhurkin, and staffers from IMEMO and ISKAN.

The two sides discussed issues that were not yet on the official agenda between the two governments but were soon to be. The Soviets knew that people on the U.S. side would someday return to government and be among the decision makers, and the Americans knew that their views would be presented to high Soviet officials. In this manner, the meetings were used by both sides to raise trial balloons on future policies of the two governments.

The first focus of UNA in the late 1960s was on environmental issues, a growing concern in both countries and a relatively noncontroversial subject in the spectrum of U.S.-Soviet relations. The discussions, which began in 1969, helped prepare the way for the signing on May 23, 1972, of the U.S.-USSR Agreement on Cooperation in the Field of Environmental Protection, the first of eleven agreements for cooperation in various fields of science and technology that were signed during the early years of the first Nixon administration.

A second focus was on nuclear nonproliferation. A joint paper on the need for nonproliferation prepared by the two UNA delegations laid the groundwork for the intergovernmental negotiations that followed and the signing, on July 1, 1968, of the U.S.-Soviet Agreement on Nuclear Non-Proliferation.

Conventional arms transfers (CAT) was another subject for which a special UNA panel was created. The Soviets had not previously studied arms transfer, and what they heard from the American panelists was completely new to them and resulted in their initiating studies of their own at ISKAN and IMEMO. Among the Soviet panelists were Andrei Kozyrev and Vladimir Petrovsky, who both became strong supporters of U.S.-Soviet arms control and nonproliferation efforts.

When the Carter administration came into office in 1977, seven members of the CAT panel joined it, including Cyrus Vance, who became secretary of state, and

Paul Warnke, director of the Arms Control and Disarmament Agency (ACDA) and chief U.S. negotiator at the Strategic Arms Limitation Talks (SALT). At talks with the Soviet Union on CAT in 1977 and 1978, the administration made several proposals that had originated with UNA-USA, but the talks were terminated when they did not lead to significant results.

Another service provided by UNA-USA was to bring high-level Soviet delegations to the United States after presidential elections to acquaint them with the politics and personalities of the new administration. One such delegation came in November 1976 to learn about the Carter administration's positions, and another in November 1980 after Reagan was elected. Like many foreign observers, the Soviets were apprehensive about new U.S. administrations and the changes they might bring, and such briefings served to reduce some of the uncertainty they had about U.S. intentions and policies every four years, a problem encountered by many other countries as well.

A panel on economic issues helped to get the Soviets to think more about their role in the world economy. Among the subjects discussed were international trade organizations, monetary systems, energy markets, and the role of Soviet Union in the global economy. The U.S. delegation was headed for a time by Andrew Trowbridge, head of the National Association of Manufacturers and former commerce secretary. Other U.S. participants included Robert Roosa (Brown Brothers Harriman), Michael Blumenthal (treasury secretary in the Carter administration), Marshall Shulman (Columbia University), Marshall Goldman (Harvard Russian Research Center), and Robert Clymer (*New York Times*).

The UNA seminars developed a cadre of people on both sides who saw issues in the same way and understood what the other side was saying. The two sides often produced parallel reports that often converged in their conclusions. Participants also developed personal relationships during their three-day meetings and put each side in touch with people on the other side who were making decisions. For the Russians, meeting and talking with Americans became normal, and with time the quality of their written and spoken presentations improved. Earlier meetings had usually opened with recriminations on both sides, but after a while the Russians and Americans stopped trying to score points and settled down to achieving something. The Americans, however, recognized that when some Russians spoke, they were speaking for the government, while others were merely spreading disinformation. Nevertheless, a good working relationship developed, and when the Russians said they would do something, they did it. If they could not, they would say so.

UNA-USA inputs at times reached the highest levels of the Soviet government. Shortly after Gorbachev addressed the United Nations General Assembly on December 7, 1988, with a speech that signaled a new Soviet approach to foreign relations, a high-level Soviet official told an American UNA-USA delegate that he had drafted the Gorbachev speech and had drawn heavily on a paper that the American had prepared several months earlier.

U.S. contributions at the seminars also had a bearing on Soviet internal debates. The Soviets would suggest topics in which they were interested so they could use the American papers as arguments for or against a particular position of their own government. On one occasion, for example, the Soviets asked the Americans to bring scholarly papers showing that there were no peaceful uses for nuclear explosions. On another occasion, they asked the U.S. side to prepare a position paper on changing the flow of Siberian Rivers, a subject of intense debate within the Soviet Union at the time. Soviet scientists themselves could not write such a paper, but they could show the paper to their political leaders and say, "Here is the American position." In such a manner, and in many other similar cases, the U.S. side was able to make significant inputs into Soviet decision making.

When the Soviets came to the United States, after their formal sessions UNA-USA took them for a week to other cities where they stayed with UNA-USA members in their homes, not only to save money but also to see American home life firsthand. On those visits, they exchanged views with local people, were interviewed, and began to see the United States as not just Washington and New York. The Russians, in turn, took the Americans to Kiev, Minsk, Leningrad, and Novgorod, and after meetings, the Russians would arrange two days of meetings with high officials and decision makers. Such meetings also served to give the Soviet participants contacts with high-level people in their own government which they otherwise might not have.

When, after the breakup of the Soviet Union, the newly independent states of Central Asia became members of the United Nations, UNA-USA played an important role in briefing their delegations on the workings of the United Nations. The briefings were especially important because, with the predominance of Russians in Soviet delegations to the UN, the new Central Asian states had little experience in international affairs.

The Quakers and "Friendly" Assistance

For decades, the AFSC [American Friends Service Committee] has worked to maintain a dialogue with Soviet officials and people through reciprocal seminars, high school teacher exchanges, and a work-study program for youth leaders. Many who participated in these programs in the 50's and 60's were deeply affected by them. Many of these people are now in positions of some influence in their respective countries.

—AFSC REPORT, *The Dialogue Continues with the Soviets*

Of all the transnational exchanges with the Russians, the Quakers (Society of Friends) get the prize for longevity.[32] Quaker contacts with the Russians date from the seventeenth century, when English "Friends," as they are more correctly called, traveled to Russia to appeal for better treatment for the peasants. This connection received a new impetus when, as noted earlier in these pages, Tsar Peter the Great arrived in London in 1697 on his travels through Western Europe. While in London, Peter attended several Friends meetings and spent many hours in conversation with a Quaker, William Penn, the same William Penn who later made a name for himself in North America.

In the eighteenth century, an English Quaker physician, Thomas Dimsdale, visited Russia at the invitation of Catherine the Great to inoculate Russians, including the *tsarina* herself, against smallpox. The Friends' contacts with Russia continued in 1818 when an English Friend, Daniel Wheeler, went to Russia with his own and two other farmer families in response to a request from Tsar Alexander I for help in reclaiming the marshes around St. Petersburg. It was an early instance of Western technical assistance to Russia. By 1819, Quaker-reclaimed land was producing healthy crops of vegetables, grain, and grass, and by 1826 the reclamation project had been completed. During their years in Russia, Daniel Wheeler and his fellow Friends had drained some 100,000 acres of marshland and rid St. Petersburg of the scourge of its toxic miasma.

During the Crimean War, Quakers provided relief to victims of the war they had tried to prevent. In the famine which followed World War I, large-scale American and British Quaker relief helped to feed Russia and, after the war, to reduce the incidence of typhus, malaria, and cholera. A Quaker center was maintained in Moscow until 1931 when the last staffer there was given ten days to leave the Soviet Union. In 1948, Quakers provided streptomycin to counter a massive epidemic in the Soviet Union.

In 1955, two years after the death of Stalin, the AFSC invited the Soviet Union to participate in its semi-annual Conferences for Diplomats in Europe and its International Student Seminars in Europe. In 1960 the AFSC also initiated a series of reciprocal seminars for young leaders with the Soviet Union's Committee of Youth Organizations. Also in 1960, the AFSC embarked on three long-term reciprocal exchanges with the Soviets—a secondary-school teacher exchange, a continuation of its youth leader exchange, and reciprocal seminars for academic and professional leaders. The latter seminars, alternating between the two countries, brought

32. For Quaker exchanges with Russia the author is indebted to Laurama Pixton, formerly with the American Friends Service Committee, Everett Mendelsohn, of Harvard University, and William B. Edgerton, "Adventures of an American Slavist in Soviet Russia," in Marietta Omarovna Chudakova, ed., *Tynyanovskie Chteniya* (Riga: Znayete; Moscow: Imprint, 1994).

together eight Americans and eight Soviets for a week of dialogue and a week of travel and meetings in the host country to discuss such issues as arms control and disarmament, the Arab-Israeli dispute, China and Southeast Asia, U.S.-Soviet relations and the Third World, and the role of the individual in public and political life of the two countries. Other AFSC initiatives included reciprocal exchanges of disarmament specialists and the hosting of various Soviet visits to the United States.

Several factors contributed to the success of AFSC efforts to promote a dialogue. The Quaker exchanges were continuous, regardless of the international political climate; they were credible, since they promoted no ideological line; and they were confidential, in that the Quakers reported on the substance of the discussions but did not mention the names of participants.

Quakers are few in the world but they often make an impact in small but important ways. Their Soviet programs were not deliberately aimed at westernizing the Russians—although they helped do so—but simply at normalizing relations between two countries with opposing ideologies.

9 | OTHER NGO EXCHANGES

Visiting the Soviet Union tranquilized the hawks. They saw, immediately, a totally unexpected third-world poverty and longstanding, deeply felt Russian fear of war. At the same time, visiting the Soviet Union disabused the doves. Nothing about the undemocratic and totalitarian way in which Russia operated could do anything but stir the apprehensions of dovish visitors.

—JEREMY J. STONE, *Every Man Should Try*

The U.S. government was the major sponsor of exchanges with the Soviet Union, but scores of nongovernmental organizations (NGOs) also participated, some with and others without financial support from the U.S. government. Among them were the Alley Theater (Houston), American Bar Association, American College of Cardiology, American Conservatory Theater (San Francisco), American Council of Teachers of Russian, American Council of Young Political Leaders (ACYPL), American Economic Association, American Field Service, AFSC, American Library Association, Chautauqua Institution, Communication Association of America, Esalen Institute, Eugene O'Neill Theater Center, Guthrie Theater (Minneapolis), Institute for Soviet-American Relations, the U.S. Center of the International Theater Institute, League of Women Voters, National 4-H Council, Metropolitan Museum of Art, National Gallery of Art, Smithsonian Institution, National Governors Association, Salzburg Seminar in American Studies, Opera Company of Boston, Sister Cities International, U.S. Conference of Mayors, YMCA, and many American universities, colleges, and sports associations.

These and other NGOs brought to the United States a wide range of Soviets, including, among many others, mayors of major cities, prime ministers of republics, members of parliament, leaders of women's organizations, university presidents, journalists, librarians, theater directors, lawyers and judges, teachers, and young political leaders. A few of those reciprocal exchanges are described here.

Young Political Leaders

The Komsomol, the Young Communist League, was the first official organization to be infected with the spirit of change.

—JONATHAN STEELE, *Eternal Russia*

The American Council of Young Political Leaders (ACYPL), which represents young Democrats and young Republicans, began an exchange in 1971 with the Committee of Youth Organizations (CYO), which represented the Komsomol, the youth organization of the Communist Party and the stepping-stone to Party and government positions. Supported by grants from the State Department, USIA, and corporate funding, the exchange was sustained through the demise of the Soviet Union and continues today with the Russian Federation and other independent states of the former Soviet Union.

Each exchange consisted of a five-day seminar with young (under forty-one) political leaders of the two countries discussing—actually debating—domestic and foreign policy issues, followed by a study tour of one to two weeks in the host country, including, for the Soviets, stays in American homes. The CYO, as host, emphasized showing the visiting Americans how young people lived, were educated, and grew up in the Soviet Union; the ACYPL, as host, concentrated on U.S. politics and the American way of life. Through those visits, a generation of future political leaders gained firsthand experience in the other country that served most of them well in their future careers. As one American delegate reported after a seminar in the Soviet Union, the conservatives in the U.S. delegation found that they had more in common with the Soviets than they had anticipated, while the liberals discovered that they had less.

On the U.S. side, participants included federal legislators; officials at the national, state, and local levels; state legislators; and political journalists. Among the more prominent participants (and their future positions) were Senator Richard J. Durbin; Congressional representatives Steny Hoyer, Wyche Fowler, Don Ritter, Dana Rohrabacher, Curt Weldon, Gerald C. Weller, and Michael Wise; Governors George F. Allen (Virginia), Robert A. Taft (Ohio), Donald K. Sundquist (Tennessee), and Winthrop Rockefeller (Arkansas); Mayor Michael R. White (Cleveland); Martin Anderson (Hoover Institution); Bernard W. Aronson (assistant secretary of state), Patrick J. Buchanan (candidate for president), Hodding Carter III (State Department spokesman and president, Knight Foundation), Frank Fahrenkopf (chair, Republican National Committee), Edwin J. Feulner (president, Heritage Foundation), M. Peter McPherson (president, Michigan State University), R. Spencer Oliver (director, OSCE Parliamentary Assembly), and Olin Robinson (president, Middlebury College).

Soviet participants were mostly from the Komsomol, the media, scholarly institutes, and industrial and agricultural enterprises, with an occasional representative of the arts and letters. They are more difficult to trace in the post-Soviet period, but among those who are known to have achieved prominence are Geydar Aliyev (president of Azerbaijan), Aleksei G. Arbatov (deputy head, Duma Defense Committee), Tedo Z. Dzhaparidze (Georgian ambassador to the United States),

Andrei A. Kokoshin (deputy minister of defense under Yeltsin), Andrei V. Kortunov (president, Moscow Public Science Foundation), Andrei Y. Melville (Moscow State Institute of International Relations), Aleksandr Zorin (journalist), and Sergei Karaganov (foreign policy adviser to Yeltsin, and chair, Council on Foreign and Defense Policy). Another alumnus of the exchange is Gennadi Yanaev, who signed the first exchange agreement with the ACYPL and rose to become a vice president of the Soviet Union, a leader of the unsuccessful August 1991 coup against Gorbachev, and president of the Soviet Union for three days until the coup failed.

What did the young Komsomols learn from their visits to the United States? As R. Spencer Oliver, a former ACYPL executive director, tells it: "The moment of cumulative impact on the Soviets occurs when they no longer argue about the merits and demerits of the two societies. This usually happens near the end of the visit when they fall silent, then offer a comment about 'what a wonderful country the United States is,' or 'how lucky Americans are to live as well as they do.'"[1]

"The main contribution of the exchanges to the Soviet participants," says Hodding Carter III, the former State Department spokesman and participant in several of the exchanges, "was to hasten the deterioration of their faith in the regime they served."

> We showed them everything, from slums to palaces. They saw a large number of places and interacted, if only superficially, with a mixed bag of Americans. They witnessed firsthand our inability to present a united front; they heard our disagreements, often as vehement as those we had with them. And products though they were of the system that had rewarded them with those coveted slots on the exchange delegations, they had to come away privately shaken by the disconnect between the reality of life in the Soviet Union and the reality of life in the United States. On this, I do not believe I am being naive.

> Some of them were such princes of communism that they were more than able to deal with cognitive dissonance. But even the most orthodox could not screen out all of the evidence before their eyes. And when I saw that the ostensible leader of the anti-Gorbachev coup was our old, cynical apparatchik friend, the former CYO head who initiated the first exchange agreement, I knew the counter-revolution was going to be a failure. He and his mates simply didn't have the true belief necessary for

---

1. R. Spencer Oliver, "Political Exchange Programs: An Overview" (a talk at Airlie House, Warrenton, Va., June 16, 1976).

the bloody work a successful coup would have required. Part of the reason lay in the effect of exchange programs—of all openings to the outside world—on their belief systems.

> Our formal exchanges around the conference table reflected none of this. But our private exchanges repeatedly did. Not in some simpleminded "I do not believe in communism" kind of way. More in the things they asked, the favors they sought, the particular sights they wished to see. In our cups (of which there were plenty) we got closer than that. Andrei Kokoshin (to name one who did okay for himself) was both a sophisticated slickster and a painfully honest man, and he all but said repeatedly that the game was up.[2]

Finally, the Komsomol, as noted above, was the first official Soviet organization to be infected with the spirit of change, and it was economic change. In the late 1980s, an alternative or "Komsomol economy," as it was called, began to develop. Under the Coordinating Council of Centers of Scientific and Technical Creativity of Youth, created in the 1987 and staffed by Komsomol officials, the first commercial structures were established in the Soviet Union, spawning the first generation of new Russian businessmen in such fields as banking, construction, and real estate.[3] Mikhail Khodorkovsky, one of the richest men in Russia today, began his business career in 1987 when, as a Komsomol officer, he established a collective called the Young Entrepreneurs Foundation, which started trading things such as computers. One has to wonder whether the idea for those new commercial enterprises had their origin in the earlier visits of so many Komsomol officials to the United States under the ACYPL exchange.

American Councils for International Education (ACTR-ACCELS)

The American Council of Teachers of Russian (ACTR) was founded in 1974 by a group of university and school faculty members to further the study of Russian by providing opportunities for Americans to study Russian at an advanced level in Moscow. In cooperation with Moscow's Pushkin Institute of the Russian Language, it administered summer, semester, and academic-year programs in Russia for American undergraduate and graduate students, as well as a summer exchange of high school teachers of Russian and English. With its Soviet partner, it also

---

2. Hodding Carter III, e-mail to author, December 29, 2000.
3. See Olga Kryshtanovskaya and Stephen White, "From Soviet *Nomenklatura* to Russian Elite," *Europe-Asia Studies* 48, no. 5 (1996): 716. See also Olga Kryshtanovskaya, "Young Oligarchs," *Vremya MN* (Moscow), January 18, 2002.

developed a series of Russian-language textbooks and cosponsored, with the Russians, conferences on the teaching of Russian.

The exchanges began in 1976 when 18 American students from 14 colleges and universities were placed at the Pushkin Institute for four months. Between 1976 and 1991, the ACTR placed 1,682 American students from 238 colleges and universities in semester, academic year, and summer programs in Moscow and Leningrad/St. Petersburg. During the same period, more than 120 Russian-curriculum consultants, textbook authors, teachers of Russian, researchers, and conference participants came to the United States for periods of two weeks to ten months, and some 250 Russian curriculum consultants were received in the United States as visiting lecturers or instructors in Russian language and literature.

Beginning with the 1988–89 school year, the ACTR has been part of a consortium which, on behalf of the U.S. government, has conducted an exchange of American and Soviet high school students. In the first year, thirty pairings of U.S. and Soviet schools were made, and 370 American and 402 Soviet students were exchanged for a minimum of one month. By 1990–91, that exchange had grown to sixty-six school pairings, and the exchange of 645 American and 833 Soviet students.

With the gradual opening of the Soviet Union, the ACTR's scope expanded beyond student exchange to include other training and exchange activities sponsored by the U.S. government. To administer those programs, the ACTR, in 1987, created the American Council for Collaboration in Education and Language Study (ACCELS), which has become a leader among U.S. organizations in the administration of government-funded exchanges in the humanities, social sciences, economics, business, law, public administration, and educational administration in the countries of Eastern Europe, Russia, and Eurasia.

The Councils, as it is now known, manages over forty educational programs in and with the regions of the former Soviet Union, and has forty-six offices in Armenia, Azerbaijan, Belarus, Georgia, Kazakhstan, Kyrgyzstan, Moldova, Russia, Tajikistan, Turkmenistan, Ukraine, and Uzbekistan, and a full-time staff of over 270. Among its diverse activities, it develops educational and training programs for U.S. and NIS government agencies, educational institutions, and businesses; conducts in-country professional development programs for alumni of exchange and training programs, including conferences and workshops; recruits for and manages more than fifteen major sponsored exchange programs with the countries of the former Soviet Union; manages student advising centers in Russia, Kazakhstan, Tajikistan, Turkmenistan, Ukraine, and Uzbekistan; administers standardized testing for the Educational Testing Service; and publishes textbooks and materials for the teaching of Russian and English as foreign languages.

Through its multifaceted exchanges and other activities, the ACTR has played a key role in improving U.S. relations with the countries of the former Soviet

Union, as well as the study of Russian in the United States. Thousands of its alumni are now serving in academia, industry, business, government, and various professions.

Center for Citizen Initiatives

Since 1983, the San Francisco-based Center for Citizen Initiatives (CCI) has conducted two-way exchanges with Russia and other former republics of the Soviet Union to help empower citizens to take responsibility for societal change. The brainchild of Sharon Tennison, who has been organizing citizen-to-citizen networks between Americans and Russians for more than twenty years, one of its major programs has brought more than three thousand fledgling entrepreneurs from some three hundred Russian towns and cities to the United States for four- to six-week internships with American businesses. The Russians, who live with American families, study marketing, financial management, product innovation, quality control, labor organization, and other aspects of modern business. Their hands-on experience has proven successful in encouraging Russian business development at the grassroots. In exchange, American consultants have traveled to Russia, on a pro bono basis, to advise Russian firms.

The new entrepreneurs brought to the United States by the CCI, have been described by journalist Trudi Rubin: "These are not the so-called 'oligarchs' who ripped off Russia's natural resources for a song and put little back into the country. Just the opposite, they are the nucleus of Russia's future middle class. They overcame incredible odds (no loans, no laws, no experience, no protection from shakedowns) to build successful businesses that employ anywhere from 4 to 950 people."[4]

The CCI is funded by private donations and grants from the U.S. Department of State and the Agency for International Development. In the year 2000, it had a budget of $5 million, in-kind contributions of another $2.5 million, and a team of over ten thousand U.S. volunteers.

Student Debaters

One novel U.S.-Soviet exchange was a series of annual debates between university students of the two countries. They began in 1976, sponsored by the Communication Association of America (now the National Communication Association) and the Soviet Committee on Youth Organizations. The debates, held before student audiences in the two countries, were conducted in the United States in English, and in the Soviet Union in Russian. Audiences in the Soviet Union numbered, on

4. Trudy Rubin, in *Philadelphia Inquirer,* March 14, 2001.

average, about five hundred but the number of persons reached was much larger, since videos of the debates were sent to other Soviet universities.

Russian debaters who came to the United States were mostly *spetsshkoly* (special schools) graduates who spoke good English, wore Western clothes, and were familiar with Western life and customs. Some were from Soviet think tanks and had studied in the United States or were in training to become diplomats. As such, they were relatively well informed about the United States and able to recognize the validity, or invalidity, of the arguments of the debaters, including their own. American debaters who went to the Soviet Union were mostly university students or recent graduates who were able to debate in Russian.

Topics for debate were selected by the two sponsors but were often loaded to favor the Soviet side and put the Americans on the defensive. One early topic, for example, was "Is Unemployment a Denial of a Human Right, and Does It Lead to Alienation of the Worker?" That topic, however, gave the American debaters an opportunity to talk about aspects of American life that were previously unknown to their Soviet audiences, such as U.S. unemployment compensation, the freedom of movement that gives unemployed Americans the ability to move to places where work may be available, and emigration as a factor in labor statistics. No matter what the topic for debate, it gave the American debaters an opportunity to offer new perspectives on the United States to their Soviet audiences. Moreover, Soviet student audiences were introduced to the novel concept that there could be two sides to every issue, and they could be debated in civil and polite discourse.

In the pre-glasnost years, the American debaters were quick to note that the further they got from Moscow, the more outspoken and uninhibited were the Soviet debaters and their audiences. In Tashkent, in Soviet Uzbekistan, for example, the Americans were invited to speak on the radio, where they said whatever they wished, no matter how provocative it may have been to Soviet listeners.

After one debate, recalls a former American debater, the Americans were led to a table laden with food and drink where one of the Russian debaters, after getting uproariously drunk, confided to him, "I don't believe a word of what I said out there on the podium."[5]

Sister Cities

Sister Cities International (SCI) is a U.S. nonprofit citizen diplomacy network that creates and strengthens partnerships between U.S. and foreign communities. Its Soviet program began in 1973 in partnership with the Union of Soviet Friendship Societies but, because of caution on the Soviet side, by 1986 there were only six

5. Donald J. Raleigh, author's telephone interview, June 28, 1999.

twinnings, the most active of which were Seattle-Tashkent, Detroit-Minsk, and Baltimore-Odessa. In 1986, after Gorbachev had come to power and after his successful summit with Ronald Reagan in Geneva, the Soviets agreed to add ten more; by 1989 there were twenty-three twinnings, and by 2002 ninety-four.

The Baltimore-Odessa twinning boasts a number of accomplishments over its more than twenty-five years of existence. Johns Hopkins's Wilmer Eye Institute has had an active exchange with Odessa's Filatov Institute, a leading center of eye research. In a joint venture, International Harvester and the Salvation Army raised $25,000 to build a Children's Diagnostic and Rehabilitation Center in Odessa, which has an exchange with Johns Hopkins' Pediatrics. Baltimore's McDonough and Friends Schools have conducted exchanges with Odessa secondary schools. And Baltimore has adopted the second grade of Odessa's Internat No. 4 for abandoned street children, funding two teachers, two administrators, a psychologist, and supplementary meals.

More recently, the La Crosse (Wisconsin)-Dubna relationship, with a focus on health, has demonstrated what city twinnings can do in medicine. The twinning has transformed medical care in Dubna, where the death rate is now 20 percent below the Russian national average. Thanks to help from La Crosse and the exchange of some one thousand residents of the two cities in each direction during the 1990s, Dubna now boasts a rebuilt maternity hospital, a kidney dialysis center, a diabetes education center, two women's wellness clinics, and a rehabilitation center for disabled children. New and streamlined medical procedures have resulted in a fivefold drop in hospital admissions of patients in diabetic comas. A contraception program has cut the city's abortion rate to two-thirds the national level. And after Dubna doctors studied how Wisconsin hospitals treated the five most common ailments in Dubna, they found that they were admitting too many patients and prescribing too much medicine. The resultant elimination of 190 Dubna hospital beds has saved hundreds of thousands of dollars annually.

The La Crosse-Dubna experience has been replicated, and by 2002 there were eight partnerships between American and Russian hospitals.

Trust for Mutual Understanding

The Trust for Mutual Understanding, a New York-based organization, makes grants to American nonprofit organizations collaborating with partners in Russia and East Central Europe through professional interaction in the visual and performing arts and environmental conservation. Its first grant was made in 1985 to the American Association of Museums to help fund an exchange of American and Soviet museum experts. Many of the partnerships formed in the course of that exchange subsequently led to collaboration on art exhibitions in the two countries.

With the phasing out and eventual withdrawal of U.S. government funding of performing arts exchanges, the Trust stepped in to fill the breach. Projects it has funded include, among many others, exchange visits of the Manhattan String Quartet and Leningrad's Tanyeyev Quartet; concerts by the American Russian Youth Orchestra in the two countries; theater exchanges between the Eugene O'Neill Theater Center and the U.S. Center of the International Theater Institute, and various Soviet and Russian theater organizations; and Making Music Together, a three-week festival of Soviet music, opera, and dance, which brought 250 Soviet performing artists, directors, and technical personnel to Boston in 1988, and a reciprocal Festival of American Music held in Moscow and Leningrad in 1991.

The Trust has emphasized the award of small grants to American grassroots organizations in the arts and environmental protection that have enabled them to conduct cooperative activities and exchanges with partners in the Soviet Union and Russia. Its grants in environmental protection have been particularly effective in providing support to the growing environmental movement in Russia and its efforts to halt and reverse severe environmental degradation.

Esalen Institute

A convergence of mountains and sea, mind and body, East and West, meditation and action.

—ESALEN INSTITUTE

Founded at Big Sur in 1962 as an alternative educational center to explore the full realization of the human potential, Esalen became known for its blend of Eastern and Western philosophies. Situated on twenty-seven acres of spectacular California coastline and blessed with natural hot springs, Esalen has experienced a steady influx of artists, philosophers, psychologists, and religious thinkers. And to Esalen, beginning in 1980, also came the Russians for what some have derisively called "hot tub diplomacy" but others have praised as an exemplary example of citizen diplomacy.

Esalen's Soviet-American Exchange Program was intended as an alternative to the adversarial U.S.-Soviet relationship. Emphasizing citizen exchanges as a complement to government diplomacy, its activities have included, among others, the first U.S.-Soviet televised space bridges; collaboration between novelists, playwrights, and poets; symposia on the political psychology of Soviet-American relations; cooperation with the Soviet Ministry of Health on health promotion, stress reduction, and health programs in the workplace; and hosting a variety of Russian visitors in politics, science, and the arts.

Esalen's Soviet program also helped to fill the void created when the United States suspended cultural exchanges with the Soviet Union following the invasion of Afghanistan in late 1979. Prominent Soviets were only too pleased to accept invitations to visit "sunny California" and participate in seminars with Americans in the pleasant ambiance of Big Sur and to continue relationships with Americans begun under other auspices.

10 | PERFORMING ARTS

I personally attach . . . high importance to cultural contact as a means of combating the negative impressions about this country that mark so much of world opinion. What we have to do, of course, is to show the outside world both that we have a cultural life and that we care something about it—that we care enough about it, in fact, to give it encouragement and support here at home, and to see that it is enriched by acquaintance with similar activity elsewhere. If these impressions could only be conveyed with enough force and success to countries beyond our borders, I for my part would willingly trade the entire remaining inventory of political propaganda for the results that could be achieved by such means alone.

—GEORGE F. KENNAN

If the public doesn't want to come, nothing will stop them.

—SOL HUROK

The importance of cultural exchanges in international relations was recognized by George Kennan, dean of American diplomats, but Sol Hurok, the legendary American impresario, knew what the public would come to see in both the United States and the Soviet Union, and he became one of the important middlemen who made cultural exchanges a success, both artistically and financially, despite the chill winds of the Cold War.

The performing arts were one of the most visible of U.S.-Soviet exchanges. In the United States, few of the cognoscenti failed to hear of, if not see, the Soviet dance groups, symphony orchestras, operas, ice shows, and circuses, as well as the many outstanding, individual artists who visited the United States each year, often on extensive coast-to-coast tours. American ensembles and soloists that went to the Soviet Union in exchange invariably played to full houses and were likewise appreciated by both the intelligentsia and the general public. For Duke Ellington's Moscow performances in 1971, tickets were sold on the black market for as much as eighty rubles, when the usual price for a theater ticket was seldom higher than four.

Performing arts exchanges between the two countries began in 1955, two years after Stalin's death, when an eighty-five-member company of *Porgy and Bess*, on tour in Western Europe, was invited to perform in Leningrad, Moscow, and

Stalingrad, where they were a smash hit. Similar successes were enjoyed the following year by the Boston Symphony, violinist Isaac Stern, and tenor Jan Peerce.

Pianist Emil Gilels was the first Soviet artist to appear in the United States in decades, when he performed to rave reviews on a month-long tour in 1955. Violinist David Oistrakh followed with similar success that same year, as did renowned cellist Mstislav Rostropovich in 1956. All three were presented in the United States by Columbia Artists Management.

With the signing of the Lacy-Zarubin Agreement in 1958, performing arts exchanges became a recurring feature in U.S.-Soviet relations.[1] However, as with the scholarly exchanges, they were subject to quotas imposed by the agreement, starting, in 1958, with three major ensembles on each side over a two-year period, and eventually rising, in 1985, to ten over a three-year period. Exchanges of individual artists were subject to similar quotas, which, however, were not always enforced, and Soviet artists in the United States far outnumbered Americans in the Soviet Union.

Soviet favorites in the United States included the Moiseyev Folk Dance Ensemble and the Bolshoi and Kirov Ballets, whose repeated coast-to-coast tours received glowing press reviews as well as handsome fees. But their visits also brought gains for the United States. "There is universal agreement," wrote Hurok's biographer Harlow Robinson, "that Hurok did more than any other single individual in the arts to introduce America to the riches of Soviet/Russian culture, that he played a major role in creating an American audience for ballet and modern dance, and that his pioneering work in bringing the performing arts on tour to the provinces led indirectly to the rise of regional dance and theater companies."[2] *Saturday Review* music critic Irving Kolodin wrote in the same vein: "Hurok has contributed as much, perhaps, as any university in educating not only a dance public in America, but also a corps of critics."[3]

Tours across the United States were also an eye-opener for the Soviet artists. "America was for us simply another planet," said Galina Ulanova, star of the Bolshoi Ballet and one of the greatest Russian ballerinas of modern times, after her first visit to the United States in 1959: "We knew so little about the outside world, and we were just amazed by the scale of the country. All those huge stores five and six floors high, with all these clothes on sale, and entire apartments on display—we just didn't have anything like that."[4] Equally revealing was the remark

---

1. For details of how the exchanges were negotiated and conducted, see Richmond, *U.S.-Soviet Cultural Exchanges*.

2. Harlow Robinson, *The Last Impresario: The Life, Times, and Legacy of Sol Hurok* (New York: Viking, 1994), 468.

3. Irving Kolodin, "Sol Hurok, Adventurer in the Arts," *Saturday Review of Literature*, May 30, 1959, 37.

4. Galina Ulanova, in Robinson, *The Last Impresario*, 376.

of choreographer Igor Moiseyev: "I'm amazed that all your workers are fat and all your millionaires are thin."[5] It was exactly the opposite of what he had been led to believe from the caricatures of Americans in Soviet political cartoons.

For Soviet performing artists and audiences, isolated from the West since the 1930s, the visits by American and other Western performers brought a breath of fresh air as well as new artistic concepts in music, dance, and theater to a country where orthodoxy and conservatism had long been guiding principles in the arts. As a West German official described it:

> While the Soviet Union was the source of considerable creativity in literature, drama, and motion pictures in the 1920's, the Stalin era brought such a decline that when contacts were reestablished, the USSR had nothing to offer but an urgent desire for inspiration from abroad. This is the reason for the immense success of Western cultural presentations in the Soviet Union, which began in 1954 with the triumphal guest appearances by the *Comédie Française*. A specific German contribution to the regeneration of the Soviet theatre was the guest performance of the *Hamburg Schauspielhaus* with Gustaf Gründgens in 1959, which was in line with similar theatrical tours from other Western states.[6]

When George Balanchine took his New York City Ballet to Leningrad in 1962, the reception was revolutionary. As Solomon Volkov, a cultural historian of the city of St. Petersburg wrote: "I remember the overwhelming impression created by the tour. Older people rejected it: 'The Americans aren't dancing; they're solving algebra problems with their feet.' But the young saw in Balanchine's productions the heights that the Petersburg cultural avant-garde could have reached if it had not been crushed by the Soviet authorities. Leningrad's aspiring musicians, writers and dancers were inspired."[7] The intense interest of the Soviet public in Western performing artists was amply demonstrated by sold-out halls, lines of ticket seekers hundreds of yards long, and the storming of gates by those without tickets. One Russian recalls how he stood in line all night to buy tickets for a performance by London's Royal Shakespeare Theater.

Among the American ensembles and individual artists that performed in the Soviet Union under the cultural agreement were the Philadelphia Orchestra, New York Philharmonic, Cleveland Symphony, and San Francisco Symphony; in

---

5. Igor Moiseyev, in Robinson, *The Last Impresario,* 355.

6. Wolfgang Kasack, "Cultural Relations with the USSR: A German View" (paper presented at the conference "Russia and the West: Cultural Contacts and Influences," Schloss Leopoldskron, Salzburg, Austria, October 30–November 3, 1973).

7. Solomon Volkov, *New York Times,* September 9, 2001, trans. Antonina W. Bouis.

dance, the American Ballet Theater, New York City Ballet, Joffrey Ballet, Alvin Ailey Dance Theater, Jose Limon Dance Company, and Paul Taylor Dance Company; in jazz, Benny Goodman, Woody Herman, Earl Hines, Duke Ellington, the Preservation Hall Jazz Band, the New York Jazz Repertory, Dave Brubeck, and the Thad Jones–Mel Lewis Jazz Orchestra; in theater, the Arena Stage, The American Conservatory Theater, and Jessica Tandy and Hume Cronyn in *The Gin Game*. Benny Goodman's highly successful thirty-two-concert tour in 1962 seemed to signal Soviet official acceptance of jazz, but old habits died hard, and only two years later the government daily *Izvestiya* suggested that four of the band's musicians were really secret agents.[8]

The Arena Stage's sixteen performances of Thornton Wilder's *Our Town* and Lawrence and Lee's *Inherit the Wind* in Moscow and Leningrad in 1973 are examples of what performing arts exchanges can accomplish. The Washington D.C. company, the first U.S. permanent dramatic theater to visit the Soviet Union, was a resounding success. All performances were sold out weeks in advance, thousands of would-be spectators had to be turned away, and to accommodate some of the demand, Arena opened its dress rehearsals to students and other theater people. *Our Town* touched on human experiences common to Russians and Americans, and one Soviet cultural official likened Wilder to Anton Chekhov.[9] The cheering audiences, the rave press reviews, and the offstage rapport with the visiting Americans all made for a very satisfying experience. On her return to Washington, Zelda Fichandler, the Arena Stage's artistic director summed up the trip cogently, "If we didn't transcend politics, we circumvented or cut through it."[10]

"There was widespread astonishment," said Fichandler, "that the kind of theater represented by Arena Stage even existed in America. They had always thought of American theater as being made up of musical comedies, Broadway hits produced by pick-up companies with the aim of making profits, and what they called 'sexual clownery.' But the first performance proved that there are other professional theaters in the United States besides those of New York and Broadway. We were, as one Soviet writer put it, 'something totally unexpected.'"[11]

For both plays, the audience cheered, applauded rhythmically, stood and shouted bravos, and called the company back many times for stage bows. They loved us, wrote Fichandler, for "the realism of our acting, the theatricality of our productions, for the humanism, the humanity of our theater, for its concern with contemporary ideas and life, they loved us for, 'our serious and humane art' [as

8. *New York Times*, August 7, 1962.

9. Viktor P. Sakovich, Soviet cultural counselor, in conversation with author after a performance of Arena's "Our Town," Washington, D.C., 1973.

10. Zelda Fichandler, in address to National Press Club, Washington, D.C., November 26, 1973.

11. Ibid.

Pravda put it] and for the closeness of our theater to the ideas and ideals of Stanislavski [*sic*] and the Moscow Art Theater, and no higher compliment was available for them to give us."[12]

Inherit the Wind reenacted the "Scopes monkey trial" of 1925, in which John Scopes, a young teacher in Dayton, Tennessee, was charged with teaching evolution to his high school students. The play had been published in Russian, and a film based on the trial had been shown in the Soviet Union, so the audience, which heard the Arena presentation through simultaneous translation, was familiar with the story. Soviet ideologists may have seen the play as a struggle between religion and science in which religion won, but the play is also about freedom of speech, and the message of a state trying to impose its ideology was not lost on the Soviet audience. *Inherit,* moreover, was performed while writer Aleksandr Solzhenitsyn and physicist Andrei Sakharov were being harassed in the Soviet Union for their views.

Summing up the visit, Fichandler said:

> There are times when you meet another human being on terms that are neither yours nor his—you simply show something you have made and it pleases him. This is when we are at our best. At these times, the optimistic element in life takes over. That conscious tendency to synthesize, harmonize, reconcile, organize the conflicts that we find in life is in the ascendency and we are, for a moment, fully human and most alive. For that moment, what we all too lightly call "cultural exchange" is taking place.[13]

But did such cultural exchanges really change the Soviet Union? One answer is given by a Russian cellist who studied at Moscow's elite music schools during the 1960s. We were raised, he explained, on propaganda which portrayed Soviet society as the wave of the future, while the West was decadent and doomed. And yet, he continued, "From that 'decadent' West, there came to the Soviet Union truly great symphony orchestras with sounds that were electrifying, and they came year after year, from Boston, Philadelphia, New York, Cleveland, and San Francisco. How could the decadent West produce such great orchestras," we asked ourselves. "Cultural exchanges were another opening to the West, and additional proof that our media were not telling us the truth."

12. Zelda Fichandler, "Homecoming Notes on Inherit the Wind," *Washington Star-News,* October 28, 1973.

13. Zelda Fichandler, in address to Woman's National Democratic Club, Washington, D.C., November 5, 1973.

11 | MOVED BY THE MOVIES

Of all the arts, the most important for us is the cinema.

—LENIN

Lenin was correct in predicting that the cinema would be an important medium for indoctrinating people, but the father of the Soviet state could not have foreseen the influence that foreign films would have on the Soviet public. From foreign films Soviet audiences learned that people in the West did not have to stand in long lines to purchase food, did not live in communal apartments, dressed fashionably, enjoyed many conveniences not available in the Soviet Union, owned cars, and lived the normal life so sought by Russians.

As Thomas L. Friedman has pointed out, that had unforeseen consequences: "The single most underestimated force in international affairs today is what happens—thanks to globalization—when we all increasingly know how everyone else lives. People everywhere start to demand the same things, and when they can't get them, they get frustrated."[1]

Soviet audiences saw Western films as a window on another world, and they indeed got frustrated. Through foreign films Russians were able to see aspects of life in the West that invalidated the negative views promulgated by the Soviet media. Audiences were not so much listening to the sound tracks or reading the subtitles, as watching the doings of people in the films—in their homes, in stores, on the streets, the clothes they wore, and the cars they drove. One Russian woman recalls how, on seeing *The Apartment,* starring Shirley MacLaine and Jack Lemmon, she was impressed by watching Lemmon warm up his TV dinner, unknown at that time in the Soviet Union, and lighting his kitchen stove without a match. And when refrigerators were opened in Western films, they were always full of food. Such details, which showed how people lived in the West, were most revealing for Soviet audiences. When they saw films about Westerners and their problems, their reaction was, as one Russian put it, "I wish we had their problems."

U.S.-Soviet film exchanges have a long history, going back to 1921 when D. W. Griffith's *Intolerance* was shown in the Soviet Union under the title, *The World's Evil,* although in an edited version which deleted the Christ's Passion episode.

1. Thomas L. Friedman, *New York Times,* June 16, 2000.

That was the start of the Soviet practice of doctoring foreign films to conform with ideology, a practice continued in the ensuing years.[2]

In the years following World War I, the Soviet film industry was nascent, and foreign films were imported to meet the entertainment needs of the masses. From 1923 to 1933, 956 American films were purchased, mostly silent films by D. W. Griffith, Charlie Chaplin, Harold Lloyd, Cecil B. DeMille, Eric von Stroheim, and Buster Keaton. Soviet audiences also thrilled to the adventures of Tarzan and Zorro, and the most popular matinee idols of those years in Soviet Russia, surpassing even Soviet film stars, were Charlie Chaplin, Mary Pickford, Douglas Fairbanks, and Conrad Veidt.[3] During the 1930s, however, when the Soviet film industry began large-scale production, only a few American films were purchased.

World War II brought a new need for entertainment, and showings of American films resumed with such hits as *Bambi, The Thief of Baghdad, The Three Musketeers, The Jungle Book,* and *Charlie's Aunt,* all of which enjoyed great success.

In the immediate postwar years, American films were again shown to Soviet audiences, the so-called trophy films captured by the Red Army from film archives in Berlin and other European capitals. The films were subtitled, credits were deleted, titles were changed, and the films were shown without compensation to their American producers, which was of no concern to the audiences, who enjoyed them immensely. However, conflict between the U.S. and Soviet film industries over those pirated showings led to a suspension of film sales until 1958 and the signing of the Lacy-Zarubin Agreement.

During the years of the cultural agreement, four or five American films, on average, were purchased by the Soviets each year. Most were pure entertainment—comedies, adventure stories, musicals, and science fiction—which met the interests of Soviet audiences. Among the more popular were *Some Like it Hot, The Apartment, The Chase,* and *Tootsie.* Also purchased, however, were films of social protest and realistic portrayals of contemporary American life which Soviet propagandists considered ideologically correct in portraying the ills of capitalist society. Many of those films, however, were made in the social protest tradition of American literature and had been screened by the State Department and given a "no objection" stamp of approval prior to being sold to the Soviet Union.[4] Such

2. Much of the material on motion pictures here is from Valery Golovskoy, "U.S. Film Showings Up in Russia," in *Variety,* January 12, 1983, and author's interviews with Golovskoy, Washington, D.C., April 12, 2000; Mikhail Sulkin, Newton, Mass., May 25, 2000; Svetlana Boym, Cambridge, Mass., May 25, 2000; and Oleg Sulkin, New York, N.Y., June 20, 2000.

3. Richard Stites, *Russian Popular Culture: Entertainment and Society Since 1900* (Cambridge: Cambridge University Press, 1992), 56.

4. In the early years of the cultural agreement, it was common practice for the State Department and the USIA to screen American films before they were offered to the Soviet Union for purchase.

films, nevertheless, helped to satisfy the great curiosity and hunger for information about the United States. They showed much about American contemporary life and its high standard of living. What may have appeared as poverty to Americans seemed like affluence to Russians. The directors with the largest number of films purchased in those years were Stanley Kramer with seven and William Wyler with six. Although the number of purchased films was small, hundreds of copies were made for distribution in cinemas throughout the Soviet Union.[5]

Financial considerations also played a role in the purchase of foreign films, and price as well as "progressive" subject matter were the primary criteria for purchase. B and C films came at reduced prices, and many were purchased years after their initial release in the United States. But regardless of their age, quality, and social message, foreign films were always a hit with Soviet audiences and a financial success for *Sovexportfilm,* the government agency responsible for the purchase of foreign films and the sale of Soviet films abroad.

French and Italian films were the most popular, and as many as ten of each were purchased each year. Also popular were Polish and Czech films, which opened another window on the West for Russians. Andrei Piontkovsky, a Russian political analyst, recalls that the only film he saw several times over in his youth in the Soviet Union was *Ashes and Diamonds,* by the Polish director Andrzej Wajda, which because of its representation of the challenge by Poland's younger generation to the communist regime, became a cult movie in Poland. "Those among us," writes Piontkovsky, "who couldn't force ourselves to love Big Brother, despite all the efforts made by our school education, were enraptured by *Ashes and Diamonds* and by what we saw as its anti-communist and anti-Soviet message."[6]

Another channel for Soviet citizens to see American films, and outstanding ones, was the Moscow International Film Festival, held biennially since 1959, where foreign films were screened for the public in Moscow and Leningrad. Moreover, many festival films, although not purchased by the Soviets, were clandestinely copied and screened at closed showings for members of the Politburo and other high officials and their spouses on what was called the dacha circuit.

The intelligentsia were also able to see a wide variety of foreign films at "members-only" showings at the professional clubs of writers, scientists, architects, journalists, cinematographers, and other privileged people of the Soviet Union. Thursday night, for example, was film night at Moscow's House of the Journalist, where foreign and Soviet films not released for general distribution could be seen by Soviet journalists and their guests. At such closed showings, two American

5. See William Benton, "Should We Continue the Cultural Exchanges with the USSR?" *Saturday Review of Literature,* October 27, 1962, 18.

6. Andrei Piontkovsky, "Different Directions for Poland, Russia," *The Russia Journal* (Moscow), April 14–20, 2001, in JRL 5202.

films on the possibility of a nuclear holocaust, *On the Beach* and *Dr. Strangelove*, were screened and, as one viewer has described it, "They absolutely shocked us. . . . We began to understand that the same thing would happen to us, as to them, in a nuclear war."[7] Films that were high on the banned list, such as *The Russians Are Coming* and *Doctor Zhivago*, were screened for only a limited number of people.

Another venue for screening foreign films were the lecture tours conducted by the Union of Cinematographers. Soviet filmmakers and critics would tour the provinces with foreign films from the state archives, giving talks on the films, showing excerpts, and then the entire film. Shown on those tours were such films as Fellini's *8½* and the James Bond films. The Bond films, although not released for public showing, were extremely popular and aroused the public's curiosity because they had been denounced in the press as anti-Soviet.

Yet another outlet for Western films were the *Kluby liubitelei kino*, the film fan clubs which gave members an opportunity to not only see foreign films but discuss them afterwards in free-ranging give-and-take discussions. Supported by *Gosfilmofond* (the State Film Depository), the clubs were able to borrow films that were not cleared for public showing but could be screened for limited audiences. (During the 1980s, under glasnost, the film clubs were also able to borrow films from similar clubs in Western Europe and Western embassies in Moscow.) The film clubs were very active in places distant from Moscow—Southern Russia, the Ural region, Ukraine, and cities with high concentrations of intellectuals and scientists, such as Leningrad, Novosibirsk, Obninsk, and Dubno, as well as the many secret scientific cities.

Foreign films were selected by a special commission of *Goskino* (the State Committee on Cinematography) with the participation of Central Committee representatives, and censorship took place after the dubbing with Russian-language subtitles.[8] Destined for the cutting room floor was footage which contained criticism of communism; scenes with homosexuality, sexual perversion, or eroticism; and references to Jews. And in some cases, the traditional American "happy ending" was deleted.

Dubbing was a more subtle form of censorship. Moscow's Gorky Studio, where the dubbing was done, was adept in composing subtitles that could radically change the meaning of a sound track. In Stanley Kramer's *Ship of Fools*, for example, based on Katherine Anne Porter's book of the same name, which tells the tale of Germans returning by ocean liner to Nazi Germany in the 1930s, all mention of Jews was deleted. It is difficult to imagine how that could have been done, but the

7. Vitaly Goldansky, in English, *Russia and the Idea of the West*, 279 n. 136.

8. Marianna Tax Choldin and Maurice Friedberg, eds., *The Red Pencil: Artists, Scholars, and Censors in the USSR* (Boston: Unwin Hyman, 1989), 143 n. 33.

dubbers were very talented, and the film which was seen in closed showings was much different from the original. In *The Life of Emil Zola,* which highlighted the French novelist's defense of Alfred Dreyfus in a trial that captured world attention, the dubbers made no mention of Dreyfus having been a Jew. Foreign films, however, were shown mainly in large cities where audiences did not mind the dubbing, were more sophisticated, and could read between the lines.

Despite the best efforts of the dubbers and censors, much of the West's message did get through. Soviet cinemagoers were indeed moved by the foreign movies they saw, but not in the direction Lenin had anticipated.

12 | EXHIBITIONS—SEEING IS BELIEVING

Exhibits brought a whole generation of Soviets into contact with the West and the United States in particular. They were one of the best investments the United States made.

—MICHAEL DOBBS, in lecture at the Kennan Institute, February 3, 1997

"Better to see once than hear a hundred times," advises an old Russian proverb, and Russians heeded that advice in thronging to see the twenty-three major exhibitions brought to the Soviet Union by USIA under the cultural agreement from 1959 to 1991. What they had heard a hundred times about the United States from their own media was negated by a visit to one of the USIA touring exhibitions, which gave them a glimpse of the United States, its people, and how they lived. The exhibitions also provided a rare opportunity for Soviet citizens to talk with Russian-speaking American guides and ask questions about the United States.

The exhibition exchange began in 1959 with Soviet and U.S. national exhibitions at Moscow's Sokolniki Park and New York City's Coliseum. That exchange received wide publicity because it was at Sokolniki that Richard Nixon and Nikita Khrushchev, while touring a model American home, engaged in what has come to be known as the "kitchen debate."[1]

The two exhibitions were contrasted by Norman Cousins, who saw both:

> The Soviet exhibition features its vast new industrial capabilities, its jet planes, its automobiles and tractors and trucks, its hydro-electric power installations, its state farms. True, the life and habits of the individual are not ignored in the fair; far from it. But the major theme has to do with energy and a vast industrial forward thrust.
>
> By contrast, the American exhibition focuses on the individual citizen—how he goes shopping, how he has his hair cut, what the inside of his home is like, what he does for work and what he does for fun. In short, what everyday is like for many millions of people who live in the U.S.[2]

1. For a firsthand account of the kitchen debate, see the letter to the editor by Hans N. Tuch in the *Washington Post*, August 31, 1987.

2. Norman Cousins, "Tale of Two Exhibitions," *Saturday Review of Literature*, August 1, 1969, 24.

The two 1959 exhibitions were the first in a series of exchanges that continued over the next thirty-two years and gave millions of Soviet and American citizens a look at the achievements of the two countries and how their people lived.

The cultural agreement provided for month-long showings of thematic exhibitions in three cities (later increased to six, and then nine) over the two (later three) years of each agreement, to portray life in the United States and the latest developments in a number of specialized fields. Among the U.S. exhibition themes were medicine, technical books, graphic arts, architecture, hand tools, education, research and development, outdoor recreation, technology for the home, photography, agriculture, information, and industrial design. The American exhibitions drew huge crowds, with lines stretching for blocks awaiting admittance, and were seen, on average, by some 250,000 visitors in each city. All told, more than 20 million Soviet citizens are believed to have seen the twenty-three U.S. exhibitions over the thirty-two-year period.[3]

The exhibitions were staffed with twenty or more Russian-speaking Americans who demonstrated the items exhibited and engaged in spirited conversations with the Soviet visitors. As Eisenhower wrote of the American guides at the 1959 U.S. exhibition at Sokolniki:

> I was particularly impressed with reports of the group of outstanding United States college students who served as guides and who day after day stood up and in fluent Russian fielded questions of the greatest diversity about life in the United States. In fact, those bright young men and women so impressed their hearers that when some trained Communist agitators began infiltrating the crowd and throwing loaded questions, friendly Russians in the audience would help out by supplying answers in loud whispers.[4]

What Eisenhower could not have foreseen was that many of the young Russian-speaking American guides would go on to make careers in the Soviet area as scholars, professors, diplomats, and journalists. With their firsthand knowledge of life in the Soviet provinces, they became a national asset during the Cold War years when U.S. knowledge of the Soviet Union as it really was was minimal. Americans in those years could travel to Moscow, Leningrad, and Kiev, but the exhibit guides also went to places seldom visited by Americans, such as Volgograd, Alma Ata, Baku, Tashkent, Ufa, Zaporozhye, Tselinograd, Rostov, and Novosibirsk.

3. These statistics are from the file, "Special International Exhibitions," in the Historical Collection, Bureau of Public Diplomacy, Department of State, Washington, D.C.

4. Eisenhower, *Waging Peace*, 410.

Visitors to the U.S. exhibitions were mostly male and in their early- to mid-twenties. They asked a variety of questions about life in the United States and listened to the guides' responses with great interest and apparent open-mindedness. Many questions were put to the guides on international issues and world affairs but that depended to some extent on the city—more in Moscow, Leningrad, and Kiev, and fewer in provincial cities—as well as the degree to which local authorities harassed visitors or sought to limit attendance.

Another high-visibility activity that attracted large numbers of viewers in both countries was the exchange of art exhibitions between U.S. and Soviet museums. The major partners to these exchanges, which began in the mid-1970s during détente, were the Metropolitan Museum and the National Gallery of Art on the U.S. side, and the State Hermitage and Pushkin Museums on the Soviet side. Museum exchanges were given a further boost in 1975 when the Metropolitan Museum and the Soviet Ministry of Culture signed an agreement for an exchange of five exhibitions on each side during the following years. As the exchanges developed, some of the Soviet exhibitions were also shown at the Los Angeles County Museum of Art and other American museums. Working relations were also established between museums of the two countries that involved exchanges of personnel as well as artistic material.

13 | HOT BOOKS IN THE COLD WAR

Ever since the *Lay of Igor's Campaign* and Nestor's *Primary Chronicle,* the written word has had a special, almost magical quality for Russians. . . . Precisely because the literate were a minority, books were objects of awe and veneration. . . . This aspect of literature is at least as important today as it was a hundred years ago.

—KLAUS MEHNERT, *The Russians and Their Favorite Books*

The *knigonoshi* were the book bearers of the tsarist era, Russians who traveled to the West on business or pleasure and returned home with forbidden books, often by bribing border guards to avoid government controls on the import of foreign literature. This chapter, however, is about modern *knigonoshi* who brought Western literature to the Soviet Union, circumventing the strict controls imposed by communist ideologists.

Books played an important role in the westernization of the Soviet Union and the winning of the hearts and minds of many Russians. Russians love books, and they are widely read and treasured in a country where people were largely illiterate less than a century ago. James R. Millar, now professor of Russian studies at George Washington University, recalls how a Russian student came to his dormitory room at Moscow State University one night in 1966 on a mission that could have gotten him into serious trouble with the authorities. The student had an English-language copy of Vladimir Nabokov's autobiography, *Speak, Memory,* a forbidden book, which he was translating into Russian, and he needed help with some of Nabokov's colloquial English terms.[1]

The Soviet Union published more copies of books than any other country, and yet there was always a book hunger there. The simple explanation is that publishing was a state monopoly, and the state was publishing many books that Russians did not want to read, or the ones they wanted to read were not published in sufficient numbers to meet popular demand. Soviet censorship was depriving readers of books that would have become bestsellers. Moreover, while censorship of books has a long history in Russia, the Soviet Union had eliminated illiteracy, and book hunger was no longer limited to the intelligentsia but had become a mass phenomenon. It is, therefore, ironic that a regime which had dramatically raised the cultural and educational level of its citizens, could not supply the books that they wanted to read.

1. James R. Millar, author's interview, Washington, D.C., June 10, 1999.

After the death of Stalin an underground system of typed and retyped manuscripts, mainly works by dissident Russian authors at home and abroad, began to circulate among the intelligentsia. To meet the demand for such books in Russian that could not be printed or purchased in the Soviet Union, two employees of Radio Liberty, Isaac "Ike" Patch and Betty Carter, modern day *knigonoshi*, came up with the idea for the *Book Program*, as it was called in 1956. Its purpose, writes Patch, was "to communicate Western ideas to Soviet citizens by providing them with books—on politics, economics, philosophy, art, and technology—not available in the Soviet Union."[2]

Patch's proposal got the enthusiastic support of Howland H. Sargeant, president of the Radio Liberty Committee, who approached the CIA with a request for funding. The Agency came through with a modest initial grant of $10,000, which as the book program grew, eventually came to more than a million dollars a year.

The Bedford Publishing Company, headed by Patch, was established as a private venture, funded by the CIA but separate from Radio Liberty, to publish Western works never before translated into Russian. From its main office in New York and branch offices in London, Munich, Paris, and Rome, Bedford distributed books to Soviet visitors to the West and Western visitors to the Soviet Union.

Among the translated books were such classics as James Joyce's *Portrait of the Artist as a Young Man*, Vladimir Nabokov's *Pnin*, George Orwell's *Animal Farm*, and Robert Conquest's *The Great Terror*. Over the years, Bedford and its successor organizations distributed to readers in the Soviet Union more than a million books, most of which are believed to have reached their destinations as evidenced by letters to the distribution centers. According to Patch, 35 percent of the books were given to Soviet travelers in the West—engineers, teachers, artists, students, and journalists. Another 40 percent were given to Western travelers to the Soviet Union—doctors, lawyers, teachers, and engineers. Ten percent were mailed to people in the Soviet Union authorized to receive book packages from the West, and the remaining 15 percent found their way to the USSR by "special routes."[3] Moreover, with the possible exception of a few books confiscated by Soviet customs officials, Patch says there is no evidence that the Soviet authorities made any concerted effort to disrupt the distribution. Alexander Solzhenitsyn's wife, Natasha, for example, has told Patch that, during the 1960s and early 1970s, she and her husband regularly received books supplied by Bedford Publishing through an intermediary.[4]

2. Isaac Patch, *Closing the Circle: A Buckalino Journey Around Our Time* (Wellesley: Wellesley College Printing Services, 1996), 256. The book was published privately, in a limited edition, without Library of Congress cataloguing or an ISBN number.

3. Ibid., 261.

4. Ibid., 261–62.

One of those special routes for distribution was the American Embassy in Moscow, where a supply of the books was maintained. Embassy officers preparing to travel within the Soviet Union or hosting Russians for dinners in their apartments in Moscow could pick up books to be passed on to their Soviet acquaintances. The books were also made available to American students and other visitors to the embassy to be given to their Soviet colleagues. In a society where foreign literature was strictly controlled, such books, especially those in Russian translation, were highly prized.

Soviet diplomats stationed abroad were also conduits for introducing forbidden books into the Soviet Union. As Victor V. Karyagin has written: "We in London (like our colleagues in other foreign capitals, I suppose) had a rare opportunity to read samizdat and emigre publications . . . hardly anybody withstood the temptation of tasting the forbidden fruit. I myself collected an entire library . . . the Bible, the Koran, Pasternak, Solzhenitsyn, Okujava [sic], Daniel, Sinyavsky, Allilluyeva [sic], and much else."[5]

There were also reverse *knigonoshi*, foreign visitors to the Soviet Union who facilitated the transmission of Soviet dissident literature to the West. During the 1970s and 1980s, as the Soviet dissident movement emerged, exchangees and other Western visitors or travelers were often asked by their Russian friends to help in sending samizdat literature abroad, which they were able to do through contacts in their Moscow embassies. Through those channels, many works by Soviet dissidents—articles, letters to the editor, and books—reached publishers and readers in the West.

Other modern day *knigonoshi* were the Western publishers who brought their books to the Moscow International Book Fair, held in alternate years beginning with 1977, two years after the Helsinki Accords were signed. At the 1979 fair, more than 170,000 books were displayed from more than seventy countries, including some 15,000 British and 13,000 American titles. The intent was to sell books or translation rights to Soviet book importers or publishers, but the public was also admitted to the fairs, although not allowed to make purchases. Thousands of visitors, however, pored over the books during the week-long fairs, and some stood at the Western stands for hours reading books that were almost impossible to obtain in the Soviet Union.

The fairs, however, did not provide for the free flow of information as provided by the Helsinki Accords. At each fair, Soviet authorities would confiscate books they found objectionable, including those by banished dissident writers, histories of Russia and China, and works on politics or philosophy. In 1979, forty-four American titles were removed from the shelves by the Soviets, including a collection of political cartoons by New York caricaturist David Levine, Henry Kissinger's memoirs, works by exiled Nobel laureate Aleksandr Solzhenitsyn, two

5. Victor Karyagin, quoted in English, *Russia and the Idea of the West*, 105. Karyagin was one of the 104 Soviet officials expelled from Britain in 1971.

books about Soviet defector and ballet star Mikhail Baryshnikov, and one by dissident humorist Vladimir Voinovich. The Voinovich book. *The Life and Incredible
Adventures of Private Ivan Chonkin,* was a satire on contemporary Soviet life that
later became a bestseller in Russia. Also confiscated in 1979 was George Orwell's
Animal Farm, as it had been in 1977, although his *1984* passed muster.

Among the most popular Western stands at the fairs were those of the [Ameri-
can] Association of Jewish Book Publishers (AJBP) and Israeli publishers. The
AJBP booth displayed hundreds of titles about Jewish life and history. The Israeli
exhibit proved equally popular, with shelves of books published in Israel in Russian, Hebrew, Georgian, Arabic, and English editions.

Book censorship presented a dilemma for American publishers—to exhibit their
products to book-hungry Russians or to boycott the fairs as a protest against Soviet
persecution of dissident writers and others who could not publish. As the *New York
Times* put it in an editorial urging American publishers not to participate in the 1977
fair: "This Moscow book fair will be an insult to the courageous Soviet writers who
are silenced in their own land. That is reason enough for the Americans to stay away."[6]

Some American publishers did stay away but many more went, at least in the
first few years of the fairs, attracted by the prospect of several hundred thousand
Russians perusing their books on history, social sciences, psychology, art, and
management. As Vasily Aksyonov recalled the fairs, they gave Soviet writers and
intellectuals "their only access to the Western book world."[7] Eventually, however,
U.S. interest declined for economic reasons, as low sales to Soviet booksellers and
publishers did not cover the costs of going to Moscow and exhibiting there.

A more pressing problem was the theft of books by the Soviet public, either for
personal use or sale on the black market. Thefts were a big problem in the first few
days of the fairs, when the publishers wanted to have all their wares available to
show to prospective Soviet buyers, but toward the end of the week most of the
exhibitors did not object as their books disappeared. Those most pleased to see
them go were the Christian and Jewish book publishers. Whatever was left after
the pilferers had performed was sold at deep discounts or given to Soviet libraries,
academic institutions, or favored Russian friends.

Tamizdat

Certainly nothing is more worthy of our attention than finding ways to reach out and
establish better communication with the people and the government of the Soviet Union.

—RONALD REAGAN, in his address to the Conference on U.S.-Soviet Exchanges,

JUNE 27, 1984

6. *New York Times,* July 11, 1977.
7. Vasily Aksyonov, in *Christian Science Monitor,* September 2, 1983.

Many Americans know about *samizdat* (self-published literature), the clandestine publishing in the Soviet Union which circumvented Soviet censorship, but few know about its first cousin, *tamizdat* (published over there), the publication abroad of works in Russian that could not be published in the Soviet Union but which found their way to readers there. As Anatoly Chernyaev, Gorbachev's foreign policy adviser writes, Gorbachev himself was a serious reader of both *samizdat* and *tamizdat*.[8]

There were many such publishing ventures abroad, and a few of them will be described here.

Ardis Publishers

Ardis was started on a shoestring by a young American couple, Carl and Ellendea Proffer, students of Russian literature at the University of Michigan who had studied at Moscow State University in 1969 under the IREX exchange. Carl had published a book on Nabokov, and Ellendea was writing her dissertation on Mikhail Bulgakov, two Russian writers who could not be published in the Soviet Union. From the Proffers' interest in Russian literature and the contacts they had made with writers in the Soviet Union came their idea for a journal, the *Russian Literature Triquarterly*, published in Ann Arbor where Carl was teaching at the University of Michigan. When the Proffers had learned to operate their IBM Composer, their *tamizdat* endeavor was born, and they began to publish books by Russian writers who were banned in the Soviet Union. Manuscripts were obtained from writers in the Soviet Union or in exile abroad, and the books eventually found their way back into the Soviet Union where they had a ready audience and became collectors' items.

For ten years the Proffers had the usual problems of foreigners on visits to the Soviet Union—constant surveillance, interrogation of friends, body searches on leaving the country—but it was not until 1979 that they were officially barred from entry. Carl never saw Russia again; he died from cancer in 1984, at age forty-six. Under the direction of Ellendea, however, Ardis continued its publication of Russian works, and in 1994 it moved to California where it publishes today.

How successful, one might ask, was Ardis in bringing change to the Soviet Union? The answer is simply that Ardis made the Soviet authorities publish works that they did not want to publish. Ellendea Proffer, for example, recalls that when Ardis began to publish the collected works of the long-banned Bulgakov, Vladimir Lakshin, the major Soviet critic of Bulgakov, wrote in *Literaturnaya Gazeta* that Bulgakov might as well be published in Moscow, since he was being published *za*

---

8. Chernyaev, *My Six Years with Gorbachev,* 138.

okeanom (overseas), and shortly thereafter he was indeed published.[9] And so it continued with other writers published by Ardis—Andrei Bitov, Fazil Iskander, Lev Kopelev, and Osip Mandelshtam, among others. The Soviet rationale was that they were being published "over there," so they might as well also be published here. With the advent of Gorbachev's glasnost, the restrictions on publishing began to be lifted.[10]

Yevgeny Yevtushenko, speaking at the 1985 Congress of the Russian Republic Writers' organization, argued for a loosening of restrictions on the publication of literary works, including the publication of older works banned for decades. It would be better, argued the popular poet and frequent visitor to the United States, to publish such works in the Soviet Union than have them published abroad and used as anti-Soviet propaganda by foreign radio stations.[11] A similar call for publication of forbidden works was made at the Eighth Writers' Union Congress in 1986 by Andrei Voznesenky, another poet and frequent visitor to the United States.

Problems of Communism

Problems of Communism was a *Time*-sized bimonthly publication of USIA that provided analysis and information on the Soviet Union, China, and other communist states and political movements.[12] From its inception in 1952 until its closure in 1992 it was recognized as the leading worldwide journal on international communism. Its 25,000 copies were distributed by USIA overseas posts without cost in more than one hundred countries, where it was regarded as the principle academic publication on Soviet affairs. It was read by scholars, the media, research departments of international banks, and analysts who briefed government decision makers. Thanks to a special dispensation by the U.S. Congress, USIA was also able to distribute it in the United States, where an additional 5,500 copies were sold to individual subscribers by the U.S. Government Printing Office.

Abraham Brumberg, who edited *P of C*, as it was popularly known, for its first seventeen years, has attributed its success to the high quality of its authors and his determination not to turn the publication into a simple organ of anticommunist propaganda.[13] Among its distinguished contributors were such luminaries as

9. Ellendea Proffer, in e-mails to author, November 3 and 19, 2000.

10. Anatoly S. Chernyaev, in memoir *My Six Years with Gorbachev*, 38, makes it clear that publication abroad was a factor in permitting previously forbidden works to be published in the Soviet Union.

11. See John Garrard and Carol Garrard, *Inside the Soviet Writers Union* (New York: The Free Press, 1990), 199–200.

12. Much of the material on *Problems of Communism* here, including the quotations, is from Howard Oiseth, *The Way It Was* (Washington, D.C.: USIA, 1977), a history of the USIA's Press and Publication Service, in the State Department's Public Diplomacy files.

13. Abraham Brumberg, in address at Oxford University, England, July 9, 2000.

Raymond Aron, Abram Bergson, Zbigniew Brzezinski, Merle Fainsod, George F. Kennan, Richard Lowenthal, Hans Morgenthau, Harrison Salisbury, Arthur Schlesinger Jr.; Marshall D. Shulman, Stephen Spender, and Hugh Trevor-Roper. Several Soviet institutes were known to have acquired it and kept it on file, and the official Soviet government newspaper *Izvestiya* once paid it tribute by calling it "a serious journal designed to inform major elements of the bourgeoisie."

Problems of Eastern Europe

Russia has a tradition of "thick journals," as they are called, the monthly and quarterly periodicals on weighty subjects that are so prized by the Russian intelligentsia. One of the more influential of such journals, published in the United States but distributed in the Soviet Union from 1981 to 1996, was *Problemy vostochnoi evropy* (*Problems of Eastern Europe*), an independent quarterly that published Russian-language translations of articles by American and European political and economic analysts, policymakers, and scholars, as well as the writings of people from within the Soviet Union and Eastern Europe.

Among the authors published were Adam Ulam, Abraham Brumberg, Zbigniew Brzezinski, Paul Goble, Samuel Huntington, Elie Kedourie, Henry Kissinger, Irving Kristol, Walter Laqueur, Daniel Moynihan, Alec Nove, Richard Pipes, Peter Reddaway, Stephen Sestanovich, Robert Tucker, and Enders Wimbush. To readers in the Soviet Union, for whom normal access to such authors was forbidden, the journal was a treasure.

Problems was a labor of love of two people, František and Larisa Silnicky, who founded the journal and edited it from their apartment, first in New York and later in Washington, D.C. František, a historian, was educated in Czechoslovakia and the Soviet Union; his wife Larisa, a journalist and economist, born in Odessa, was an editor with the Russian desk of Radio Liberty in Washington, D.C.

The idea for *Problems* was born in the late 1970s when the Silnickys emigrated to the United States, ending an odyssey that had taken them from Russia to Czechoslovakia and, after the 1968 Soviet invasion there, to Israel. In New York, they met many Russian dissidents and, in reading their writings, found that the theoretical level of their work was rather low compared to that of East Europeans. In Poland, Hungary, and Czechoslovakia, there had been several efforts by elites to reform their Soviet-type societies by working within government structures. Economic and political change in those countries began at the top and then slowly spread from the communist party to the public. By contrast, most of the Russian *samizdat* dealt with human rights issues and served as a form of protest but was neither an attempt at reform nor directed toward the ruling apparatus. In the Soviet Union, most dissidents recognized that something was wrong with their society but their critiques, the Silnickys believed, were based on emotion rather than analysis.

After studying what Soviet dissidents were writing, the Silnickys believed it would be useful to show them what East Europeans had done in their attempts to change their Soviet-imposed societies. *Problems* did not aspire to be an émigré publication but to educate and fill the gap in Russia created by decades of isolation from the West, and to bring the East European experience to the reform movement in the Soviet Union. The Silnickys sought to analyze, without emotion, developments in Eastern Europe and the Soviet Union, and facilitate an exchange of ideas between the two. Also treated in their journal were nationality questions, a specialization of František Silnicky, and a special issue was dedicated to this question in response to a request from Emil Pain, Yeltsin's adviser on nationalities. Another special issue was dedicated to Juan J. Linz's *The Breakdown of Democratic Regimes*.

Together with Boris Shragin, Ludmilla Alexeyeva, and other Russian human rights activists in the United States, the Silnickys worked without compensation to publish the first issues of *Problems*, and they paid all costs until 1984, when a series of grants from the National Endowment for Democracy put the publication on a firmer financial basis.

When Gorbachev came to power in the mid-1980s, he brought to his government many people who had been in Prague in 1968, had witnessed the Prague Spring, and had begun to formulate ideas on how to reform Soviet society. Several members of the Russian parliament at that time told the Silnickys that they were trying to build something in the Soviet Union that they knew little about. So, in addition to their quarterly journal, the Silnickys also began to publish Russian translations of political science works by Western writers. Among the books published were George Orwell's *Animal Farm;* Walter Laqueur's *Russia and Germany* and *The Black Hundreds;* Silnicky's *Natsional'naya politika KPSS, 1917–22* (The Nationality Policy of the Communist Party of the Soviet Union, 1917–22); Zdeněk Mlynář's *Nightfrost in Prague;* Anatoly Marchenko's *To Live Like Everyone;* and a Russian-language edition of *Robert's Rules of Order* with an introduction by Senator Bill Bradley.

Distribution to Soviet readers was made through a network of personal contacts in the Soviet Union and Eastern Europe as well as several private American organizations that distributed or exchanged books in the region, among which were the Sabre Foundation, the Columbia University Library, the Russian-American Bureau of Human Rights, and the International Book Exchange Fund. With the advent of perestroika, copies were sent directly to Duma members and the Duma library. Addressees in the Soviet Union confirmed that all copies were received and distributed.

Responses from readers in the Soviet Union and Eastern Europe were enthusiastic. But even before perestroika, the Silnickys had received from readers in the Soviet Union several articles which they arranged to have published anonymously in the West. Three articles, one of them titled "Afghanistan Is Our Vietnam," were published in the *Washington Post* and reprinted in many European newspapers.[14]

Lilia Shevtsova, writing on behalf of scholars in the foreign affairs institutes of the Russian Academy of Science, has stated: "During the last years, we have welcomed and come to depend upon the Washington journal *Problems of Eastern Europe,* edited by Larisa and František Silnicky. . . . Under the communist regime, this publication was extremely important for our community because it was one of only a few sources which dealt with theoretical analysis of the problems of democracy and freedom."[15]

Progress Publishers

Many of the authors published by *Problems of Eastern Europe* were also published by the Soviet Union during the coldest years of the Cold War. In a classified operation, Western nonfiction works, many of them by American Sovietologists and public figures, were translated into Russian in Moscow and distributed to a limited list of two to five hundred highly placed people.[16] The program began at the Foreign Language Publishing House, but after several reorganizations, ended up at Progress Publishers. One of the translator-reviewers there was Georgi Arbatov, who would later become director of ISKAN; another was Yegor Gaidar, a future acting prime minister of Russia.

Subjects of interest to Progress included economics, politics, international affairs and diplomacy, history, and military affairs. Among the translated authors were George W. Ball, Chester Bowles, Zbigniew Brzezinski, Allen Dulles, John Foster Dulles, Samuel Huntington, Herman Kahn, George F. Kennan, Edward Kennedy, Henry Kissinger, Walter Lippmann, Richard M. Nixon, Paul Samuelson, Adlai Stevenson, and Adam Ulam. Also translated were transcripts of U.S. congressional hearings bearing on the Soviet Union, including many that the U.S. government itself would have been pleased to distribute in the Soviet Union.

The Progress operation helped mitigate some of the consequences of the Soviet Union's self-imposed isolation from Western thought and research. As Arbatov

14. S. Khovansky [pseud.], "Notes from the Soviet Antiwar Movement: Afghanistan Is Our Vietnam," *Washington Post,* March 23, 1986.

15. Lilia Shevtsova, in letter to Carl Gershman, president, National Endowment for Democracy, May 30, 1995.

16. The author has drawn here from Vladimir G. Treml, "Western Economic Sovietology and Soviet Authorities," in *The National Council for Eurasian and East European Research, 1978–1998: An Annotated Bibliography of Its Publications* (Washington, D.C.: The National Council for Eurasian and East European Research, 1999).

himself admitted years later: "Soviet specialists, scholars, scientists, and students missed several important decades of world socio-political thought . . . including the publication of works, teachings, and concepts of the leading Western philosophers, economists, sociologists, psychologists, and political scientists of the twentieth century."[17]

The books published by Progress enabled high-level Soviet leaders and policymakers to keep abreast of developments and thinking in the West, and one of their most avid readers was Mikhail Gorbachev. "He was so interested," says former Soviet ambassador to Washington Anatoly Dobrynin, "he had read so many books about the United States. Gorbachev took all the books he could find about the United States and read them all."[18]

As Gorbachev has confirmed: "As a member of the Central Committee I had access to books by Western politicians, political scientists, theoreticians published by the Moscow publisher Progress. . . . Reading these sources allowed me to familiarize myself with different views of history and on contemporary processes taking place on both sides of the ideological fault line."[19]

In economics, the books also proved to have an impact. According to Vladimir Treml, professor emeritus of economics from Duke University:

> There is sufficient . . . evidence to suggest that Western economic Sovietologists did influence the Soviet economic profession and higher authorities. There is no doubt that in the last twenty years, the Soviet economic profession and policymakers have gradually become less ideological and intolerant of Western views as well as more pragmatic, respectful of factual information, and balanced in its assessment of the Soviet economy. A number of different factors have contributed to these changes—one of them has been the exposure to Western Sovietology.[20]

But high Soviet officials were not the only readers of those forbidden books. They were brought home by senior officials and often read by their relatives and children, who passed them on to friends. Andrei Znamenski, a graduate student in history at MSU in 1985, recalls how a fellow student lent him, for one day, a copy of Wolfgang Leonhard's *The Future of Soviet Communism,* which had been lent him by another student whose father was a KGB colonel. "The book absolutely crashed me," writes Znamenski, now a professor at Alabama State University, "it

17. Arbatov, *The System,* 9.

18. Anatoly Dobrynin, quoted in Stein, "Political Learning by Doing," 240.

19. Mikhail S. Gorbachev, *Zhizn' i reformy, Kniga 1* (Moscow: Novosti, 1995), 144–45; quoted passage translated from the Russian by Vladimir Treml.

20. Treml, "Western Economic Sovietology," 44.

eliminated all remnants of the faith in Soviet socialism which I had at the time. The next day I roamed the streets of Moscow thinking about what I had read, and looked at everything with different eyes."[21]

How many such unauthorized readers of those books there were is not known but it can be presumed that the Soviet intelligentsia was better informed about the West than was believed at the time.

Library Exchanges

The Library of Congress and several American university libraries had for many years an active exchange of publications with Soviet libraries. The Library of Congress exchanges began in the 1920s, after Lenin had instructed Russian libraries to conduct exchanges with foreign libraries in order to acquire materials that would assist in the development of the new communist state. Those exchanges continued through the 1920s, even before the United States had recognized the Soviet Union, and into the 1930s until they were interrupted by World War II. They were resumed in 1946 and continued through the Cold War years when universities joined in, prompted by the growth of Slavic studies in the United States.

Collections in both countries were enriched, but many of the publications sent by American libraries ended up in Soviet *spetskhrany* (literally, books under special preservation), where access was restricted.[22] Nevertheless, American and other Western publications were available to individuals who had the proper connections, as well as university students who had authorization from their professors. Moreover, many of the exchange arrangements were with provincial Soviet libraries, where control was not so strict as in Moscow, and consequently, more Western publications were placed in open collections.

Book exchanges between libraries of Russia and the United States began even earlier, in 1772, when Benjamin Franklin, from his post in London, acted as intermediary for the transfer of the first edition of the proceedings of the Philadelphia-based American Philosophical Society to the Russian Academy of Sciences in St. Petersburg. It was the first exchange of publications between the two countries.

To protect Russians from Western influences considered harmful, tsarist Russia had four general categories regarding the circulation of foreign publications. The four categories, as described by American scholars, were "those permitted by the censorship authorities to circulate freely; those banned absolutely; those under a ban 'for the public,' accessible only to individuals who applied at the Foreign

---

21. Andrei Znamenski, e-mail to author, May 10, 2001.

22. By the 1980s, the number of foreign periodicals ending up in the *spetskhrany* reached a six-digit figure. See Dennis Kimmage, ed., *Russian Libraries in Transition: An Anthology of Glasnost Literature* (Jefferson, N.C.: McFarland, 1992), 112.

Censorship Committee offices and were approved by the authorities; and those permitted for circulation only after the excision (by blacking or pasting over or by cutting out) of specified words, lines, or pages."[23]

In further support of the theory of continuity in Russian history, during the Soviet period there appear to have been four analogous categories restricting access to foreign publications. One of those categories, the equivalent of the tsarist "banned for the public," led to establishment of the *spetskhrany*—special collections of books, journals, and other material generally designated as anti-Soviet. That depended on the whim of the censor, but could also include Bernard Malamud novels, Tom Stoppard plays, John le Carré thrillers, and copies of the *New York Times, Times Literary Supplement,* and *Vogue.*[24] Access to the *spetskhrany* and their restricted reading rooms in libraries and institutes was tightly controlled, and only authorized individuals were admitted.[25]

That system of controlled access to Soviet library collections, wrote Harrison Salisbury, veteran Russian correspondent of the *New York Times,* was organized like the three circles of hell:

> The outer circle with the general catalog is available to recognized students and scholars possessed of requisite passports, certificates of identity, and papers certifying to their need and right to examine these books. . . . The second circle is for more qualified scholars, those who are aspirants for a higher degree, those with special security clearance, those with party documentation. . . . The third circle is an inner citadel in which some restricted documents and books are available to those with senior credentials and high party and political validation. But within that are other circles, other catalogs, some of whose very existence is known only to the most trusted scholar-bureaucrats. . . . Here is the memory hole of Soviet history (and of Russian history as well). Here trespass is seldom granted.[26]

Trespass, however, was granted, as noted above, to those with a "need to know" and a letter of authorization from their institution or place of study, including graduate students recommended by their professors. Anatoly Chernyaev, Gorbachev's principal foreign policy adviser, recalls having access to books by Zbigniew Brzezinski and Raymond Aron.[27] Another reader of the Western books was

23. Choldin and Friedberg, *The Red Pencil,* 30.
24. *New York Times,* September 5, 2001.
25. Ibid., 31.
26. Harrison E. Salisbury, *The Book Enchained* (Washington, D.C.: Library of Congress, 1984), 7.
27. Chernyaev, *My Six Years with Gorbachev,* xxi.

Yegor Gaidar, later an acting prime minister of Russia and liberal reformer. Gaidar writes that his horizons were considerably broadened when, as an economics student at Moscow State University, he gained access to the university library: "It opened up enormous opportunities for self-education—Ricardo, Mill, Bohm-Bawerk, Jevons, Marshall, Pigou, Keynes, Schumpeter, Galbraith, Friedman, and many more. Getting to know these primary sources was not particularly encouraged, but neither was it prohibited."[28]

All that ended in 1988 when *Glavlit,* the Soviet censorship organization, announced that many books, including foreign publications previously held in the special collections, would henceforth be available to the general public.[29] By the early 1990s, access to the *spetskhrany* had been considerably liberalized, and some collections completely dismantled.

Another, less conventional, site where Western publications were freely available in the late Soviet period indicates how porous the Iron Curtain could be. That site was located in Kuibyshev (now Samara), the big industrial city on the Volga, in a region closed to foreigners. As related by Andrei Znamenski, there was a huge dump on the edge of the city where magazines, newspapers, and books discarded by elite Moscow institutes and government agencies were brought for reprocessing at a nearby paper plant. In 1978, Znamenski, then a student at the local university, was introduced to this "library," as it was called, by some friends. For the next five years, he and his fellow students would visit the "library" periodically and pick up relatively recent copies of the *International Herald Tribune,* the *New York Times,* the *Financial Times, Newsweek, Time,* and Germany's *Stern* and *Spiegel.* That bonanza ended, however, in 1983 when a drunk fell asleep at the dump, dropped a cigarette, and started a fire, which led to tighter control over access to what the students had previously regarded as their public library.[30]

Amerika Magazine

Another Western publication available to the Soviet public, and sanctioned by the Soviet government, was *Amerika* magazine, published by USIA. Agreement for its distribution was reached in 1956, one year after the Foreign Ministers' Conference in Geneva, when the Soviet Union consented to the reciprocal distribution of illustrated monthly magazines about life in the two countries, *Amerika* in Russian in the Soviet Union, and *USSR* (later renamed *Soviet Life*) in English in the United States.

28. Yegor Gaidar, *Days of Defeat and Victory,* trans. Jane Ann Miller (Seattle: University of Washington Press, 1996), 17.

29. For the full text of the announcement in *Izvestiya,* see Kimmage, *Russian Libraries in Transition,* 88–89.

30. Andrei Znamenski, e-mail to author, May 10, 2001

Amerika (*America Illustrated,* in English) had previously been distributed in the Soviet Union. During World War II, U.S. ambassador to Moscow Averell Harriman had made repeated efforts to obtain Soviet consent for distribution of a monthly publication on the United States. But it was not until March 25, 1944, that Molotov finally wrote Harriman agreeing to a bimonthly illustrated magazine, and by October 1945 the first two issues of *Amerika* had been distributed.[31] Published at that time by the Office of War Information (OWI) and intended to meet the high interest of Soviet citizens in information about the United States, *Amerika* achieved great popular success. As *Time* reported, "*America Illustrated* was hot stuff. They [the Russians] liked its eye-filling pictures of Arizona deserts, TVA dams, the white steeples of a Connecticut town, Radio City, the Bluegrass country, the Senate in session, Manhattan's garment district."[32] It also had a special attraction for women who, in making their own clothes, as many Russian women did in those years, copied the fashions they saw in the pages of *Amerika.* The magazine's success, however, was too much for the Soviet authorities; and in 1952, when the return of "unsold" copies escalated and it became clear that the Soviet Union was not honoring its agreement on distribution, it was reluctantly discontinued by the U.S. side. The signing of a new agreement in 1956 provided for the renewed distribution of the magazine.

The new *Amerika,* a prestige product, was a sixty-page, large-format, glossy, Russian-language monthly full of articles portraying life in the United States, with lots of color photos but no advertising. Designed to show the best U.S. journalistic practices in telling America's story to the Soviet people, its articles were acquired initially from *Life, Look, Fortune,* and other U.S. publications but later augmented with articles by freelance writers and *Amerika*'s own Washington staff. *Soviet Life* was of similar format, with articles culled from the Soviet press by the Novosti Press Agency and translated into English.

The agreement provided for each side to sell 50,000 copies of its magazine monthly—5,000 distributed through subscriptions, and the remaining 45,000 at newsstands in more than eighty cities. Each side was also authorized to distribute gratis an additional 2,000 copies, later increased to 5,000, through its embassy.

The first issue of the new *Amerika* appeared in October 1956. Although written for a mass audience, its graphics and text descriptions of life in the United States appealed to Soviet citizens at all levels of society. Particularly popular was its coverage of how Americans lived, worked, and played, from their kitchens to their cars. Moreover, its photo treatment and editorial style were new to the Soviet print media and served as models for similar Soviet photo magazines

---

31. *Foreign Relations of the United States, 1945* (Washington, D.C.: U.S. Government Printing Office, 1946), 5: 880–81.

32. *Time,* March 4, 1946.

Because of its popular appeal, *Amerika* proved far more successful than *Soviet Life*, since, with the exception of the communist *Daily World*, it was the only U.S. publication on sale in the Soviet Union at that time. By contrast, *Soviet Life* had to compete with a wide variety of U.S. and foreign publications, and its contents were not always of interest to American readers. *Amerika* soon became a collector's item, and many Russians, even today, prize the issues they saved over the years.

To counter the popularity of *Amerika* and limit its distribution, the Soviet distributor began to return "unsold" copies to the American Embassy, and it became obvious that the Soviets, in a gross distortion of reciprocity, were limiting sales of *Amerika* to the approximate level of sales of *Soviet Life*. To ensure the limitations on *Amerika*, the Department of Propaganda and Agitation of the Community Party's Central Committee issued a top secret directive.[33]

Party units were advised to organize subscriptions to *Amerika* for "politically literate and ideologically stable people," Soviet bureaucratese for people who could be trusted. It was further advised that subscriptions should be entered, not in the usual manner at Soviet post offices but rather through "social organizations" at work enterprises and institutions, which also ensured party control.

Regarding retail sales, the Central Committee recommended that the magazine be sold, not at kiosks in places open to the public, such as bazaars, parks, and railroad stations, but at "closed" kiosks located in enterprises, institutions, and other government buildings. Sales could be made at kiosks on main streets but only in limited numbers. The instruction also noted that there was no need to make efforts to sell all copies because, according to the U.S.-Soviet agreement, the Soviet distributor had the right to return unsold copies to the publisher. Party organizations were also advised to take precautions that in the distribution of *Amerika* there be no "unhealthy situations or commotions." For distributors of the magazine throughout the Soviet Union, the message from the Party's Central Committee was clear.

Despite such extreme measures, there is ample evidence that *Amerika* magazine had a wide readership in the Soviet Union. On days when the magazine went on sale in Moscow, American Embassy officers would check kiosks where they learned that the few token copies found there were usually held under the counter for preferred customers. On trips around the country, embassy officers found that Soviet citizens they encountered knew about the magazine, and many had seen

33. The recommendations on limiting distribution and entering subscriptions for *Amerika* are in "*O rasprostranenii v CCCP zhurnala* 'Amerika'" (On the distribution in the USSR of *Amerika* magazine), July 30, 1956, signed by F. Konstantinov, head, Department of Propaganda and Agitation, Central Committee of the Communist Party of the Soviet Union. This document can be found at Harvard University's Lamont Library in *fond* 89, "Declassified Documents of the Communist Party, 1956," no. 191, *opis'* 46, *delo* 11 (and at http://psi.ece.jhu/~Kaplan/IRuss/BUK/GBARC/pdts/usa/us56-6.pdf).

copies whose covers they were able to describe. Moreover, judging from the dog-eared copies they did see, embassy officers concluded that each copy was read by many readers.

Averell Harriman recalled that in his visits to Soviet homes over the years, he also saw many dog-eared copies of *Amerika* and was told by his hosts that the magazines were indeed read by many people. He also confirmed that women were copying the fashions they saw in the magazine.[34] Such multiple readership led the publisher to use heavier coated paper and thicker binding staples than usual for a magazine of its size.

The Party's instruction that subscriptions be entered at social organizations and institutions was intended to make it more difficult for the average Soviet citizen to purchase the magazine but it also ensured that the magazine would reach high-ranking officials. Moreover, the complimentary copies distributed gratis by the American Embassy were mailed to officials and other prominent people throughout the Soviet Union. One such official on the embassy mailing list was a young party secretary in Stavropol named Mikhail S. Gorbachev. To dispose of the "unsold" copies returned to the embassy, they were distributed to embassy contacts and to visitors at the U.S. exhibitions shown in the Soviet Union under the cultural agreement.

The effectiveness of *Amerika* can best be assessed by the extreme measures taken by the Soviet authorities to limit its distribution. There is no doubt that readers were impressed with the standard of living and everyday life in the United States portrayed in the magazine, and they made the inevitable comparisons with their own lives. Produced by a Washington staff of no more than thirty-five at an annual cost of one million dollars (exclusive of salaries), *Amerika* was a minor expense, but a major success, in the cold war of ideas.[35]

Dialog USA

An even more minor cost in the cold war of ideas was *Dialogue,* a USIA quarterly journal which, as its title indicates, was intended to open a dialogue with a world-wide audience interested in ideas and social problems. As its editor, Nathan Glick, put it in the first issue (which came out in spring 1968):

> *Dialogue* addresses itself to what one writer recently called "the intellectual public," those readers who have a compelling interest in ideas, social

---

34. Averell Harriman, cited in USIA memorandum, Sherwood H. "Woody" Demitz to Robert Poteete, August 3, 1977, State Department Public Diplomacy files.

35. The cost estimate of *Amerika* Magazine is from John Jacobs, a former chief editor of the magazine, personal communication with author, September 11, 1999.

problems, literature, and art. We hope to avoid facile popularization and irrelevant scholarship, and to publish articles that link special knowledge to wider cultural influences or pressing human needs. Our title refers primarily to the continuing discussion among Americans of matters ranging from education and culture to politics and economic development.[36]

There was also a reciprocal character to the intellectual discourse sought by *Dialogue* that transcended barriers of geographical frontiers and political systems. Glick spoke of the international fraternity of intellectuals with its common concern for humane values and its responsiveness to imaginative art, and he expressed the hope that the magazine would contribute to an international dialogue of ideas and aspirations.[37]

Dialogue began with a basic English-language edition from which other editions were adapted in French, Spanish, Portuguese, Greek, Polish, and Russian. Copies were distributed gratis by USIA's overseas posts in more than a hundred countries. Printed in its early years without color and with only a few black and white photos, it was a low-cost production.

The Russian edition, *Dialog USA,* began publication in fall 1969, and five thousand copies were distributed each quarter through 1988 by the American Embassy in Moscow and the Consulate General in Leningrad. In contrast to *Amerika,* there was no agreement with the Soviet Union on the distribution of *Dialog,* and when the Soviet authorities raised the issue with the American Embassy, they were told that there was also no agreement for the Soviet magazine *Sputnik,* which was being distributed in the United States. The matter was dropped and never raised again.

Most of the articles in *Dialog USA* were abridged versions of articles acquired from other publications and translated into Russian to explain issues that were of concern to American intellectuals. Among the works published were articles by such celebrities as Kenneth Clark, John Kenneth Galbraith, Randall Jarrell, George F. Kennan, Clark Kerr, Irving Kristol, Seymour Martin Lipset, Robert Lowell, and David Riesman, as well as interviews with Saul Bellow, Ralph Ellison, and Archibald MacLeish.

Dialog USA was accepted by its Soviet readers as another of the "thick journals" so prized by the Russian intelligentsia for whom the magazine was written. Moreover, the description of the worldwide audience sought by its editor, as described above, sounds very much like the Russian intelligentsia. Comments received from Russian readers were uniformly favorable, and one Russian reader described it as one of the best-written Russian journals.

36. Nathan Glick, "USIA's 'Little Magazine,'" *Cultural Affairs* 12 (fall 1970).
37. Ibid.

14 | THE PEN IS MIGHTIER . . .

Crooked letters, but straight sense.
—RUSSIAN PROVERB

Writers are respected, honored, and widely read in Russia, where they have long been regarded as the conscience of the nation. Because of the strict controls on what could be published, under tsars as well as commissars, Russian writers attempted to treat in their works subjects of political and social import that could not be discussed openly. That explains, in part, their importance in a nation that reveres the written word. Until the 1920s, the vast majority of Russians were illiterate, and it seems as if the Russians of our time are trying to make up for all the books their ancestors were unable to read.

Writers were privileged people in the Soviet Union, especially those who were members of the Union of Soviet Writers. Membership in the Union, as in the case of other professional unions, brought a number of perks, including access, in major cities, to the Houses of Writers with their good restaurants, bars, and coffee shops, at low, subsidized prices; the screening of foreign films; vacations at rest homes; month-long no-cost stays at rural retreats where they could write in peace and quiet; preference in assignment of housing; financial benefits; quality medical care; access to special food stores; and that highest privilege of all for the favored few—travel to the capitalist West.

Foreign travel, especially to Western countries, was a special treat for writers, as it was for all Soviet citizens. In the early years of the cultural agreement, a few Soviet writers came to the United States, usually in groups accompanied by the Union's English-speaking Freda Lurye, whose official role was listed as interpreter but who also served as political chaperone.

Edward Albee and John Steinbeck spent a month in the Soviet Union in 1963 under the cultural agreement, and Albee later recalled that they had had "freewheeling discussions with an entire spectrum of writers—from the brilliant, outspoken revisionist young to the stony-faced elders who had, with some honor or not, survived Stalin . . . and we had more than one night of vodka-drinking, table-thumping arguments with Stalinist holdovers in the bureaucratic apparatus of the Soviet Writers Union. It was an exciting time."[1] In a press conference with

1. Edward Albee, in Mel Gussow, *Edward Albee: A Singular Journey, A Biography* (New York: Simon and Schuster, 1999), 206.

American correspondents before departing Moscow, Albee described the Soviet writers he had met as "not depressed and not optimistic, but ironic" about their situation, and living in "isolation from the mainstream of contemporary writing."[2]

Another American writer, Ted Solotaroff, had a somewhat different reaction when he spent a month in the Soviet Union on the exchange:

> What I sensed they got out of visiting American writers was, to them, our spectacular freedom to speak our minds. I mean, there we were, official representatives of the U.S.—sort of the equivalent of their Writers Union apparatchiks—who had no party line at all, in most cases, except the party of humanity, and who had the writer's tendency to speak out on controversial issues. I did so often in the month I was there, and each time I could see how much I was envied. In other words, the exchanges enabled Soviet writers, intellectuals, students et al. to see that the "Free World" wasn't just political cant.[3]

Other American writers who visited the Soviet Union in an attempt to end that isolation included, among others, John Cheever, James Dickey, E. L. Doctorow, Arthur Miller, and William Jay Smith.

The isolation of Soviet writers was partly eased during the détente years of the 1970s, when controls on travel to the West were somewhat relaxed and exchanges expanded. Some writers were allowed to accept invitations from American universities and to travel individually, rather than as members of a delegation, and without a Writers' Union watchdog.

Chingiz Aitmatov, the celebrated Kyrgyz writer, came to the United States in 1975 on a State Department grant to attend the American premiere at Washington's Arena Stage of *The Ascent of Mount Fuji,* a play he coauthored. As a sign of his status in the Soviet Union, he was accompanied, not by a political chaperone but by one of his English-speaking sons, Sanjarbek, who was then an analyst at Arbatov's institute. (Another son, Askar, later became a deputy foreign minister in the independent Kyrgyzstsan, and is currently a senior adviser to the Kyrgyz president.)

Aitmatov's controversial play, first staged in Moscow in 1973 to great acclaim, is about four men and their former school teacher, a convinced communist, who meet on a mountain top and reminisce about their past. As an examination of conscience during the Stalinist and post-Stalinist years, the play revolves around what they did, or did not do, to a fifth classmate who was betrayed to the authorities, apparently by one of them, and suffered severely for an indiscretion he had

2. Ibid., 209.
3. Ted Solotaroff, e-mail to author, September 17, 2000.

committed during the war. As Robert G. Kaiser reported, "The play's authors leave the audience with the conclusion that those who were silent about Stalin's crimes share the guilt for them."[4]

Subsequently, Aitmatov and his son traveled throughout the United States as guests of the State Department, and several months after his visit he sent me, through a personal messenger, a handwritten letter of thanks, thus avoiding Writers Union control. In his letter he wrote, "You are performing a great, necessary, and useful piece of work for cultural cooperation between our two countries. You have helped us to know your country in the best possible way."[5]

Writers in Residence

Lawrence, Kansas, was the destination of many Soviet writers during the 1970s and 1980s. In another example of cooperation between the public and private sectors, the University of Kansas brought more than twenty-five, mostly Russian, writers to its Lawrence campus for periods of several days to several weeks for lectures and informal meetings with students and faculty. International travel was paid by the Soviet Writers Union; Kansas covered the local costs in Lawrence; and the State Department paid for side trips to other universities and other parts of the United States. The program was conceived and directed by Gerald Mikkelson, professor of Slavic languages and literature at Kansas.[6]

Among the writers who came to Kansas were such luminaries as poets Bella Akhmadulina, Oleg Chukontsev, Aleksandr Kushner, Bulat Okudzhava, and Yevgeny Vinokurov; prose writers Vasily Aksyonov, Grigori Baklanov, Daniil Granin, Valentin Rasputin, Vladimir Soloukhin, Yuri Trifonov, and Sergei Zalygin; playwrights Edvard Radzinsky and Viktor Rozov; and critic Marietta Chudakova.

Those visits to Kansas, writes Mikkelson, "not only broadened their horizons culturally and ideologically, and gave them plenty of food for thought that sometimes got translated into specific literary works or images, but it added to their prestige and emboldened them at home in their efforts to make the Soviet Union a more livable place for writers and people in the other creative and performing arts."[7]

Kansas also benefited from having such distinguished writers in residence. They lectured in Russian to audiences of twenty to fifty people and had informal meetings with faculty and students. Several of the Kansas graduate students wrote

4. *Washington Post,* February 4, 1975.
5. Chingiz Aitmatov, letter to author, September 8, 1975 (translator not known).
6. For much of the information on Soviet writers at Kansas, the author is indebted to Gerald E. Mikkelson, University of Kansas.
7. Gerald E. Mikkelson, e-mail to author, April 21, 2000.

their doctoral dissertations on the works of the writers they had met at Lawrence and went on to careers teaching Russian literature.

As for the Russians, their best benefit was the opportunity to spend a few quiet weeks on an American university campus, observing the work of faculty and students, conversing with people interested in Russia and its literature, spending time in a good library, and getting to see the Midwest, the heartland of America not usually visited by Russians. Several of the writers wrote about Kansas in their subsequent works.

Trifonov, in his posthumously published cycle of stories, *Oprokinutiy Dom (Topsy-Turvy House)*, wrote about his visits to Kansas, Las Vegas, and California. Rozov included a chapter in his memoirs called "Kansas City," and wrote about how one of his plays was performed in the University of Kansas Theater. Chukontsev published a poem in which he compared Kansas and Wisconsin to his native Moscow; "It's frightening here" [in Russia], he wrote, "and boring there" [in America].[8]

Rozov and Soloukhin, in the late 1970s, agreed to be interviewed by the Voice of America and spoke well about American hospitality and the value of such contacts to them as writers. Soloukhin, after his stay in Kansas, and at some personal risk, made contact with Solzhenitsyn at his exile retreat in Vermont. Akhmadulina, in another display of courage, stopped off on her way home to visit Vladimir Nabokov, the famous Russian writer living in exile in Switzerland.

Yuri Trifonov, in an interview with a Soviet newspaper, described his three weeks at Kansas in 1978, where he lectured to students and faculty on contemporary Soviet literature, and his travels to ten other universities as a guest of the State Department. In New York, he met with his publisher, Simon and Schuster, and signed contracts for two of his books, one of which, *The House on the Embankment,* is an acute description of life in the Soviet Union as it really was. When asked in the interview why he was subjected to so much criticism and abuse in the Soviet press, Trifonov replied that his main concern was to write about the defects of Soviet society, especially its moral shortcomings, and that irritates some critics.[9] In Washington, Trifonov called on me at the State Department, and he came alone, without a Soviet Embassy escort, contrary to the practice of most Soviet visitors.

A similar program, the Iowa Writing Program (IWP) at the University of Iowa at Ames, was conceived and directed by Paul Engle and his wife Hua-ling. Founded in 1967, the IWP was the first international writers residency at a university. Still in existence, it brings writers of the world to Ames, where they become

8. Gerald E. Mikkelson, e-mail to author, October 12, 1999.
9. Yuri Trifonov, "Intervyu o kontaktakh," *Inostrannaya literatura,* no. 6 (1978).

part of the literary community on campus. Over the years, more than a thousand writers from more than a hundred countries have completed residencies in the program.

East European writers, Poles and Romanians in particular, attended the Iowa Writing Program regularly, but the Soviet Union for many years did not respond to repeated invitations. When it finally did send a writer in 1986, it was Boris Zakhoder, a children's poet and the celebrated translator of *Alice in Wonderland, Mary Poppins,* and A. A. Milne's *Winnie the Pooh* and *The House at Pooh Corner.* Generations of Russian children have grown up with *Vinny Pookh,* as the lovable bear is known in Russian, and the Zakhoder translations of the Milne books sold more than 3.5 million copies in a single year. Joseph Brodsky described Zakhoder as "a legend."[10]

When Writers Meet

Russia has always had a tendency to borrow culturally from whomever it was opposing politically.

—JAMES H. BILLINGTON, *Russia Transformed*

American and Soviet writers held a series of meetings during the 1970s and 1980s at the initiative of Norman Cousins, editor of the *Saturday Review of Literature.* The meetings were an adjunct of the Dartmouth Conference series, which, as noted above, had also been initiated by Cousins. Cochairs of the writers' meetings were Cousins and Nikolai Fedorenko, chief editor of *Inostrannaya literatura (Foreign Literature)* magazine, a sinologist and former Soviet ambassador to the United Nations.[11] The meetings were funded by the Kettering Foundation and the State Department.

At the first meeting, held in Moscow in 1977, the list of Soviet participants reads like a Who's Who of Soviet writers. Among the thirty participants were Chingiz Aitmatov, Vasily Aksyonov, Yuri Bondarev, Genrikh Borovik, Konstantin Chugunov, Valentin Katayev, Tatyana Kudryavtseva, Maurice Mendelson, Yuri Nagibin, Boris Pankin, Yuri Trifonov, Andrei Voznesensky, Yevgeny Yevtushenko, and Sergei Zalygin. (Another two dozen writers had wanted to attend, the Americans were told, but space at the conference table was limited.) The American writers were Edward Albee, Norman Cousins, Vera Dunham, Leo Gruliow, Elizabeth Hardwick, Robert Lowell, Nathan Scott, and William Styron.

10. Daniel Weissbort, e-mail to author, September 6, 2000.

11. Detailed accounts of these meetings, written by Norman Cousins, and from which the author has drawn, can be found in "When Writers Meet," *Saturday Review of Literature,* September 17, 1977, and June 24, 1978, and "When American and Soviet Writers Meet," June 24, 1978.

The Americans focused much of their presentations on the treatment of dissident writers in the Soviet Union, some of whom they visited after the meeting, while the Soviet writers belabored the disparity between the large number of American authors published in the Soviet Union and the much smaller number of Soviet authors in the United States. Despite their differences, the two sides agreed to continue their dialogue, and a second meeting was scheduled for New York the following year.

The New York meeting focused on the art of the novel and the place of the author in the world literary community. At the table were Edward Albee, Vera Dunham, Elizabeth Hardwick, Arthur Miller, Joyce Carol Oates, Harrison Salisbury, William Jay Smith, William Styron, John Updike, and Kurt Vonnegut, with Norman Cousins as cochair and Leo Gruliow as rapporteur.

The Soviet writers were Nikolai Fedorenko as cochair, Grigori Baklanov, Nodar Dumbadze, Valentin Katayev, Aleksandr Kosorukov, Freda Lurye, Mikola Slutskis, Sergei Zalygin, Yasen Zasursky, and Isabella Zorina. Three of the Soviet writers—Fedorenko, Kosorukov, and Lurye—were officials of the Union of Soviet Writers.

After presenting their polemics about the differences between the publishing industries of the two countries, the Americans and Soviets discovered how much they had in common as writers. Harrison Salisbury, the former *New York Times* correspondent in Moscow, thought it highly significant that, once the writers had completed their polemics on publishing and started to talk about writing, they discovered that they were on common ground. Salisbury, a Russian speaker, added that if he had not known the identity of the writers at the table, he would have been unable to tell, from their discussion of literary principles, who were Russian and who were American.[12]

Nevertheless, as evidence of the gulf remaining between the two sides, at the close of the meeting one of the Soviet delegates, an official of the Writers' Union, suggested to Cousins that if the United States would establish a state publishing house, it could ensure that books by foreign writers would be published in the United States in sufficient numbers.

To that proposal, wrote Cousins, "We responded that we wouldn't trust government to select and publish any books, foreign or domestic."[13] And when one of the Soviet writers later asked Cousins privately whether the American writers weren't running the risk of getting into trouble with their State Department by speaking of their distrust of government, Cousins replied that there was a far greater likelihood that anyone in the government who objected to such observations would be in trouble himself.[14]

12. Cousins, "When American and Soviet Writers Meet," 44.
13. Ibid., 45.
14. Ibid.

What was learned and what was gained from such meetings, asked Cousins. From the American standpoint, he replied,

> Perhaps the most important thing we learned is that it is no longer accurate to say that Soviet writers can be divided into only two categories—the out-and-out dissidents and the hard-line party members. There is a wide octave between the two, with varying intensities, shadings, and leanings. We learned that Soviet literary rubber-stamping of political purpose has gone out of style and that authors are dealing increasingly with questions of corruption and abuses of power, although they are adroit enough to know what lines not to cross. We learned that the renewed and enlarged respect for classical Russian literature has been accompanied by a sharpening of literary and human values.[15]

Cousins thought it presumptuous to say what the Russians had learned from the Americans but he hazarded a guess: "They were certainly aware of our convictions that as members of a world literary community, we are deeply troubled about the conditions of the dissident writers and that we want to be able to communicate with them in a meaningful and helpful way. They were also made aware of our desire to find out more about contemporary Soviet literature."[16]

What such meetings meant to the Soviet participants was exemplified by what Soviet poets privately told Stanley Kunitz, the American poet, at the third meeting in the series, held at Batumi, a Black Sea resort. "Bear with us," the Russians said with foresight. "It's difficult. We have to learn how to survive. But we are trying. Eventually, the old hard-liners will die off. Time is on our side. Keep coming."[17] Time was indeed on their side, and the American writers kept coming, well into the 1980s when change had come to the Soviet Union.

Several of the Soviet writers who attended those meetings were to play prominent roles in the changes that occurred after Gorbachev's accession to power in 1985. Sergei Zalygin, a member of the Secretariat of the Union of Soviet Writers, in 1986 was appointed editor of the prestigious literary journal *Novy Mir,* where he published long-banned works by Boris Pasternak, Joseph Brodsky, and Aleksandr Solzhenitsyn. In the same year, Grigori Baklanov was appointed chief editor of *Znamya,* a leading literary and political monthly, and Chingiz Aitmatov was appointed chief editor of *Inostrannaya literatura,* replacing hard-liner Nikolai Fedorenko. Aksyonov settled in the United States and became a professor at

15. Ibid.
16. Ibid.
17. Stanley Kunitz, quoted by Herbert Mitgang in "Book Ends," *New York Times Book Review,* December 23, 1979.

George Mason University where he continued his writing. Aitmatov, Aksyonov, Baklanov, and Zalygin had all been in the United States earlier under various exchange programs, the last three at Kansas.

Aitmatov, as editor of *Inostrannaya literatura,* began to publish more Western writers, and in an article in *Izvestiya,* the Soviet government daily, he condemned Stalin for the horrors he had inflicted on the Soviet people and the Soviet economy. In the article, Aitmatov noted how Germany and Japan had emerged from the ashes of World War II with higher living standards and industrial development, while the Soviet Union, a victor in the war, lagged behind. Aitmatov blamed this on the isolation Stalin had imposed on the Soviet Union, and in a paragraph that reflected his own extensive foreign travels, he wrote: "I believe that Stalin's stygian isolationism and alienation from the outside world were not least to blame for this retrogression. To live with one's neighbors in enmity and threats is not a very clever thing to do; far more intelligence and flexibility are required to understand the interaction between different world structures with the aim of deriving mutual benefits."[18]

This is not to imply that all those writers became reformers after attending the U.S.-Soviet writers conferences or being in residence at Kansas. However, most of the writers at those conferences had previously been to the United States, and many of them would come again in later years. Foreign travel played a role in broadening their perspectives and creating a better understanding of the United States and its people, as well as its literature.

The benefits of closer contacts between Soviet and American writers were illustrated in the mid-1970s when two prominent personalities from the Moscow theater came to the United States under the State Department's International Visitor Program. Oleg Yefremov was one of Russia's most revered actors and theater directors, as well as artistic director of the Moscow Art Theater (*Mkhat*), and Mikhail Roshchin was a promising young playwright. The two began their visit in San Francisco where they worked with the American Conservatory Theater in staging a play by Roshchin that Yefremov had directed in Moscow. Moreover, as a result of that visit, the promising playwright literally got a new lease on life and went on to write many more plays. Roshchin, it was later learned, had heart trouble, and during a subsequent visit American friends arranged to have his heart valves replaced by a renowned American cardiologist.

One final vignette illustrates how Soviet writers were affected by their visits to the United States. In 1988, I was in Minsk for three weeks with a U.S. book exhibit. Minsk, then the capital of the Soviet republic of Byelorussia (today's independent

---

18. Chingiz Aitmatov, "Are the Foundations Being Undermined?" *FBIS-Soviet Union,* May 12, 1988, translated from *Izvestiya,* May 4, 1988.

Belarus), was not the most exciting city in the Soviet Union to visit, and for a little diversion, I asked my hosts if they could arrange a meeting with some local writers. And so, one afternoon, I was driven to a villa on the edge of the city—one of those writers' retreats found in most large Soviet cities—where ten of the leading writers in Byelorussia were seated around a table awaiting my arrival.

I wanted to talk about life, literature, and current issues in Byelorussia, but the writers wanted to talk about New York and the wonderful times they had there as "public members" of Byelorussian delegations to meetings of the United Nations General Assembly.

When the United Nations was founded in 1945, the Soviet Union was given three seats in the General Assembly—the Soviet Union, Ukraine, and Byelorussia—and for each General Assembly meeting there were three delegations, each of which usually included a few writers, dancers, singers, or other cultural figures, whom most of us in the State Department regarded as window dressing. But the month those writers spent in New York was a revelation. Window dressing they may indeed have been, but after the UN daily meetings they stepped out of their show windows and onto the sidewalks of New York, where they apparently had the time of their lives.

15 | JOURNALISTS AND DIPLOMATS

The intelligentsia was used to thinking one thing, saying another, and writing something else again.

—ALEKSANDR N. YAKOVLEV, "Setting Russia's History Straight"

Gorbachev, me, all of us, we were double-thinkers. We had to balance truth and propaganda in our minds all the time. It is not something I am particularly proud of, but that is the way we lived. It was the choice between dissidence and surrender.

—GEORGI SHAKHNAZAROV

Among the Russians accustomed to thinking one way but writing another were journalists and diplomats stationed outside the Soviet Union. During the Cold War, thousands of them worked in the United States and other countries around the world, and it is fair to ask if they too were influenced by their years abroad.

This is complicated somewhat by the commonly held belief that all Soviet correspondents abroad, as well as many of the diplomats, had intelligence connections or obligations to report to the GRU or KGB, a factor that colored their written perceptions of the West and their reporting to Moscow.

That view is voiced by Raymond Anderson, a former *New York Times* Moscow correspondent; who wrote about his subsequent assignment in Egypt:

> I did get to know some very competent Russians in Cairo, half of them listed later in John Barron's book [on the KGB] as "operatives." but there was no clue at the time. They did their journalism jobs. They were good colleagues and none ever lied to me. They gave me some bits of information that helped me at critical moments on deciding what was going on in Egypt. The information was correct. No one ever tried to recruit me. but I always assumed that each and every one was staff KGB or at least reporting to the KGB so I kept my distance.[1]

According to Mikhail Kroutikhin, a former TASS bureau chief in the Middle East, TASS reporters abroad were a mixed crowd, "some 50% were 'pure' journalists,

---

1. Raymond Anderson, e-mail to author, October 24, 1999. John Barron, *The KGB Today, The Secret Work of Soviet Secret Agents* (New York: Reader's Digest Press, 1974).

another 45% belonged to the GRU (Main Intelligence Department, General Staff), and 5% were with the KGB."[2] "None of us," adds Kroutikhin, "was under any illusion about the difference in life in the USSR and in the Middle East, meaning both the conditions of everyday life and human rights and freedoms":

> Cynicism was a natural part of our existence, as well as hypocrisy (active participation in the Communist Party, which made us eligible for foreign assignments). That was the way educated people in the USSR survived in the totalitarian environment. Very few of us seemed real hardcore believers in the advantages of Soviet-style socialism. This is why membership of intelligentsia in the CP was limited (while workers could enroll easily, quotas existed for admitting people with university educations).

Recalling his youth in Moscow, Kroutikhin continues:

> All contacts with foreign culture were instrumental in forming a new mentality in the Soviet people and bringing closer the fall of the totalitarian empire. We were eager to grasp at anything foreign that came our way—the 1957 World Youth Festival, foreign films, the first foreign entertainers such as Yves Montand who visited Moscow in the late 1950s, etc. Few people in my youth traveled abroad, but those who did almost immediately abandoned most of their illusions.

In his own case, says Kroutikhin, his views were not changed by his service abroad. They changed earlier, at age seventeen, when he began to study English and "was carried away by the cultural vistas the knowledge of that language opened for me. I spoke English better than my schoolteacher and read lots of foreign books." As a consequence, he continues, "We did not see the Soviet Union differently from our stations abroad, simply because we saw it with the same eyes when we were at home."

For his daughter, however, he adds, "the revelation came as the light on the Damascus road for St. Paul: "She was six. It was her first evening abroad, in Tehran in 1971, and she had been tasting such beverages as 7 Up and Coke and Fanta for the first time in her life. When we were falling asleep, we heard her whisper, from her bed in the next room, the names of the beverages. I guess it was the moment her patriotism ended forever."

As noted above, Oleg Kalugin, the KGB officer who studied at Columbia University in 1958–59, returned to New York as a correspondent for Radio Moscow,

2. The following quotations and comments by Kroutikhin are from his e-mails to the author, November 24 and 26, 2000.

and former student Boris Yuzhin returned to California as a TASS correspondent. But, as Max Frankel, former executive editor of the *New York Times* and a former *Times* Moscow correspondent, writes of the Soviet journalists he has known: "[Those] KGB connections (or obligations) did not preclude their absorbing the free spirit of our press and, indeed, of our political life, and I am sure it affected them deeply in ways they could never express. Many of their smartest people in journalism, as in the arts, lived external and internal lives, one that sustained careers, and the other shared only with close relatives and friends, lest they lose their 'permission' to fraternize with the West."[3]

After the Soviet invasions of Hungary in 1956 and Czechoslovakia in 1968, many of the Soviet correspondents abroad as well as some of its diplomats, disillusioned with Soviet policy but unwilling to express their views openly and jeopardize their careers, became mental defectors, sharing their innermost thoughts only with family and close friends.

One of those disillusioned diplomats shared his despair with an American diplomat. The two were attending a Quaker Conference for Diplomats and became quite close. The night before the conference ended, the American and the Soviet spent the entire night together drinking whiskey and sharing their innermost thoughts. As dawn was breaking, the Russian became sentimental and his "soul" emerged, as it often does when Russians imbibe. He regretted that the two would never meet again because he planned to return to Moscow and resign from the diplomatic service.

The American was shocked by this disclosure and asked why his Russian friend would give up a promising career. Becoming quite serious and, looking the American straight in the eye, the Russian said in his fluent English that he could not take it any more, the double thinking—saying one thing to his colleagues in the embassy and the opposite to his foreign acquaintances. You have no idea, he continued, what it means to have two different ways of thinking—one for your colleagues, and the other for the outside world. He wanted to go back to Moscow and find a job where he did not have to be on guard every minute of his life and remember to whom he was speaking. He enjoyed the diplomatic life, he concluded, and all the things to which he had access, but the price was too high.

The two parted, and the American thought he would never see the Russian again. Years later, however, to his great surprise, he encountered the Russian in a Western capital to which the two were assigned. "I thought you were going back to Moscow and resign," said the American. The Russian shrugged his shoulders and raised his hands, palms up, as if to say "What can you do? It's fate."

It was a classic case of a man who recognized the contradictions between his political indoctrination and the world beyond the Soviet borders in which he

3. Max Frankel, e-mail to author, September 13, 1999.

worked, where the reality of daily life did not conform to the principles of Marxism-Leninism he had been trained to regard as inexorably valid everywhere. How many such cases there were in the diplomatic service is not known, but it can be safely assumed that this was not an isolated one.

That it was not an isolated case has been confirmed by Alexandra Costa, who defected from the Soviet Embassy in Washington in 1978. In a book that relates the how and why of her defection, she tells how an embassy friend explained to her why Soviet diplomats who had served in Washington were changed by that experience and returned to Moscow much different from when they had left it:

> Your perspective has changed because of your exposure to all this information; and by being a part of the embassy you got used to thinking about things in more global terms. Your friends cannot understand you because their concerns are confined to their own local world of internal politics in Moscow, and it bothers you because you know there are more important things in the world. They don't understand many things you mention in your conversation because they don't know what these things are. . . . Your change is permanent. When you return to Moscow, you will continue to socialize with people you met here at the embassy, rather than with your old friends, because we know the same things, we think the same way. You will feel like a foreigner in Moscow for many years to come, and the only people you will be comfortable with are those with the same experience.[4]

Until well into the 1960s, virtually all of the reporting from the United States in the Soviet press was predictably stereotyped. Dispatches to Moscow from Washington and New York typically opened with such lines as "Progressive American circles warmly applauded the Soviet initiative on . . . " But a big change came with Stanislav Kondrashov, a veteran *Izvestiya* correspondent in the United States, who, as the late Lars-Erik Nelson of the *New York Daily News* recalled, "instead of quoting *The Daily Worker* as representative of the American press, began quoting *The New York Times* and *The Washington Post*."[5] Kondrashov was in the United States during the Cuban missile crisis, and many years later, during glasnost, he criticized the Soviet government's secrecy in denying that it had placed missiles in Cuba when the United States had photographic evidence of their deployment.[6]

4. Alexandra Costa, *Stepping down from the Star: A Soviet Defector's Story* (New York: G. P. Putnam's Sons, 1986), 100.

5. Lars-Erik Nelson, e-mail to author, September 13, 1999.

6. See Andrei Melville and Gail W. Lapidus, *The Glasnost Papers: Voices on Reform from Moscow* (Boulder, Colo.: Westview Press, 1990), 49.

Kondrashov called for the creation of a state based on the rule of law, which would eliminate the Soviet mania for secrecy. How can we explain, he asked, "the distinctive vow of silence that our leaders—from generation to generation—imposed upon themselves? Or by the clandestineness, which became second nature, that was institutionalized by Stalin so that he could keep in his own hands all elements of power that was not accountable to the people?"[7]

One of the real pushes for change on the part of Soviet foreign correspondents, continued Nelson,

> was seeing the Far East—Japan, South Korea, and the Asian Tigers— move into the modern world economy of miniaturized electronics, computers, world-class automobiles, etc. The Russians were always prepared to lag a step or two behind Britain, Germany, and America but . . . it was a real shock for them to realize that even China might be leaping ahead of them, with the military threat that such progress implied. No country is prepared to commit national suicide for the sake of an ideology. Exposure to the outside world told them how badly communism had failed to provide a decent living and also to protect them.[8]

Gennadi Gerasimov was a *Novosti* correspondent in the United States from 1972 to 1978, and during the Carter administration he attended White House and other U.S. government press conferences. When the urbane Gerasimov returned to Moscow and became the spokesman for the Foreign Ministry in the Gorbachev years, he began holding regular press conferences twice a week, answering questions on subjects previously considered off-limits, a revolutionary innovation for a Soviet government agency and a radical departure from the Brezhnev years. Gerasimov seemed to be modeling his style after Jody Powell, Carter's press secretary, and his wit and repartee were a welcome change from the dour pronouncements of previous Soviet spokesmen.

When Mikhail Gorbachev, in 1989, renounced the so-called Brezhnev doctrine, which had sought to justify the Soviet invasion of Czechoslovakia, Gerasimov declared that Hungary and Poland were going their own way, and the Brezhnev doctrine had been replaced by the Sinatra doctrine, a play on the Frank Sinatra hit tune, "My Way." But conservative communists did not appreciate Gerasimov's wit and spontaneity, and in 1991 he was packed off to Portugal as ambassador plenipotentiary. After the fall of the Soviet Union, Gerasimov became a frequent visitor to the United States, where he was a guest professor at several universities.

7. Ibid., 50–51.
8. Lars-Erik Nelson, e-mail to author, September 13, 1999.

Gerasimov had served earlier in Prague, 1961–64, on the staff of *Problems of Peace and Socialism,* although his major interests were political science and international relations. As an exchange journalist in the United States in the mid-1960s, he was influenced by the work of Thomas Schelling and heard lectures on game theory at Columbia and Princeton. Years later, he recalled the benefits of his American studies of foreign policy and national security, and his listening to discussions and debates in American universities. He had already done some reading in U.S. foreign policy literature but being there and discussing it with the professors, he said, was more meaningful.[9] After his return to Moscow, he wrote articles introducing Soviet readers to the work of Schelling and other American scholars on game theory, acquainting them for the first time with U.S. strategic thinking of those years. Through his writings, Gerasimov became known as a critic of ABM defensive systems.

Vitaly Korotich first came to the United States in 1966 as a secretary of the Ukrainian Writers Union and was best known then as a poet. Fluent in English, he became a regular on the U.S.-Soviet exchange circuit, where he soon developed a network of American friends and supporters. From those visits came several books on the United States, some fictional but based on his encounters with Americans, which gave him poetic license to show how biased Americans were against Ukrainians and Russians, and how hostile toward the Soviet Union. One of his books, *The Face of Hatred,* was described by the *New Yorker's* John Newhouse as "an anti-American diatribe." Published in Russian in 1984 and reissued in 1989, it sold two million copies and was translated into German and Spanish. "It was a slimy book," wrote Vasily Aksyonov, "and it surprised me."[10]

Korotich never joined the Communist Party but in his earlier years was a staunch supporter of Brezhnev and the Soviet system. Nevertheless, in 1986 he became chief editor of *Ogonyok* (*Little Flame*) and one of Gorbachev's most ardent advocates in the media. With his attacks on opponents of change—party bosses, the KGB and the Soviet Army—he raised the weekly's circulation, during his four and one-half years as chief editor, from 260,000 to 4,600,000.[11] In describing his war against the Stalinist system, Korotich wrote:

> We are learning to say out loud words we were afraid to voice for decades. In the past it was difficult for *Ogonyok* to decide to publish just a one-sentence reference to the need for public control over the Soviet military and the KGB. Now we can publish everything that we can vouch for, which is how it should be. That is how *Ogonyok's* stories on the

9. English, *Russia and the Idea of the West,* 279 n. 142.
10. Vasily Aksyonov, quoted by John Newhouse in "Profiles," *New Yorker,* December 31, 1990, 44.
11. Ibid., 38.

crimes of Stalin and modern corruption originated. That is how we examine such things as the decline of the Bolshoi Ballet, the rise of non-party organizations in the Baltic republics, the problems of the poor and attempts to use anti-Semitism to restore a dictatorship of fear.[12]

Korotich is "clearly comfortable" in America, wrote Newhouse who speculated that he might want to live here some day.[13] Indeed, Korotich spent seven years in the United States as a visiting lecturer at several universities before returning to Russia in 1999 where he now resides.

Another apologist in the United States for the Soviet Union was Genrikh Borovik, a talented and popular writer who later became a strong supporter of Gorbachev and his reforms. Although not positively identified as an intelligence agent, Borovik is believed to have been close to the KGB. Kalugin describes him as "one of our 'pet' Soviet journalists who always did our bidding."[14]

In the 1960s, Borovik was stationed in New York as head of North American operations for the *Novosti* news agency. Raymond Anderson, the former *New York Times* Moscow correspondent who knew Borovik in those years, describes him as "a reasonable person, even when Brezhnev was still around, with no baloney about socialism, and not afraid to talk with Americans."[15] "An original and venturesome reporter," adds Anderson, "Borovik took chances to get a good story. He appeared on a TV talk show, attended a tsarist officer's ball in Manhattan and wrote a feature story about it, and visited the military recruiting center in Times Square and wrote about it, but without the usual propaganda virulence of other Soviet journalists. An amiable and outgoing type, even in the worst days of the cold war, people he met in the States seemed to like him."[16] A man with good connections in all times, Borovik eventually chaired the Soviet Peace Committee, became a participant in the Dartmouth Conference; and thirty years later he was still making news but whistling a different tune, as Michael Wines, the *New York Times* Moscow correspondent reported: "When Genrikh Borovik was running the *Novosti* news agency's North American operations from New York in the late 1960s, he was a frequent critic of the United States and the Vietnam War. But Borovik's friends back in the Soviet Union saw it differently. 'America was a role model,' Borovik recalled years later, 'there were plenty of emotions, sure. But at the same time, people said, Nevertheless, America is a very free place.'" "Thirty years and 180 degrees later," continued Wines, "Mr. Borovik is a playwright and television anchor in Moscow, and a man

12. Vitaly Korotich, "Typing Out the Fear," *Time,* April 10, 1989, 124.
13. Newhouse, "Profiles," 44.
14. Kalugin, *First Directorate,* 157.
15. Raymond Anderson, e-mails to author, October 21 and 24, 1999.
16. Ibid.

with some sympathy for the United States' decision to join the war against Yugoslavia. And now he defends America to friends who believe the United States is bent on world domination—and that Russia was its unwitting ally in the Kosovo peace accord."[17]

New York was a choice assignment for Borovik but the closest many Soviet journalists got to the West was Prague, culturally the most Western of the Soviet satellite capitals and a very pleasant place for Russians and others from points further east. From 1959 to 1990, Prague was the site of the editorial offices of *Problemy mira i sotsializma* (*Problems of Peace and Socialism*), the journal of the world communist movement, published in many languages but staffed mainly by Soviets as well as a few other Europeans, Americans, and representatives of Third World communist parties.[18]

An assignment at the Prague journal gave Russians a broader view of the world, a better understanding of their foreign comrades and their countries, cultures, and especially their ideological differences, which would be regarded as heretical in Moscow. Gennadi Gerasimov has described the interplay there between Soviet staffers and their communist comrades from Western Europe: "Communists at the journal who came from capitalist countries and were ideologues at home, brought to the Prague collective a many-voiced struggle of ideas. There, in conditions sufficiently free for that time, they discussed Marx and Solzhenitsyn, and argued about Gramsci and Orwell."[19]

Among the staffers, in addition to Gerasimov, were Georgi Arbatov, Vadim Zagladin, Yuri Zhilin, Yevgeni Ambartsumov, Lev Sheydin, and Mikhail Kremnev. Moreover, adds Gerasimov, on the staff of *Problemy* were many future staffers of *Novoye Vremya,* the liberal journal that became a prophet of perestroika.[20]

As one American scholar has described the *Problemy* scene: "*Problemy mira i sotsializma* certainly featured much orthodoxy, but also published a whole host of heretofore heretical perspectives. These included the diverse views of West European Marxists on issues from integration and the Common Market to the benefits of a multiparty electoral system."[21]

Anatoly Chernyaev, a principal Gorbachev adviser and confidant who earlier served at *Problemy* in Prague, goes further: "Our journal, above all, helped to create cadres within the Communist Party of the Soviet Union, those same people who brought heresy to Stalinist dogmatism. Those people, and there were many of

17. *New York Times,* June 6, 1999.

18. The English-language edition of *Problemy mira i sotsializma,* published in London, was titled *World Marxist Review.*

19. Gennadi Gerasimov, "Kak Razedelas Stal," *Novoye Vremya,* March 5, 2000, 38 (author's translation).

20. Ibid.

21. English, *Russia and the Idea of the West,* 101.

them, who were formerly schooled at the journal, became grafts of freedom on the decrepit tree of Soviet Marxism-Leninism that years later was destined to participate in the dismantling of the communist pattern of thought and behavior."[22]

Among *Problemy*'s Soviet staffers in the 1960s, in addition to those mentioned above, were such young intellectuals as philosophers Ivan Frolov and Merab Mamardashvili, historian Yuri Karyakin, economist Oleg Bogomolov, and foreign policy specialists Nikolai Inozemtsev, Georgi Shakhnazarov, and Anatoly Chernyaev, who in later years became active in the Soviet reform movement and advisers to Gorbachev.[23] Many of the Soviet scholars and journalists who served in Prague also gained a better understanding of, and even sympathy for, the Czechoslovak reform movement, which came to be known as the Prague Spring. One of the journal's staffers, Vladimir Lukin, was recalled to Moscow in 1968 for his criticism of the Soviet invasion of Czechoslovakia and, as noted above, was given shelter at Arbatov's institute. Lukin later served as Russian ambassador to Washington and in the Russian *Duma* as a deputy speaker and member of the democratic Yabloko Party.

Aleksei Rumyantsev, who served as *Problemy*'s chief editor from 1958 to 1964, was chief editor of *Pravda* from 1964 to 1965 until his liberal views caused him to be transferred to the Academy of Sciences in Moscow. There, as a vice president, he was instrumental in establishing ISKAN in 1967, the Institute of Applied Social Research in 1968, and the Institute of Scientific Information on the Social Sciences in 1969.[24]

Yet another "Praguer," as they were known, who would later play a role in the Soviet Union's glasnost and perestroika was Yegor V. Yakovlev, a professional journalist who spent three years at *Problemy* (1972–75), and returned to Prague in the early 1980s as an *Izvestiya* correspondent. In 1985, Yakovlev was offered the job of chief editor at *Moskovskiye Novosti* (Moscow News), a weekly tabloid newspaper published in Russian and eight foreign languages, including English. His instructions were to publish articles that other Soviet newspapers would not touch. The author of a dozen books on Lenin and the son of a secret police officer, Yakovlev turned the once dull weekly into the "flagship of glasnost." As British journalist Jonathan Steele described it: "It reported on crime and corruption. It discussed drug abuse, prostitution, and police brutality. It reopened the controversies of Soviet history for a new generation, revealing details of the Gulag's prison camps, and publishing, for the first time since Khrushchev's period, the fierce warning about Stalin which Lenin wrote before his death."[25]

22. A. S. Chernyaev, *Moya zhizn' i moye vremya* (Moscow: Mezhdunarodniye otnosheniya, 1995), 234.
23. Ibid., 71.
24. English, *Russia and the Idea of the West*, 270 n. 26.
25. Jonathan Steele, *Eternal Russia: Yeltsin, Gorbachev, and the Mirage of Democracy* (Cambridge: Harvard University Press, 1995), 3.

Yelena Khanga, a *Moscow News* staffer at the start of glasnost, recalls that Yakovlev called his staff together and asked if they knew the similarity between a fly and a president. "They can both be killed by newspapers," he said, and he advised his staff to be like watchdogs over government activities.[26] Under Yakovlev's direction, *Moscow News* became indispensable reading for Russians interested in public affairs. Its total print run was 1.2 million but copies of its Russian edition of only 350,000 became hot items on the black market, where they were resold at high prices.

26. Yelena Khanga, author's telephone interview, December 29, 1998.

16 | FATHERS AND SONS

The rise to maturity of an educated postwar, post-Stalinist generation is the fundamental socio-political change that Gorbachev, Yeltsin, and all other political figures of the older, sixty-plus generation have had to deal with.

—JAMES H. BILLINGTON, *Russia Transformed*

Conflict between fathers and sons is a well-known theme in the literature of many nations. Russians know it from Ivan Turgenev's masterful novel, *Fathers and Sons* (titled in Russian as the more politically correct *Fathers and Children*). Stalin himself would have experienced such a conflict had he been alive when his daughter, Svetlana Alliluyeva, defected to the West in 1966 and became a U.S. citizen. Nikita Khrushchev also would have known it when his son Sergei became a U.S. citizen in 1999.

Earlier, in the 1950s, the father-son conflict took another form in the *stilyagi* (style-hunters), the Soviet "zoot suiters." As described by S. Frederick Starr: "The early *stiliagi* were the inverse image of the Stalinist society of their fathers' generation. The fathers wore baggy trousers, so the sons cut theirs narrow; the fathers were careless in dress, so the sons waged a clean-cut protest; the fathers denounced the wicked West, so the sons embraced it; the fathers sacrificed for the future, so the sons indulged in the present. The *stiliagi*, in short, rebelled against the officially sponsored mass culture of the Soviet Union."[1]

The *stilyagi* also had a female counterpart. As described by *Sovetskaya kultura*, the newspaper of the Soviet Ministry of Culture, "This species wears dresses which cling to the point of indecency. Her skirts are slit. Her lips are brightly painted. She wears 'Roman' sandals during the summer."[2] "The media ridiculed these "disgusting girls," writes Rodger Potocki, "with their 'a la garçon' haircuts—pitiful bristles of cropped hair—and their shoes that remind one of caterpillar tractors. These Soviet youth not only dressed in what they thought to be the latest in American fashion, but adopted English names, drank *kokteili*, dropped American slang, smoked Lucky Strikes, and danced to hot *dzhaz*."[3]

1. S. Frederick Starr, *Red and Hot: The Fate of Jazz in the Soviet Union* (New York: Oxford University Press, 1983), 239.
2. "Stilyagi," *Sovetskaya kultura*, January 18, 1955, 2 (translated by Rodger Potocki Jr.).
3. Rodger Potocki Jr., "The Stilyagi: A Love Affair with the American Dream" (manuscript, Georgetown University, 1991).

Our pages here, however, are about the children of high-ranking Soviet officials and members of the intelligentsia a generation later whose parents sent them to the prestigious English-language *spetsshkoly* (special schools) where English was taught intensively. In such schools, students began their study of English at an early age and graduated with near fluency. The intention was to prepare them for good jobs with the Foreign Ministry, Intourist, Soviet banks, or the KGB, but the parents did not realize that, in the process of learning a Western language, their children would also be westernized, and many would support changes and reform. Foreign language study not only introduced them to new words but also to new cultures, values, and ways of thinking.

The *spetsshkoly* began as an effort to provide intensive schooling in foreign languages, mathematics, science, and the arts. Intended originally for the gifted and talented, such schools in the late Soviet period were filled with the children and grandchildren of high officials and members of the nomenklatura and intelligentsia, the "golden youth," as they were called. The schools, as a sign of their prestige, were assigned low numbers, from 1 to 100, whereas ordinary schools were given four-digit numbers. That changed when Yeltsin, in his populist mode, attacked the special schools as havens for the privileged, some of whom were grandchildren of his opponents in the Politburo, although Yeltsin's own grandson attended a Moscow English-language *spetsshkola* before he was sent to school in England.[4]

School No. 5, an English-language *spetsshkola*, was located on Moscow's Kutuzovsky Prospekt, a broad avenue where many prominent Russians resided. Among the students there in the 1960s were girls with such names as Viktoria Brezhneva, Tatyana Suslova, and Irina Aristova, granddaughters of high-ranking communist party officials. They married well but, like most Soviet women, did not become active politically, unlike many of their male classmates.[5]

Among the male *spetsshkoly* students in the 1960s was Vyacheslav A. Nikonov, who, as noted earlier, went on to study American history at Moscow State University. Named after his grandfather, Vyacheslav Molotov, the Old Bolshevik and Stalin confidant, Nikonov became a prominent democrat in the 1980s and 1990s as the leader of the Party of Russian Progress and Accord, member of the Russian Duma (lower house of parliament), campaign analyst for Yeltsin, member of the Advisory Council of the Moscow Center of the Carnegie Endowment for International Peace, member of the Russian President's Human Rights Commission, and president of the *Fond Politika* (Politics Foundation).

---

4. Under Yeltsin, the special schools lost their low numbers and were given new four-digit numbers.

5. In 1987, Moscow newspapers began an exposé of the special schools, reporting on their special facilities, how some pupils would arrive in chauffeur-driven cars, and noting that only 6 percent of first-year students came from working-class families.

Aleksei Arbatov, another *spetsshkola* graduate, is the son of Georgi Arbatov, former director of the prestigious ISKAN, foreign policy adviser to every Soviet leader since Brezhnev, and well known in the West as a preeminent spokesman for the Soviet regime. The younger Arbatov, today a member of the democratic Yabloko Party, is also a deputy in the Russian State Duma, where he serves as deputy chair of the Committee on Defense. Prior to service in the Duma, he was a visiting scholar at the John F. Kennedy School of Government at Harvard University as well as a visiting professor at the RAND Corporation.

Igor Runov, deputy director for policy at the American Chamber of Commerce in Moscow, is a graduate of Moscow's School No. 9. He is the son of Boris A. Runov, who studied at Iowa State University in 1960–61 in the third year of the graduate-student exchange and later became the Soviet Union's deputy minister of agriculture and a frequent participant in the Dartmouth Conference. The elder Runov, as related earlier in these pages, first came to the Dartmouth Conference in 1974, and his importance increased in the following years as the world food problem gained prominence on the conference agenda. As the deputy minister of agriculture, he was also Soviet cochair of the U.S.-USSR Joint Commission on Agriculture.

Yegor Gaidar, the liberal and West-leaning reformer, and Yeltsin's acting prime minister and minister of finance and the economy in the early 1990s, is a grandson of Arkady Gaidar, a communist hero of the Russian Civil War and World War II, and noted writer of children's books. Yegor is also a son of Timur Gaidar, a military correspondent in Cuba and Yugoslavia for *Pravda,* the Communist Party newspaper. Yegor recalls that even as a boy of seven living with his father in Cuba, then still a very Western country just after the Cuban Revolution, he could see that socialism was not working.[6] He also accompanied his father to Yugoslavia, where permissible reading went far beyond Soviet limits, and he was able to read communist revisionists Eduard Bernstein, Roger Garaudy, and Ota Šik; Milovan Djilas's *The New Class;* and even Paul Samuelson's *Economics,* whose "pragmatic analysis and presentation of the laws of market mechanisms," he says, "I found persuasive. Although I remained an orthodox Marxist in my understanding of how societies develop, in other areas doubts began to creep in."[7] Gaidar's readings in Western economic literature served him well when he became Yeltsin's acting prime minister and took the first steps in Russia's economic reforms. As a Russian economist describes it: "It's not just that it was under Gaidar's direction that Russia took its first steps toward real market reform and that subsequent leaders have

6. Yegor Gaidar, interview with Harry Kreisler, Institute of International Studies, University of California, Berkeley, November 20, 1996. http://globetrotter.berkeley.edu/conversations/Gaidar/gaidar-con2.html.

7. Gaidar, *Days of Defeat and Victory,* 16.

only continued what Gaidar began, with a greater or lesser degree of success. It's also that in his practical political steps and in his theoretical works, Gaidar defined the philosophy and essence of the modern reforms that Russia needs."[8]

Viktor V. Erofeyev is another Russian who was changed by foreign travel and language study. The son of a high-ranking Soviet diplomat and convinced communist who had served as a political aide to Molotov, Viktor accompanied his father to Senegal and France where he perfected his French.[9] Of his return to Moscow from Paris at the age of twelve, Erofeyev writes: "I did not convert to Soviet ways. . . . I took advantage of all the privileges of my father's position: I wore expensive French sweaters and suede jackets and looked like a Western playboy. But I also used my Soviet diplomatic passport to smuggle into the country the forbidden books of Nabokov, Orwell, and Solzhenitsyn."[10]

Erofeyev wrote his candidate's degree thesis on the Marquis de Sade, a subject which, in the Russia of Leonid Brezhnev, marked him as a future dissident writer. He was not raised to be a dissident, he writes, but his father showed him the world, "and that was enough."[11]

In 1977, at age thirty, Erofeyev set out to publish an anthology of works banned by the Soviet censors. His coeditors of *Metropol,* as the anthology came to be known, were fellow writers Vasily Aksyonov, Andrei Bitov, Yevgeny Popov, and Fazil Iskander. By late 1978, they had assembled a collection of works by twenty-three writers from four generations to the present. As Erofeyev describes it, "an honest portrait of Russia, with its religious quests, sexual disasters, drunken brawls, wild humor, national feuds, and intellectual potential. The portrait respected no taboos. It was an image of Russia straining toward self-knowledge." But it was also an image that aroused the opposition of the authorities, and the five editors were summoned to the Writers Union, where they were warned of dire consequences if their anthology were published in the West, as it indeed soon was. Ardis, the American publisher of "forbidden" Soviet literature, published it in Russian, W. W. Norton in English, and Gallimard in French.

Punishment was swift. Books by the Metropol editors were banned, and those already published were withdrawn from libraries, the editors lost their jobs, and Erofeyev and Popov were expelled from the Writers' Union. But the chief victim, writes Erofeyev, was his father, who was threatened with recall from his post as ambassador to Vienna unless the son wrote a letter of recantation. When the father refused to force the son to write such a letter and was demoted to a "do-nothing" job at the Foreign Ministry, his career was effectively ended.

8. Otto Latsis, "Russia, the West and Gaidar," *The Russia Journal,* March 23, 2001.
9. See Victor Erofeyev, "A Murder in Moscow," *New Yorker,* December 27, 1999, 48–59.
10. Ibid., 49.
11. Ibid.

A telegram of support from Kurt Vonnegut, William Styron, John Updike, Arthur Miller, and Edward Albee, published in the *New York Times*, had no effect on the Soviet authorities, and the board of the Writers Union voted unanimously against the reinstatement of Erofeyev and Popov. Other collaborators remained in the Union, as Erofeyev and Popov had urged, but two others resigned and endured poverty for years. Aksyonov also quit but soon left for the United States and accepted a position at an American university after he was stripped of his Soviet citizenship.

Artyom Borovik was the son of Genrikh Borovik, mentioned above, the long-time correspondent in New York and prominent apologist for the Soviet Union. The younger Borovik, who attended school in New York when his father was stationed there, became an investigative journalist and earned a reputation as a crusader against scandal and corruption among Moscow's political and economic elites. His book, *The Hidden War, A Russian Journalist's Account of the Soviet War in Afghanistan,* created a sensation in the Soviet Union as the first book by a Russian to bring home to the Soviet people the horrors of the war as well as the psychological problems faced by returning veterans. Artyom later spent three weeks at Fort Benning, Georgia, in 1989 and wrote a five-part series for *Ogonyok* to show that a volunteer army works better than a draft army. His report was published in the United States as a book, *A Russian in the U.S. Army.* With his fluent and idiomatic English, Artyom was also a coproducer for a Frontline TV documentary on the danger of nuclear arsenals, and a special correspondent for the CBS News program *60 Minutes.* His brilliant career came to a sudden end in 2000 when he died in a plane crash at the age of thirty-seven.

Aleksandr Lyubimov is the son of Mikhail Lyubimov, a former KGB officer in London during the 1960s and author of *The KGB Guidebook to Cities of the World,* a collection of tales of KGB escapades, many of them in posh restaurants around the world. His son Aleksandr was a star of the popular perestroika Moscow TV show, *Vzglyad (View).*

All of the above were influenced in some way by their study of foreign languages. As a former student of English at a Moscow *spetsshkola* reports:

> Our teachers in English were not like the other teachers—they were more active, intellectual, open to discussion; they were like a different society in the school. Groups of pupils were small—about seven or eight persons—and we studied not only the language itself but also English and American literature, technical translation, and spent a lot of time talking about current policy ("political information" it was called). And, in 1970 or 1971, we had a group of "real Americans" teaching in our school for several months. At first, it was very unusual, everything from

their political outlook to their "bad" (from our "British" point of view) pronunciation, but after a few months it seemed normal to us.[12]

This former student recalls how her class studied the city plan of London, which was posted on a wall of her schoolroom. The map fed her longing for foreign travel, and although she has since traveled to many parts of the world, but not to London, she still knows how to get from Trafalgar Square to Westminster Abbey. She also learned much about the rest of the world because, as she recalls, her class read and discussed articles in the *Morning Star,* the British Communist Party newspaper, and the *Daily World,* the U.S. party paper, both of which had much more international news than the Soviet press and presented it in a more objective manner. Moreover, coverage of domestic news in Britain and the United States often revealed how much higher the standard of living was in those countries. For a student with an inquiring mind, years of reading the British and American communist press, Ernest Hemingway, and other approved Western writers provided many revelations of life in the West that exposed the falsehoods of the Soviet media.

In the closed Soviet society of the Soviet Union, says Mikhail Epstein, a professor at Emory University who grew up in Russia, "Study of a foreign (especially Western) language was potentially loaded with challenges to the official canon, since it could lead to reading forbidden literature and acquaintance with foreigners."[13]

Emilia Shrayer, a former teacher of English in the Soviet Union and now a U.S. citizen, says that the study of English was an eye-opener for Russians in the years when very little was known about the West and its people:

> We wanted to learn their songs, listen to their jazz, read their books, and tune in on foreign English-language broadcasts, which opened our eyes to the differences between truths and lies. As students of English, we wanted to learn more about the countries whose language we were studying. Especially popular were the novels of Harold Robbins and his descriptions of every-day life in America—scenes in restaurants, hotels, homes, as well as the explicit descriptions of sexual encounters, which were a revelation to Russian readers.[14]

Another firsthand account of the *spetsshkoly* is provided by Mark Teeter, an American who was a teacher at two of Moscow's special schools in the late 1980s:

---

12. The author, a university professor today, prefers not to be named. The American "lecturers" she refers to were American teachers under an exchange between the Quakers and the Soviet Ministry of Education.

13. Mikhail Epstein, in e-mail to author, May 10, 1999.

14. Emilia Shrayer, in author's telephone interview, May 12, 1999. Harold Robbins was a popular American writer of the 1960s and 1970s.

An enormous amount of Western recorded and printed material (records, tapes, posters, magazines) could be seen and heard at the schools ... and a certain amount of it doubtless came in through the front door, so to speak, in the guise of language teaching materials. ... These students were indeed the elite ... coming from families with unprecedented access to Western information and material goods of foreign origin. For these students the *spetsshkoly* represented as much a place to bring, share, and trade their newest and coolest acquisitions (tapes, rock magazines, and so on) as a place to "get Westernized" by the materials and programs already there provided by the school itself.[15]

Teeter supported that process by bringing to his English classes a Sunday edition of the *Washington Post* for his students to read. The various sections of the newspaper served well enough his pedagogical purposes but the "smash hit" sections, he adds, were the advertising supplements with color photographs of grocery store offerings, stereo equipment, furniture, and so on, all with prices which provided material for analysis and class discussion. Teeter used the newspaper supplements in class exercises:

> Often I put the students together in boy-girl pairs, giving each an imaginary $500, and telling them to use it to run their household for a month. Each pair would then have several minutes to pore over the ads and then explain and justify their purchases before their classmates who were encouraged to question the choices. This led to basic language processes and valuable practice in the use of more subtle English necessary for complex social interactions, i.e., explaining to your peers your preference in bed lamps or detergents.[16]

As the foregoing indicates, the foreign-language special schools produced a new generation of Soviet youth, relatively well informed about the West, fluent in English or other Western languages, and prepared to be supportive of Russian reforms in the years to come.

---

15. Mark Teeter, e-mail to author, December 18, 1999.
16. Ibid.

17 | THE SEARCH FOR A NORMAL SOCIETY

> When a person is out for a long time, a new person arises.
> —ALEKSANDR L. SALAGAEV, Russian sociologist

"Why do we live as we do?" was a question asked by many Soviets, all of them presumably cleared by the KGB and who visited the United States on exchanges, reports a veteran State Department interpreter who escorted many of them around the country:

> Their minds were blown by being here. They could not believe there could be such abundance and comfort. Many of them would even disparage things here. "Excess, who needs it," they would say. However, you could see that they did not believe what they were saying. When they returned home, in their own minds and in the privacy of their own trusted little circle of family and friends, they would tell the truth to themselves or to others. Over time, enough of them got out—to here and elsewhere—to make them realize how abysmal things were in the Soviet Union. However, their personal experiences abroad, their disgust with the way things were at home, and the emergence of leaders who were not so doctrinaire and did truly want to improve life there, all came together in perestroika and what happened subsequently. Those exchanges did a lot in giving people an opportunity to see how a normal life could be.[1]

One result of U.S.-Soviet exchanges often overlooked was the exposure to everyday American life that was a part of the visits of most Soviets who came to the United States. Their tours of American cities; visits to homes, schools, and farms; a university or small-town experience; and many other "extracurricular" activities were often arranged by local chapters of the National Council for International Visitors, a private organization that mobilizes the services of volunteers who give freely of their time to ensure that foreign visitors to the United States have a productive and pleasant stay in their communities and see the real America.

One such volunteer has described a visit to a typical Wisconsin dairy farm by a delegation of high-level Soviet scientists who were in Racine to attend a scientific

---

1. William H. Hopkins, e-mail to author, July 10, 2000.

conference. On a day off from their scientific sessions, the Russians were given a tour of a dairy farm operated by a farmer and his two daughters. The visitors were astonished by the range of the farm's modern equipment, the fact that it grew its own fodder, the extent to which the dairy operation itself had been mechanized, the cleanliness of the animals and their stalls, the very high milk production as compared with Soviet dairy farms, and the profit made by the family. For Russians, most of whom have a heritage in agriculture, such visits confirmed the shortcomings of Soviet agriculture.

Visitors to Washington, D.C., were astonished by the free access to the halls of Congress and the easy accessibility of constituents to their elected representatives and senators. And some Soviet visitors, awed by the high level of goods and services produced, were convinced that there had to be some secret center that directed the American economy; how else could it function so well, they figured. Travel broadens, it is said, but for Soviet travelers to the United States it was a broadening of major proportions, and it changed the way they saw their own country, as well as the United States.

Accounts of Soviet astonishment on visiting their first American supermarket are legion, from the first Russian students who came to the United States in the late 1950s and early 1960s, to Boris Yeltsin's visit in 1989. The early students, when shown their first American supermarket, thought they were being shown a "Potemkin village," a store set up especially to impress foreign visitors. When a Russian delegation came to San Francisco in the early 1960s and got caught in a traffic jam, one of its members commented, "I'll bet they collected all these cars here to impress us."

Russians saw Potemkin villages on their foreign travels because that is how they prepared to receive important visitors in their own country. Clean up everything, put "undesirable" elements out of sight, show the best, and persuade the visitors that what they are being shown is typical.

Many Soviet visitors to the United States were indeed haunted by the "Potemkin-village" theme—the idea that they were being shown things created especially to impress them. The term comes from one of Empress Catherine the Great's favorites, Prince Gregory Potemkin, who built model villages peopled by happy peasants, designed to impress the empress as she toured her vast domain. One Soviet visitor to the United States, for example, who was being shown family farms in the American Midwest, was convinced that the farms were Potemkin villages and said so to his American escort. "Okay," said the escort, "we'll drive down this road and you pick the next farm to visit." And so he did, to the surprise of a farmer, who nevertheless gave the Russian visitor a tour of the land that he farmed with his family.

The Potemkin-village analogy even reached the highest levels of the Soviet government. When Soviet president Nikolai Podgorny visited Austria in 1966 and saw the bounty of Viennese markets, he remarked, "Look how well they set things up for my visit."[2] Some thirty years later, Boris Yeltsin himself expressed astonishment at the abundance and variety of the products he saw in a Houston supermarket, an experience he described as "shattering": "When I saw those shelves crammed with hundreds, thousands of cans, cartons, and goods of every possible sort, for the first time I felt quite frankly sick with despair for the Soviet people. That such a potentially super-rich country as ours has been brought to a state of such poverty! It is terrible to think of it."[3]

Yeltsin's visit to that Houston supermarket, says Lilia Shevtsova of the Carnegie Foundation for International Peace, turned him into a reformer: "I remember when Yeltsin visited the United States, he became a reformer after he visited a grocery [sic] store."[4] But Bill Keller, a former New York Times Moscow correspondent, saw Yeltsin's visit to the United States in a broader perspective: "The prosperity, the rule of law, the freedom and efficiency he witnessed in America, catalyzed his notions about the fraud of Communism."[5]

Such impromptu visits, however, can backfire, as one did when a Soviet minister of higher education visited Princeton University in the early 1970s. The minister was most impressed by the buildings and the library but when his guide suggested a drop-in visit to a typical dormitory room, there was a reverse Potemkin effect. The room chosen was a mess—old peanut butter sandwiches on the floor, unwashed underwear strewn on chairs and desks, rancid gym shoes in a corner, and an unkempt student sleeping off a hangover in his bunk bed. The minister smiled, thinking he had seen the "real" Princeton beneath its opulent surface. But when he later remarked how few female students he saw on the campus—they had only recently been admitted—one of the Americans countered that in the entire history of Soviet-American student exchanges to that time, his ministry had nominated not one woman for study in the United States.[6] Another insight that Soviets brought back from their travels to the West may have been, not amazement at the abundance of food and consumer goods, but rather a redefinition of their understanding of the word "normal," a word with special meaning—and longing—for Russians. That redefinition covers the gamut of things like orderliness, punctuality, service with a smile, the ability to do business on the telephone, customer service, and reliability; and the fact that if someone says that something will be done, you can generally expect that it will.

2. Nikolai Podgorny, quoted in English, *Russia and the Idea of the West,* 120.

3. Boris Yeltsin, *Against the Grain: An Autobiography,* trans. Michael Glenny (New York: Summit Books, 1990), 255.

4. Lilia Shevtsova, in talk at the Carnegie Foundation for International Peace, Washington, D.C., March 30, 2000.

5. Bill Keller, "Somebody's Hero," *New York Times Book Review,* March 19, 2000.

6. Related by Daniel Matuszewski, in e-mail to author, December 10, 2001.

One American tells of a Russian he invited to the United States. The Russian, who was high in the Komsomol leadership and moving rapidly up the party ladder, was silent for the first two days of a trip they made together across the country. Eventually he said, "Now I understand the United States—it works!"

To Soviet citizens, it did seem that everything in the United States worked. U.S. agriculture feeds Americans and the people of many other countries as well, including Russians in some years. Manufacturing creates an abundance of consumer products. Telephones function, and people assume that government will provide the services expected of it.

The late Vladimir Petrov, professor of history and international affairs at George Washington University, met with many Soviet visitors who passed through Washington, D.C. To the Odessa-born Petrov with his fluent Russian, many of the visitors revealed their innermost thoughts:

> I met exchangees who arrived here already hating the Soviet system and perhaps overidealizing ours. Others came open-minded, searching for answers to their questions. I remember one four-hour-long conversation in a man's hotel room, sitting in the bathroom and his tape recorder going full blast in the room to foil CIA microphones, which he was sure were in every hotel room housing Soviet citizens. He was not shy of the CIA but assumed that the CIA cooperated clandestinely with the KGB.[7]

Petrov arranged for high-level visitors to meet distinguished senators and public figures—Averell Harriman, George Kennan, Elliot Richardson, William Fulbright—and on occasion, for having them deliver paid lectures. Through such lectures, he adds, one Soviet scholar, "collected enough to buy a decent apartment in Moscow with his U.S. loot—and he was a very doctrinaire man, currently advising Zyuganov [Russian Communist Party head] on foreign policy issues."[8] Indeed, many Soviet exchange visitors used their per diem to purchase items for family and friends or sell on the black market when they returned home. Escort interpreters tell of Soviets who arrived in the United States with suitcases full of food on which they lived for the first few days in order to save their per diem dollars.

A more graphic, as well as irate, reaction to a visit to the United States comes from Alla Glebova, a Russian journalist:

> I would describe Americans as a nation of sober and even boring professionals. But why do they, without any imagination, grow flowers in exactly the same places I would choose, while I, the essence of imagination, ideas,

7. Vladimir Petrov, letter to author, April 10, 1998.
8. Ibid.

and emotions, live in a garbage bin. . . . I was very persistent in my desire to understand American life. Nevertheless, I was not able to find an answer to my main question. Why do we [Russians], citizens of a great country known for its riches and brains, live in such deep doodoo [*v zadnitse*], while they [Americans], so simple and so far from perfect, inhabit such an America?[9]

Exposure to the West, or to people who had been there, created a ripple effect that had an enormous impact on the Soviet Union, especially in the years when there was little firsthand information about the world beyond Soviet borders. People who had seen the United States had a vision of what a better society could be like, the normal society Russians have always hoped for, and the order they have been seeking.

9. Alla Glebova, "Sindrom sirotstva," trans. Larisa Silnicky and author, *XX Vek i Mir,* no. 3–4 (1994): 60.

18 | "WESTERN VOICES"

I remember, as if it were yesterday, how enthusiastic many of us were. In a state where all information was subjected to heavy censorship, we consumed *Svoboda* [Radio Liberty] broadcasts like oxygen in a room with no air.

—YURI LURYI, in JRL no. 3309, May 27, 1999

Zapadniye golosa (Western voices), as they were called, were the forbidden foreign broadcasts that Soviet citizens listened to clandestinely on their shortwave radios, straining, above the din of Soviet jammers, to hear the news and commentary from Radio Liberty, BBC, the Voice of America (VOA), the Deutsche Welle, Kol Israel, and other international broadcasters. For those who could not travel beyond the Soviet bloc, foreign radio was their link to the outside world, breaking the Soviet information monopoly and allowing listeners to hear news and views that differed from those of the communist media.

Why shortwave rather than the medium wave (AM) or FM broadcasts that Americans listen to at home? The answer is simply that medium wave and FM do not carry well over long distances, and shortwave was therefore necessary to reach the Soviet Union from Western transmitters. In fact, the Russians pioneered shortwave when Lenin used it in 1922 to address listeners in the far corners of Russia.[1] For that reason, Soviet-produced radios, even inexpensive ones, had shortwave bands, which were needed, as they still are today in Russia, to receive broadcasts over its vast expanse.

For Soviet dissidents and human rights activists, foreign radio broadcasts provided an almost secure flow of information and encouragement from the West. The human-rightniks felt more secure knowing that reports of human rights violations were being smuggled to the West and transmitted back to the Soviet Union by foreign broadcasts. Moreover, they received moral support by learning through the radios that there were other protesters in the Soviet Union. And it was not only the dissidents and human rights activists who listened. At times of international tension or some interesting event that was not covered by the Soviet media, everyone seemed to be listening to the foreign radios. I recall being in the Moscow office of a high official of the Foreign Ministry, who had on his desk a Soviet-made VEF radio

---

1. Michael Nelson, *War of the Black Heavens: The Battles of Western Broadcasting in the Cold War* (Syracuse: Syracuse University Press, 1997), 1.

with the antenna pulled out to receive shortwave broadcasts. The Soviet Union also monitored foreign broadcasts and distributed to high-level officials a daily digest of their contents.

To counter foreign broadcasts deemed unacceptable, the Soviet Union built a vast network of jammers, which emitted noise, music, or voice on frequencies used by Western broadcasters and which made listening difficult if not impossible. The jamming was massive, and its total power was estimated at three times that of all the Western radios combined. Jammers were more effective in large cities, where they were concentrated, but less so in smaller cities and rural areas. Nevertheless, it was possible to hear Western broadcasts in the heart of Moscow, as I confirmed many times during a tour of duty at the American Embassy in 1967–69. If a listener had a decent radio, knew something about antennas, and was determined to learn what was being said in the West, it was indeed possible to hear Western broadcasts despite the jamming. Moreover, some of those who were able to hear the broadcasts recorded them and passed copies to their friends in a distribution called *magnitizdat.*

BBC began broadcasting to the Soviet Union in 1946, VOA in 1947, and Radio Liberation (later Radio Liberty) in 1953, only five days before Stalin died. But Soviet jamming began as early as 1948, targeted on different radios at different times, and continued, with some pauses, until 1988. Radio Liberty was always jammed but interference with the other radios was suspended during times of détente and reinstated during times of tension.

One of the Soviet listeners to Radio Liberty, BBC, and Voice of America was none other than Mikhail Gorbachev, who while being held incommunicado at his Crimean dacha during the attempted coup of Soviet hard-liners in August 1991, learned from Western broadcasts that the coup had failed and that he could return to Moscow.[2] "It would not have escaped Gorbachev's notice," wrote Michael Nelson, "that if he had not ended the jamming of Western Radios in 1988 . . . he might not have learned what was happening. If it had not been for the Radios, his resolve might not have been strengthened. He might have signed away all his powers and changed the course of history."[3]

2. Mikhail Gorbachev, *Memoirs,* trans. George Peronansky and Tatjana Varsavsky (New York: Doubleday, 1996), 633–38.
3. Nelson, *War of the Black Heavens,* 196.

19 | TO HELSINKI AND BEYOND

The participating States . . . [m]ake it their aim to facilitate freer movement and contacts, individually and collectively, whether privately or officially, among persons, institutions and organizations of the participating States, and to contribute to the solution of the humanitarian problems that arise in that connexion.

—HELSINKI FINAL ACT

When Premier Leonid Brezhnev traveled to Helsinki in the summer of 1975 to sign the Final Act of the Conference on Security and Cooperation in Europe (CSCE), it is not clear that he understood what he was committing the Soviet Union to do.[1] The Final Act, as the conference's concluding document is known, recognized, for the first time in an international agreement, respect for human rights and fundamental freedoms, including the freer movement of people, ideas, and information.[2]

There was considerable drama in the signing of the Final Act on August 1, 1975, by thirty-three European heads of state or government as well as the prime minister of Canada and the president of the United States. Not since the Congress of Vienna in 1815, which redrew the map of Europe and established a peace that lasted for forty years, had so many European leaders assembled to put their pens to a document outlining future relations between their states.

A European security conference had been proposed by the Soviets in 1954 as a surrogate for a World War II peace treaty. Soviet motives were clear—recognition of postwar borders in Europe (especially between Poland and the German Democratic Republic and Soviet Union), cooperation among European states, reduction of armaments, and removal of foreign (that is to say, U.S.) troops from Europe. Under the Soviet proposal, the United States and Canada would have been excluded from the conference.

The Europeans—the neutrals and nonaligned as well as NATO members—were interested in such a conference, tempted as they were by the prospects for

---

1. In the following pages on the CSCE, the author has drawn from William Korey, *The Promises We Keep: Human Rights, the Helsinki Process, and American Foreign Policy* (New York: St. Martin's Press, 1993), prologue and chap. 1, as well as the author's own experience as a member of the U.S. delegation to the Helsinki Review Conference in Madrid and staff consultant to the Commission on Security and Cooperation in Europe (U.S. Congress) from 1980 to 1983.

2. Ibid., xxi.

peace and stability in Europe, as well as increased East-West trade. The NATO states, however, stipulated that their non-European allies, the United States and Canada, must also participate in the conference. In addition, as the preliminary political positioning evolved in the late 1960s, the West Europeans maintained that the conference should also discuss fundamental human rights.

By the early 1970s, the timing for a European security conference seemed right. A Four-Power agreement on Berlin had been signed, German Chancellor Willy Brandt's *Ostpolitik* had produced rapprochement between West Germany and Poland, the two Germanys had recognized each other, the Vietnam War appeared to be approaching an end, and agreement had been reached to hold talks on troop reductions in Central Europe.

U.S. reaction to the conference, however, was decidedly cool. Henry Kissinger, as National Security Adviser and Secretary of State, was not enthusiastic about CSCE, fearing its focus on human rights, which he saw as an impediment to reaching agreement with the Soviet Union on security and other major foreign policy issues. Accordingly, the instructions to the U.S. delegation to the conference were to support our allies but not be confrontational with the Soviets. East European ethnic groups in the United States were also skeptical about any freezing of postwar borders in Eastern Europe and lending legitimacy to communist rule and Soviet hegemony there. But President Nixon was meeting Leonid Brezhnev at summit meetings in the early 1970s, and the administration could hardly object to Europeans also wanting to sit at the same table with the Soviets and discuss common interests. So the United States participated in the CSCE deliberations, although, reflecting Kissinger's caution, it played a secondary role and left the heavy lifting to its allies.

After three years of arduous and prolonged negotiations in Helsinki and Geneva, the CSCE reached agreement in 1975 on a forty-page, forty-thousand-word document. The Soviets got their inviolability of borders but had to accept language recognizing respect for human rights and fundamental freedoms as well as the freer movement of people and information.

As the date approached for signing the Final Act, domestic opposition in the United States grew. Although the Final Act was a political statement, rather than a treaty, and not legally binding, East European émigrés and political conservatives in both U.S. political parties strongly criticized the document as a sellout to the Soviets. Governor Ronald Reagan of California, in an early version of his "evil-empire" posture, urged President Gerald Ford not to sign it, as did Democratic Senator Henry Jackson of Washington. Mail to the White House ran heavily against signing, and much of the media agreed. The *Wall Street Journal*, in an editorial titled "Jerry, Don't Go," urged the president not to go to Helsinki, charging that CSCE was "purely symbolic, and the symbol is one of Soviet hegemony in Eastern Europe."[3] The *New York Times* called it a "misguided and empty trip."[4]

Ford courageously defied domestic disapproval, flew to Finland, and signed the Helsinki Accords, as they came to be known, and in doing so probably did more to bring about the collapse of communism than Ronald Reagan did years later with his Star Wars proposal. In the following years, the opposition that had been so strident turned to broad support as the Accords were embraced by human rights activists in the Soviet Union, Eastern and Western Europe, and the United States. As former CIA director Robert M. Gates, a career analyst of the Soviet Union, put it: "CSCE was perhaps the most important early milestone on the path of dramatic change inside the Soviet empire. The most eloquent testimonials to its importance come from those who were on the inside, who began their political odyssey to freedom at that time, and who became the leaders of free countries in Eastern Europe in 1989. . . . The human rights issue struck at the very legitimacy and survival of the Soviet political structure."[5] "In retrospect," added Gates, "CSCE provided the spark that kindled the widespread resistance to communist authority and the organization of numerous independent groups throughout Eastern Europe and even in the Soviet Union determined to bring change. This spark of resistance would burst into flame in Poland only months later, and spread throughout the Soviet Empire within a short time. No one expected this, least of all the Soviets."[6]

Dissidents and human rights activists across the Soviet bloc drew encouragement and sustenance from the Final Act, and they were determined to hold their governments to respecting and observing it. The Final Act also emboldened many in the East to demand observance of the human rights embraced by various United Nations declarations and covenants but not observed by their governments. In Poland, only four months after the signing of the Helsinki Accords, a group of fifty-nine artists, scientists, and writers took note of the Final Act in an open letter to Warsaw officials demanding the right of free expression and conscience. Several months later, in September 1976, a Committee for Workers Defense (KOR) was formed in Poland, which took the Final Act as a focal point for its activities. Czechoslovak intellectuals followed in January 1977 by creating Charter 77, an NGO that demanded full adherence to the Final Act by the Prague government.[7]

In the Soviet Union, dissidents and human rights activists also took heart when the full text of the Final Act, including its humanitarian provisions, was published

---

3. *Wall Street Journal,* July 23, 1975.

4. *New York Times,* July 27, 1975.

5. Gates, *From the Shadows,* 89–90.

6. Ibid., 87.

7. See William Korey, in "Special Bulletin" (Warsaw: OSCE Office of Democratic Institutions and Human Rights) 2, no. 3 (fall 1995).

in *Pravda* as mandated by a provision of the Final Act that required the signatory states to publish and distribute it as widely as possible. That had the effect of legitimizing dissent and enabled dissenters to cite the Final Act when petitioning for reunification of families (through emigration) and the freer movement of information through human contacts. The next step was the formation of Helsinki Watch Groups in the Soviet Union—NGOs to monitor Soviet compliance with the provisions of the Final Act. The first such group was established in Moscow in May 1976 by physicist Yuri Orlov and included among its members Yelena Bonner, wife of Andrei Sakharov; Anatoly Shcharansky, a prominent dissident who later became a minister in the Israeli government; and Ludmilla Alexeyeva, now president of the International Helsinki Federation for Human Rights. Similar watch groups were established shortly thereafter in other Soviet republics—Armenia, Georgia, Latvia, Lithuania, and Ukraine. The contribution of the CSCE to their mission has been described by Orlov: "To the extent that human rights pressure helped erode communism and Soviet power (and I think it did), the CSCE made an important contribution by providing the formal basis for the work of the Helsinki Monitoring Groups, and by serving as the only sustained forum where the Soviet Union encountered heavy pressure and criticism at the highest levels of government about their human rights."[8] Moreover, many Western visitors to the Soviet Union took advantage of the provisions of the Final Act to meet openly with human rights activists during visits to Moscow. Such visits, made by prominent personalities in politics, science, and the arts, provided moral support as well as facilitating the free exchange of information and ideas.

Of special note were the scientific seminars held during the 1970s and 1980s in the apartments of Soviet scientists, the so-called refuseniks, who had been denied permission to emigrate. In another form of scientific and cultural exchange, albeit not sanctioned by the Soviet government, hundreds of prominent Western scientists and public figures attended the seminars, at which scientific papers were read, to show support for their Russian colleagues and to maintain contact with them.[9] Among the American public figures who attended the seminars or met with the refuseniks were Mario Cuomo, Dennis DeConcini, Gary Hart, Edward Kennedy, Henry Kissinger, and Cyrus Vance.

To ensure compliance with the provisions of the Final Act, periodic CSCE review meetings were held, in Belgrade in 1977–78, Madrid in 1980–83, and Vienna in 1986–89. At Vienna, the concluding document went much further than Helsinki and Madrid in guaranteeing religious rights, ethnic rights, the right to receive

8. Yuri Orlov, quoted by Korey in "Special Bulletin."
9. See Yakov Alpert, *Making Waves: Stories from My Life* (New Haven: Yale University Press, 2000), 149–61.

information through foreign broadcasts, and freedom of travel. The jamming of foreign radio broadcasts ceased, and the "freer movement" of people, ideas, and information specified in previous CSCE documents actually became free movement. Everyone now had the right to leave his or her country, not only for family reunification, but for other reasons as well, and to return to that country.

MIKHAIL GORBACHEV, INTERNATIONAL TRAVELER

Foreign travel causes the Russians to see themselves differently.
—ZBIGNIEW BRZEZINSKI

Another young and upwardly mobile Russian for whom foreign travel was an eye-opener was Mikhail Sergeyevich Gorbachev, future member of the Politburo, General Secretary of the Communist Party, and president of the Soviet Union. A man with an inquisitive mind and a high respect for learning, Gorbachev came to those positions with more knowledge about the rest of the world than any top Soviet leader since Lenin. He was also the first university-educated leader to rule Russia since Lenin, and like Lenin, he had studied law, unlike most other Soviet leaders, who had been trained in construction and engineering. Gorbachev, moreover, had a university-educated wife who shared his political life and became his closest confidant and adviser. "My wife and I lived this life together," he said in an interview. "We thought things over a great deal because we were already people of a new generation."[1]

Gorbachev was indeed of a new generation, although his early years were rather typical for a Russian boy from a peasant family in the Soviet Union of the 1930s. He was born in 1931 in the village of Privol'noye in the Stavropol region of the North Caucasus, an area of fertile farmland between the lower reaches of two great Russian rivers, the Don and the Dnieper. Settled originally by free Cossack farmers, the region had never known serfdom, and there was plenty of land for everyone. Privol'noye, in fact, means "free" or "spacious." But 1931 was a turbulent year; peasants were being forced off their land and into collective farms. Resistance to collectivization in Stavropol was high, and one of those sent off to a prison camp in Siberia was Gorbachev's grandfather, Andrei, an event that made a lasting impression on the young boy and determined his later attitude toward Stalinism.

Bright and ambitious, Gorbachev completed eight years of basic schooling at the village school in Privol'noye and secondary schooling in a town twenty kilometers away, where he rented a room with other students and returned home once a week to get food for the following week. Summers were spent as a combine operator at a

1. Mikhail Gorbachev, in interview with Reuters, October 26, 1999; JRL, October 26, 1999.

Machine Tractor Station. After serving in the Komsomol, Gorbachev became a candidate member of the Communist Party in 1950, and a full member in 1952. In 1950, he was accepted at the Law Faculty of Moscow State University (MSU), the Soviet Union's most prestigious university, a rather high achievement for a peasant boy with a provincial education. Also unusual was his choice of law, a profession of low prestige in the Soviet Union.

It was at MSU that the country boy had his first exposure, not only to the big city life of Moscow, but also to the West. For five years he lived in the same dormitory with Zdeněk Mlynář, a sophisticated and urbane Czech student who later became a high communist official in his home country, one of the leaders of the 1968 reform movement known as Prague Spring, and a signatory of Charter 77, the basic document of organized dissent in Czechoslovakia. At MSU, the two young men were in the same study group, took the same examinations, were granted the same degrees, became good friends, and even married on the same day. "It is extremely likely," wrote Russian scientist Zhores A. Medvedev, now living in England, "that after five years of sharing a room with a Czech intellectual, Gorbachev must have been profoundly influenced by Zdeněk Mlynář: The personal knowledge of the culture and attitudes of a traditionally Western nation must have had almost the effect of a prolonged stay abroad in the early 1950s. If Gorbachev had become 'westernized' in his appearance, manners, dress, and the image he projects of tolerance and cordial behavior, all the small signs which mark him as different from the usual Komsomol and Party boss, it was probably Mlynář's doing."[2]

Another sign that marked Gorbachev as different from other young communist students at MSU, reports Mlynář, was his pragmatic attitude toward truth. As Mlynář wrote many years later: "From our classes of Marxist philosophy Gorbachev derived his own maxim, a phrase from Hegel—'The truth is never abstract.' None of us used it in the precise, Hegelian sense, but he would repeat it often when a teacher or student would express general ideas while ignoring how little those concepts were linked to reality."[3]

While still in his early years, Gorbachev was to travel even farther and wider from his provincial roots. During the 1970s, while in his thirties and a provincial party official in Stavropol, he visited Belgium, the Netherlands, the Federal Republic of Germany, and France. Some of those visits were study trips, while others were vacation visits at the invitation of the local communist party. All of them can be considered a form of cultural exchange.

Gorbachev's visit to France in 1976, his first to that country, was as head of a delegation of party officials in an exchange with the French communist party.

2. Zhores A. Medvedev, *Gorbachev* (New York: W. W. Norton, 1986), 43.
3. Zdeněk Mlynář, "My School Companion Gorbachev," *l'Unita* (Rome), April 9, 1985 (translated from the Italian by Ciro Franco).

He must have liked what he saw because in the following year, accompanied by his wife, Raisa, Gorbachev returned to France with two other Russian couples, and for three weeks the Gorbachevs and their friends traveled nearly three thousand miles by car, taking in the traditional sights. That trip provided them with an unusual opportunity to see a Western country, not as official visitors on a pre-arranged itinerary with Potemkin villages, but as tourists going anywhere they wished. Of that trip, Gorbachev has written, "It was a marvelous journey . . . which firmly bonded me to this great country and its people in love with life, so close to us in character."[4]

One can question whether the French and Russians are really so close in character, but anyone who has toured France will identify with Gorbachev as he recalled with obvious pleasure how he did what tourists usually do in Paris: "It was Paris unparalleled: Notre Dame, the Louvre, the Invalides, the Eiffel Tower, Montmartre, the Rodin Museum, and the Pantheon where rest Hugo and Zola, Voltaire and Rousseau, Langevin. . . . We took the traditional evening boat ride on the Seine and ate dishes which were for us exotic, like onion soup and frogs' legs, and of course the excellent French wines."[5]

Like all foreign visitors, Gorbachev fell in love with France, and France returned the affection. "Gorbachev and his wife," wrote French scholar Christine Marand, "have perhaps done more for cultural relations [with France] than all the concerts of Richter, all those of the Bolshoi, which were already more effective than the bulletins of VOKS."[6]

The following year, the Gorbachevs vacationed in Italy, visiting Sicily, Rome, Turin, Florence, and San Gimignano. "I am most intrigued," wrote Robert G. Kaiser, "by Gorbachev's long trips to France and Italy . . . when he was able to see how starkly the imperialist camp differed from the portrait of it drawn in Soviet propaganda."[7] Experiences like these, added Kaiser, "enabled [Gorbachev] to separate his own ideas from official ones, and to see the inadequacies of the official ones."[8]

On those trips Gorbachev was indeed troubled by the same things that had troubled other Russian leaders on their visits to the West, and Yakovlev and Kalugin as students in the United States twenty years earlier. As Gorbachev has put it:

4. Mikhail Gorbatchev, *Mémoires: Une vie et des réformes* (Paris: Editions du Rocher, 1997), 140 (author's translation).

5. Ibid.

6. Christine Marand, "Relations Culturelles Franco-Sovietiques (1966–1986)" (unpublished doctoral dissertation presented at the Institut d'Etudes Politiques de Paris, 1989), 541 (author's translation). VOKS was the Society for Cultural Relations with Foreign Countries, an early Soviet agency established to conduct cultural relations abroad.

7. Kaiser, *Why Gorbachev Happened*, 407.

8. Ibid., 15.

The most significant conclusion drawn from [my] journeys abroad: people lived in better conditions and were better off than in our country. The question haunted me: why was the standard of living in our country lower than in other developed countries? It seemed that our aged leaders were not especially worried about our undeniably lower living standards, our unsatisfactory way of life, and our falling behind in the field of advanced technologies. Instead of seeking ways to catch up with other countries and prevent the country and the system from sinking deeper into a state of crisis, the leadership was primarily concerned with devising new artificial ideological concepts which would sanctify the existing realities and present them as historical achievements.[9]

In 1984, as a Politburo member, Gorbachev and his wife visited London, and of their foreign travels the *London Times* later wrote, "These trips began the process in their minds of discarding Soviet stereotypes of the West."[10]

Most Soviet citizens, however, could not travel to the West, as Gorbachev himself has pointed out. "For a Soviet citizen," he wrote, "tourism [in those years] was limited to Eastern Europe: to go to the West, it was necessary to be ideologically irreproachable. . . . The 'Iron Curtain' was not a simple metaphor. It nourished fear and mistrust between us and the West."[11] Indeed, after Gorbachev became general secretary, he sought to show Soviet citizens how people of other countries lived. Soviet television began to present a more realistic view of Western living standards, and Gorbachev himself endorsed people-to-people exchanges across international borders: "It is . . . extremely important to stimulate contacts and exchanges at the citizen level. The experience of Western Europe, especially [the] Franco-German experience starting in the 1950s, confirms that there is no more effective way of overcoming mutual alienation and mistrust."[12]

Two years after returning from his visit to Canada, Gorbachev, at age fifty-four, was elected General Secretary of the Communist Party by a Politburo whose average age was sixty-six. A new generation had come to power, better educated than its predecessors and knowing more about the world beyond Soviet borders. Moreover, as Doder describes him, "Unlike previous Soviet leaders who were deeply xenophobic and suspicious of foreign influences, Gorbachev seemed genuinely interested in Western ideas and practices."[13] Nevertheless, while admiring many achievements of the West, he always emphasized the need for Russia to acquire

9. Gorbachev, *Memoirs,* 102–3.
10. *London Times,* September 21, 1999.
11. Gorbatchev, *Mémoires,* 142 (author's translation).
12. Gorbachev, in an address to Green Cross International, May 12, 1992.
13. Doder, *Gorbachev,* 259.

them in ways that respect the uniqueness of Russia's own culture, and his travels to the West did not leave him depressed or frustrated as to Russia's future.

British Sovietologist Archie Brown has described the influence of Gorbachev's travels on his political thinking: "Gorbachev did evolve from relatively orthodox Communist reformer—which he already was by 1985—to social democrat. . . . Conversations with Willy Brandt and Felipe Gonzalez, as well as with some of his advisers, played an important part in the evolution of Gorbachev's social democratic views."[14]

In Prague, on April 10, 1987, Gorbachev spoke of the interdependence of nations, comparing them to mountain climbers tethered together on a rope: "They can either climb together to the summit or fall together into the abyss."[15] And in December 1987, he again visited London, the first Soviet leader to do so in thirty years.

In a speech at the United Nations on December 7, 1988, which undoubtedly reflected his earlier travels to Western Europe and Canada, Gorbachev spoke of the need for increased international cooperation and suggested that countries could learn from each other, even if their ideologies differed: "Efforts to solve global problems require a new scope and quality of interaction of states and socio-political currents, regardless of ideological or other differences."[16] And in a major departure from Soviet ideology, he spoke of the "increasingly multi-optional nature of social development" in different countries, both capitalist and socialist, and called for

> respect for the views and positions of others, tolerance, a willingness to perceive something different as not necessarily bad or hostile, and an ability to learn to live side-by-side with others, while remaining different and not always agreeing with each other. As the world asserts its diversity, attempts to look down on others and to teach them one's own brand of democracy, become totally improper—to say nothing of the fact that democratic values intended for export often very quickly lose their worth.[17]

Of that United Nations speech, Gorbachev's interpreter and aide Pavel Palazchenko has written: "When Gorbachev embraced the idea of global interdependence and of the Soviet Union being part of an interdependent global whole,

---

14. Archie Brown, "Aron, Yeltsin, and Gorbachev," *Times Literary Supplement* (London), June 9, 2000.

15. Ibid., 211.

16. Gorbachev, in the *New York Times*, December 8, 1988.

17. Ibid.

and when that concept was approved by the Communist Party hierarchy, it was a decisive break with the past that had far-reaching and, at the time, unappreciated consequences."[18]

That view was shared by former U.S. secretary of state George Shultz: "If anybody declared the end of the Cold War, he did it in that speech. It was over."[19]

Others agreed, and in 1990 Mikhail Gorbachev received the Nobel Peace Prize.

18. Palazchenko, *My Years with Gorbachev and Shevardnadze,* 370.
19. Ibid.

21 | AND THOSE WHO COULD NOT TRAVEL

> The problem was not so much who came but who did not; there were many brilliant
> scholars who were deliberately forbidden to travel abroad because of their political views
> or because they did not have connections. There was not even the semblance of a fair
> selection system in the Communist countries, let alone open competition for the few
> opportunities for scholars and scientists to travel abroad.
>
> —ALLEN H. KASSOF, "Scholarly Exchanges and the Collapse of Communism"

Many outstanding Soviet scholars, scientists, and writers traveled to the West, but many others, equally or even more outstanding, were not permitted to travel beyond the Soviet bloc, having failed to receive the approval of the Foreign Travel Commission, a body that decided which citizens were sufficiently reliable to travel abroad. The sad story of George I. Mirsky is illustrative.

Mirsky, an expert on the Middle East and developing countries, an Arabic speaker and Iraq specialist, had worked more than forty years at IMEMO. His doctoral dissertation was on the history of Iraq between the two world wars, but he had never been there, not because of the Iraqis but because of the Soviet authorities. As Mirsky tells the tale: "Until the age of sixty-two (!) I was a 'non-exitable' [*nievyezdnoi*, i.e., not allowed to leave the Soviet bloc], and unable to travel further than East Berlin or Budapest. Over the course of thirty years invitations to visit various countries, including the Arabic, had piled up but each time the *Lubyanka* [KGB headquarters] 'cut' me for various phony reasons."[1]

The reason, explains Mirsky, was his "indiscreet tongue" as a youth. Years later he learned that his KGB dossier contained a report that in 1949, while on a smoke break as a student, he had expressed his opinion of Yugoslavia's Marshal Tito, noting that no matter how bad a role Tito was playing then—as seen by the Soviet Union—it was difficult, from a psychological point of view, to believe that during World War II, when he was commanding the Yugoslav army of liberation, he had also been an agent of the German Gestapo as charged by Soviet authorities.[2]

The irony of it all was not lost on Mirsky:

1. George I. Mirsky, "A Half Century in the World of Eastern Studies," *Vostok* (Moscow), no. 6 (1996) (author's translation).
2. Ibid., 129.

Orwell could have sized up the situation: a man who all his life had been studying "third-world" countries, holding a position as section chief and then department head in an institute of the academy, a professor teaching the history of the East at the prestigious Moscow State Institute of International Relations, was unable to visit, even as a tourist, even one of the countries which he studied and about which he wrote not only books and articles but also reports for the Central Committee of the Communist Party and Ministry of Foreign Affairs. That could only be possible in a country of victorious socialism.[3]

Mirsky could not travel to the United States during the Soviet years but many of his students did, and he describes their change of views as "truly profound," not so much in the sense that they were struck by the material standards of the West but rather in regard to Western mentality and social surroundings:

Before the exchange, people believed that Western society, no matter how wealthy and affluent, was narrowly materialistic, devoid of any humanism and spirituality, selfish and arrogant, indifferent to moral, cultural, and artistic values, full of hostility for Russians and of anti-Communist crusading spirit. What amazed them was American hospitality, warmth, willingness to oblige, civility and politeness, lack of ethnic prejudices, care for disabled, richness of artistic life, pluralism of opinions, abundance of associations. The Soviets were able for the first time in their lives to see a functioning civil society. This was a great surprise.[4]

One of Mirsky's former students reported how he was speechless when he saw disabled people in America crossing the streets and boarding buses in their motor-driven wheelchairs. Other students told him that in no country in the world could they hope to encounter such friendliness for foreigners as in the United States. And all of them were fascinated by the opportunities for scholarly research, the computers in libraries, and the unbelievable number of publications and magazines. "That was the main impression," concludes Mirsky, "and the exchange visitors would never be the same again."[5]

Mirsky's sad story, however, has a happy ending. With the accession of Gorbachev to power and the beginnings of perestroika, which Mirsky describes as "most important landmarks for the whole country as well as for myself personally," things began to change.[6] In 1988, Mirsky was told that he was free to travel

3. Ibid.
4. Georgi I. Mirsky, letter to author, May 5, 1997.
5. Ibid.
6. Mirsky, "A Half Century," 136.

and accept all those piled-up invitations. The first nonsocialist country he visited was Argentina; and as if a dam had broken, he in turn traveled to Egypt, Iran, Israel, India, and Hong Kong, as well as several European countries. His "second scholarly home," as he puts it, became the United States, where, over a period of seven years, he visited fifteen times, lecturing at the U.S. Institute of Peace, and Princeton, American, and several other universities.

22 | THE POLISH CONNECTION

For many Russian intellectuals, the Polish (or translated into Polish) literature in the social sciences and humanities was a kind of window to the West.

—EDMUND WNUK-LIPINSKI, Polish sociologist

In 1968, I made a get-acquainted call on Moscow's newly established Institute of Applied Sociological Research. Sociology had been banned in communist countries during the Stalin years, but the Soviet Union's new leaders soon learned that sociological research, if closely controlled, could be useful in revealing the failures as well as the achievements of Soviet society.

As the counselor for cultural affairs at the American Embassy, I was received coolly but correctly and was given a briefing on the work of the new institute.[1] At the conclusion of the meeting, the Russian briefer, in response to my questioning, acknowledged that the new Soviet sociology owed much to the work of Polish and Yugoslav sociologists who had studied in the United States and Western Europe during the 1950s and 1960s as Ford Foundation Fellows.

Eastern Europe has a long history of serving as remote Russia's window on the West, a tradition which continued through the Soviet period. Soviet citizens could travel more freely to Eastern Europe than to Western Europe, and scholars and scientists could more easily attend conferences in Warsaw, Budapest, and Prague than New York, London, or Paris. The editorial office of the international communist journal, *Problems of Peace and Socialism,* was located in Prague, and East European newspapers, journals, books, and films were readily available in the Soviet Union.

Eastern Europe, moreover, was more open to exchanges with the West than the Soviet Union, and much of what the East Europeans learned through exchanges, especially those funded by the Ford Foundation, eventually found its way into the Soviet Union. Ford, in 1957, began providing fellowships to Poles and Yugoslavs for study in the United States and Western Europe, and in subsequent years extended its programs to Hungary, Czechoslovakia, and other East European countries. IUCTG and IREX also had exchange programs in all the East European countries,

---

1. During a two-year tour of duty at the American Embassy in Moscow (1967–69), I called on a variety of Soviet institutes where no U.S. diplomat had previously visited. The appointments were made by telephone, and a visit was never refused.

as did, eventually, the Fulbright Program. Here, Poland will be cited as an example of Russia's "Window on the West."

The idea of Poland as Russia's Window on the West dates back to the late 1700s, when Poland was partitioned between Prussia, Russia, and Austria. Russia acquired by far the largest share, and with it, some of Catholic Poland's European culture, a situation that lasted until the end of World War I when Poland was reconstituted as an independent state.

Poland's independence, however, lasted only through the interwar period, and at the end of World War II, when it came under Russian dominance, it became one of the Soviet satellite states and found itself behind Stalin's Iron Curtain and cut off from its Western cultural roots. But when Poland's "October Revolution" of 1956 replaced a Stalinist regime with one of national communism that sought cultural and scientific contacts with the West, Poland again began to serve as a channel for Western ideas to Russia.

The Ford and Rockefeller Foundations established fellowship programs for Polish scholars, scientists, writers, and other cultural figures to study in Western Europe and the United States. And in 1959, as cultural officer at the American Embassy Warsaw, I was able to establish, with Fulbright funding, a U.S.-Polish exchange of graduate students, senior scholars, and university lecturers.[2] In the following years hundreds of Poles studied in the United States and Western Europe, and much of what they learned there eventually found its way into the Soviet Union.

Another channel for the transmission of Western ideas to the Soviet Union was Lithuania and its intellectually vibrant capital Vilnius. Lithuania and Poland were joined in a dynastic union in 1386 and remained united for some four hundred years until the Polish partitions, when Lithuania also became a part of Russia. Like Poland, Lithuania was independent in the interwar period, but in 1940 the Soviet Union annexed it and, after World War II, imposed a communist regime. Polish cultural influence in Lithuania, however, remained strong, especially in Vilnius, as a result of the common history and Catholic heritage of the two countries.

Tomas Venclova, the internationally renowned poet and Yale University professor of Slavic languages and literature, writes, "I was one of a large number of people in the USSR who learned Polish for obtaining more information on the West and Western culture."[3] Writing of his student days in his native Lithuania, then a part of the Soviet Union, Venclova adds: "We had no access to Western books and newspapers, yet we could subscribe to Polish newspapers and magazines, which from 1956 on became appreciably more informative than Soviet publications. In

---

2. For the origins of the Polish Fulbright Program, see Yale Richmond, "Margaret Schlauch and American Studies in Poland during the Cold War," *Polish Review* 44, no. 1 (winter 1999).

3. Tomas Venclova, correspondence with author, October 3, 1998.

the Lithuanian capital, Vilnius, there was also a modest Polish bookshop. And so, many of us learned Polish, initially with the express goal of cutting open a window to that unknown world."[4]

Another former Soviet citizen who learned Polish was Joseph Brodsky, the celebrated Russian poet and Nobel laureate who later emigrated to the United States. Brodsky has written that his disaffection with the Soviet Union began when he learned to read Polish in Leningrad in the 1960s. His interest in Polish also had a practical side, as he explains:

> In those days the bulk of Western literature, and of news about cultural events in the West, was not available in the Soviet Union. Poland was even at that point the happiest and most cheerful barrack in the Soviet camp. People there were much better informed and they were publishing all sorts of magazines and everything was translated into Polish. . . . I remember I was reading Malcolm Lowry, some of Proust, some of Faulkner, and also Joyce I first read in Polish. So that was the practical consideration. We needed a window onto Europe, and the Polish language provided it.[5]

A good source for Polish books in Moscow was the bookstore *Druzhba narodov* (Friendship of nations) on Gorky Street (now Tversky Street), dedicated to showcasing the literature and scholarly and scientific research of other communist countries. But the only section of the store that was always crowded was the one devoted to Polish books, and a foreign visitor had to push and elbow his way to the counter, Soviet style, to buy a book before a Russian had grabbed it.[6]

Vladimir Shlapentokh, a Russian sociologist who is now a professor of sociology at Michigan State University, has written of the influence of Polish sociologists, who had studied in the West as Ford Foundation Fellows, on the development of sociology in the Soviet Union: "In the 1950s, Poland had far greater contact with the West than did the USSR. In an attempt to fill the gap in their knowledge of the West, Soviet students sought to read Western literature in Polish translation. Especially important were the Polish sociologists Ian [*sic*] Szczepanski, Zygmunt Bauman, and Stefan Nowak, who adapted mostly Western sociological methodologies."[7]

4. Tomas Venclova, *Aleksander Wat: Life and Art of an Iconoclast* (New Haven: Yale University Press, 1996), vii.

5. Joseph Brodsky, in Anna Husarska, "A Talk with Joseph Brodsky," *New Leader,* December 14, 1987, 9.

6. Related by Daniel Matuszewski, former IREX Deputy Director, in e-mail to author, December 15, 2002.

7. Vladimir Shlapentokh, *The Politics of Sociology in the Soviet Union* (Boulder, Colo.: Westview Press, 1987), 21.

Shlapentokh has also written of his own experience as a sociologist in the Soviet Union: "The impact of Polish sociologists and in general of Polish culture in the late 1950s and in the 1960s was quite high. I myself subscribed to a number of Polish journals, and the newspaper *Polityka* was for me the best journal in this time. In Akademgorodok [the Soviet "Science City"], I delivered the first lectures on sociology using Zygmunt Bauman's popular book on sociology."[8] Of the influence of Polish sociology in the Soviet Union, Alan Kassof has written:

> Polish sociologists established a powerful basis for functional social analysis that soon became a serious challenge to official Marxism. While the Polish political authorities sometimes tended to look the other way, the more conservative Soviets were in full alarm—rightly, as it turned out—about the corrosive effect that the Polish sociologists were having on official dogma. The Soviets took drastic steps to isolate their own social scientists from the baleful influence of the Poles. They even forbade members of their research institutes from traveling to Poland and prohibited Poles from visiting Soviet research institutes. Soviet and Polish sociologists had to meet surreptitiously, with the Soviets coming to Poland on their own funds as tourists.[9]

In the 1950s and 1960s, the influence of Polish sociology in the Soviet Union was largely academic. But after the emergence of the Solidarity movement in Poland, Polish sociology began systematic research into various aspects of the radical social changes taking place in Poland. "For our Russian colleagues," writes Edmund Wnuk-Lipinski, a prominent Polish sociologist, Poland became

> a direct source of information about Polish society and the crisis of the communist system. At that time Polish sociology—at least partly—was a substitute for professional political science, since many sociological surveys (even after the imposition of martial law!) were directly focused on the issues that are usually in the area of interest of political science. A number of Polish publications (published in a limited number of copies due to censorship) went to Moscow and other academic centers. The main institutional framework for this kind of informal exchange was the Polish Sociological Association and its Russian counterpart but most of the contacts and exchange of materials stemmed from individual, informal contacts between the two milieus.[10]

8. Shlapentokh, correspondence with author, September 20, 1998.
9. Kassof, "Scholarly Exchanges," 268.
10. Edmund Wnuk-Lipinski, correspondence with author, March 31, 1999.

Wnuk-Lipinski also calls attention to the impact of the Polish press, particularly the weekly magazines, which, in spite of censorship during the years of martial law, were published widely and clandestinely, and turned up in the Soviet Union.[11] One of the most influential Polish-language journals which found its way into the Soviet Union was the political-cultural monthly *Kultura*, published and edited in Paris by Jerzy Giedroyc, a Polish émigré. Several editions of *Kultura* were also published in Russian translation.

11. Ibid.

23 | THE BEATLES DID IT

During the years of cultural resistance to Communist ideology in the countries of FSU [the former Soviet Union] and in EE [Eastern Europe], rock music turned out to be one of the most progressive modernizing art forms of the period. It found itself at the fore-front of cultural and ideological struggle, became a conduit of liberal "Western" ideas.

—MARK YOFFE, International Counterculture Archive, in H-Russia (#2001-195)

The influence of the Beatles on the youth of the West is well known. Less well known is their following among the youth of Eastern Europe and the Soviet Union, and the changes they brought about in those societies during the 1960s and 1970s in another form of cultural exchange.

"I am sure that the impact of the Beatles on the generation of young Soviets in the 1960s will one day be the object of studies," writes Pavel Palazchenko, Gorbachev's English-language interpreter and foreign policy aide: "We knew their songs by heart. . . . In the dusky years of the Brezhnev regime they were not only a source of musical relief. They helped us create a world of our own, a world differ-ent from the dull and senseless ideological liturgy that increasingly reminded one of Stalinism. . . . The Beatles were our quiet way of rejecting 'the system' while conforming to most of its demands."[1]

But the Beatles also had fans at the highest levels of the Soviet government. In 1987, Mikhail Gorbachev and his wife Raisa met with Yoko Ono, John Lennon's widow, and Raisa told her that they were Beatles' fans. "Gorbachev's endorsement of rock music," writes Timothy Ryback, ended three decades of official anti-rock policy in the Soviet Union: "Ever since the late 1940s, when Soviet and East Euro-pean youth turned to American jazz, fashion, and chewing gum as a means of overcoming the cultural isolation imposed by the cold war, Soviet-block [sic] gov-ernments . . . condemned Western youth culture as a form of 'spiritual poison.'"[2]

The rock groups that emerged from the underground during glasnost were seen by conservatives as a Western attempt to undermine the Soviet Union by sub-verting its youth. "Today you listen to rock," conservatives charged, "and tomor-row you will betray your motherland."[3] But under Gorbachev, writes Richard

---

1. Palazchenko, *My Years with Gorbachev and Shevardnadze*, 3.
2. Ryback, *Rock Around the Bloc*, 3–4.
3. *New York Times*, June 30, 1988.

Stites, "formerly proscribed rock bands were recognized and all styles of rock blossomed—hard, soft, punk, art, folk, fusion, retro, and heavy metal."[4]

"Across more than eight thousand miles of Eastern Europe and the Soviet Union," adds Ryback, "from the cusp of the Berlin Wall to the dockyards of Vladivostok, three generations of young socialists, who should have been bonded by the liturgy of Marx and Lenin, have instead found common ground in the music of the Rolling Stones and the Beatles."[5]

A similar, but more personal and heartfelt, view on the role of rock and roll in the early 1980s is given by Serge Levin, a Russian who now resides in Canada:

> Rock'n roll was the main factor that brought down the Communist regime. It was the cultural dynamite that blew up the Iron Curtain. People were bringing Western records from abroad, and they could be bought on the black market. Not everyone could afford them, but everyone had a tape recorder, so young people duplicated those records like crazy. And I'm telling you, the smell of freedom radiated by that music had a profound effect on myself and thousands, maybe millions of young people in my country. Very few knew what the songs were about in terms of lyrics, but everyone could feel the energy and was able to figure it out by themselves. So the music was the main factor in "Westernization" of the Russian people, at least of my generation.[6]

Rock taught Russians to speak more freely, to express their innermost thoughts, as singers Vysotsky and Okudzhava, and poets Voznesensky and Yevtushenko, had done a generation earlier.

Before rock there was, of course, *dzhaz,* another Western import that Khrushchev called "that noise music," and which Soviet conservatives also tried to outlaw but eventually came to co-opt. "Why did we love it so?" asks Vasily Aksyonov of jazz:

> Perhaps for the same reason the Communists (and the Nazis before them) hated it. For its refusal to be pinned down, its improvisatory nature. Living as we did in a totalitarian society, we needed relief from the structures of our minutely controlled everyday lives, of the five-year plans, of historical materialism. Traveling to Europe, especially Eastern Europe, jazz became more than music; it took on an ideology or, rather an anti-ideology. Jazz was a platonic rendezvous with freedom.[7]

4. Stites, *Russian Popular Culture,* 192.
5. Ryback, *Rock Around the Bloc,* 5.
6. Serge Levin, e-mail to author, December 7, 1998.
7. Aksyonov, *Melancholy Baby,* 203.

Aksyonov also believes that jazz was "America's secret weapon number one":

> Every night the Voice of America would beam a two-hour jazz program at the Soviet Union from Tangiers. The snatches of music and bits of information made for a kind of golden glow over the horizon when the sun went down, that is, in the West, the inaccessible but oh so desirable West. How many dreamy Russian boys came to puberty to the strains of Ellington's "Take the A Train" and the dulcet voice of Willis Conover, the VOA's Mr. Jazz. We taped the music on antediluvian recorders, and played it over and over at semi-underground parties, which often ended in fistfights with Komsomol patrols or even police raids.[8]

Conover hosted a program, "Music USA," for the Voice of America from 1955 until his death in 1996. For much of the world, and especially for the Soviet Union and Eastern Europe, he *was* the voice of America, and to his listeners he epitomized jazz. Conover was estimated to have as many as thirty million listeners worldwide, and many millions of them were in the Soviet Union, where his broadcasts are believed to have been a major factor in the revival of Soviet jazz after the death of Stalin.[9]

For two hours each night, six days a week, Conover's program—forty-five minutes of pop music and forty-five of jazz, each preceded by a fifteen-minute newscast—was said to have the largest audience of any international broadcast, although it was done completely in English. His mellifluous, slow-paced baritone voice and his theme song, Duke Ellington's "Take the A Train," were known to listeners from Leningrad to Vladivostok. One reason they listened, Conover believed, is that there is a sense of freedom they could detect in jazz. As he explained: "Jazz is a cross between total discipline and anarchy. The musicians agree on tempo, key, and chord structure but beyond this everyone is free to express himself. This is jazz. And this is America. That's what gives this music validity. It's a musical reflection of the way things happen in America. We're not apt to recognize this over here but people in other countries can feel this element of freedom."[10]

Jazz had been fashionable in the Soviet Union during the 1920s and 1930s, but after World War II, when it again became popular, it was condemned by Stalin's cultural tsar, Andrei Zhdanov, who declared it to be decadent, bourgeois music. Also condemned were the Soviet *stilyagi*, the long-haired "zoot suiters," who, as

8. Ibid., 18.

9. Serge Schmemann, in *New York Times*, July 15, 1982.

10. Willis Conover, quoted by John S. Wilson, in "Who is Conover? Only *We* Ask," *New York Times Magazine*, September 13, 1959.

recounted earlier in these pages, followed the styles of Western jazzmen by wearing black suits with broad shoulders, narrow trousers, and the then-popular narrow ties. But jazz and the *stilyagi* prevailed after the death of Stalin in 1953, despite attempts to purge them, and were given a degree of acceptance when restrictions on the arts were relaxed.

The Sixth World Youth Festival, as noted in Chapter 2, introduced rock music to the Soviet Union. Jazz musicians had been invited to the festival from both sides of the Iron Curtain, and some of them brought their electric guitars, previously unknown in the Soviet Union, and they took Soviet youth by storm. Also taking them by storm was the twist, the Western dance of the 1960s that spread its gyrations throughout the Soviet Union.

Rock recordings were not pressed in the Soviet Union in those years, and those that were brought in from Eastern Europe or the West were expensive. But Russians soon learned to "press" Western recordings on discarded x-ray films, which were plentiful and cheap, and millions of such "records" circulated until 1958 when the regime cracked down and outlawed them.

Despite the crackdown, the circulation of rock recordings and other Western music styles continued and actually increased during the 1960s, buoyed by the music of the Beatles and the resultant Beatlemania. As Trey Donovan Drake has written:

> The overwhelming popularity of the Beatles in the Soviet Union created two major social phenomena: It united people in a common spirit of popular culture totally independent of the official culture and, together with the underground record distribution, created a means of mass communication of youth values. . . . Most East European governments and the Soviet Union, viewing the youths' preference of rock 'n' roll to the socialist ideal for their cultural activities, undertook to eradicate Western rock from their countries.[11]

But it was a losing battle. Throughout the 1970s there was a gradual acceptance of rock culture by both people and government, and by the end of the decade there was a network of distribution for homemade albums, complete with printed artwork and lyrics. These were actually cassettes that were duplicated and passed on throughout the country. It was a cottage industry, and the resultant Russian-language albums established cultural heroes independent of socialist ideology, to whom their fans were more loyal than to the establishment.

11. Trey Donovan Drake, "Tusovka: The History of Rock in the USSR" (<http://www.sportos.com/tusovka/tus.ch 1.html>).

With the signing of the Helsinki Accords in 1975, more Western groups were allowed to tour in the Soviet Union, but the Beatles were still under a cloud. When Elton John, the popular British star, was invited in 1979 to perform in Moscow, he was asked to delete a Beatles' song, "Back in the USSR," from his repertoire. The best tickets to the Elton John show were distributed to party functionaries and their families, and the show was received coolly by the audience until the encore, when he played the banned song and almost caused a riot. And one year later, when Moscow university students planned a demonstration in memory of John Lennon, the KGB banned the event.[12]

The Rolling Stones never made it to the Soviet Union in their heyday, but when they finally were allowed to perform in Moscow in 1998, they filled a sports stadium with fifty thousand cheering Russians, many of them in their thirties and forties, who had waited more than twenty years to hear and see them live on stage.[13] And in another tribute to the Beatles, the city council of Chelyabinsk, an industrial city in the Ural Mountains, voted in October 2000 to rename one of their streets after Beatle star John Lennon.[14]

12. "Leadership Transition in a Fractured Bloc," Bulletin No. 10, Cold War International History Project (Washington, D.C.: The Wilson Center, Smithsonian Institution).

13. *New York Times,* August 13, 1998.

14. Even Communist Cuba did a cultural about-face on the Beatles when Fidel Castro, on December 8, 2000, led a day of homage to John Lennon, calling the former Beatles star "a revolutionary hero," although Cuba's communist authorities had once regarded Lennon's music as decadent Western influence. Castro said the tribute to Lennon made him feel young, adding, "Youth is all about thinking, enthusiasm and the capacity to dream." *New York Times,* December 9, 2000.

24 | *OBMEN* OR *OBMAN* ?

[Gorbachev's] "new political thinking" is the indirect result of a long-term process that includes both U.S. containment policy after World War II and the détente of the 1970s, which exposed an influential part of the Soviet elite to Western achievements and values.

—GAIL W. LAPIDUS AND ALEXANDER DALLIN, "The Pacification of Ronald Reagan"

What a difference an "a" makes! *Obmen* is the Russian word for "exchange," *obman* the Russian word for "deception," and some Americans saw exchanges with the Soviet Union as deceptions.

Supporters of exchanges sensed, as the late Alexander Dallin presciently put it, "that the impact of contacts and exposure, whether bread or circus, cannot fail to field a slow, perhaps imperceptible cumulation of new attitudes, perspectives, learning, borrowing. . . . It is bound to make for healthier, more open human relations, whose ultimate political expression remains moot."[1] Dallin also thought that the Soviet leadership underestimated the subtle, long-range impact of dealing with the outside world: "Whatever their severe limitations, every visit to the Soviet Union by an Albee or Steinbeck, a Böll or Stravinsky; every trip abroad by a Kapitsa or Voznesensky; every USIA exhibit in Rostov or Novosibirsk; every college glee club performing in Vilnius or Tbilisi; every Japanese trade delegation touring Soviet industry, has a subtle effect that perhaps none can fathom or weigh."[2] And, as Walter Laqueur predicted in 1971: "Even if the Soviet leaders regarded peaceful coexistence only as a tactical phase in their ultimate strategy of expanding their political power, was it not possible that a lengthy period of peaceful coexistence and collaboration would trigger irreversible changes in the Soviet system—not of course in a year or two, but in the perspective of several decades?"[3] Fifteen years later, that view was endorsed by John D. Negroponte, U.S. Assistant Secretary of State for Oceans and Environmental and Scientific Affairs: "A good case can be made that scientific exchanges provide opportunities for an articulate and politically sensitive sector of Soviet society to be exposed to Western methods, ideas, and values in ways which would not otherwise be possible. I cannot help but believe that such opportunities,

1. Alexander Dallin, "Current Frustrations and Long-Range Dividends" (paper presented at the conference "Russia and the West: Cultural Contacts and Influences," Schloss Leopoldskron, Salzburg, Austria, October 30–November 3, 1973).
2. Ibid.
3. Walter Laqueur, "Kissinger and the Politics of Détente," *Commentary* 56, no. 6 (December 1973): 51.

steadily sustained over the years, could make a contribution to the gradual opening of Soviet society, with attendant benefits for the human rights situation."[4]

But there were also critics who saw the Soviet Union as gaining more from the exchanges than the United States, particularly in science and technology. Among the more outspoken critics was Richard Perle, a long-time staffer of the Senate Subcommittee on International Security, Proliferation, and Federal Services, chaired by Senator Henry Jackson, and later Assistant Secretary of Defense for International Security Policy in the Reagan administration. Perle, in 1987, charged that "our Government has long known that the Soviet Union has had an aggressive program of acquiring American and other Western technologies and know-how. . . . In the détente of the 70's, the Soviet Union got the lion's share of benefits from exchanges that were supposed to be mutually beneficial. Soviet secrecy prevented us from learning much of interest, while American openness facilitated Soviet acquisition of American technology and know-how."[5]

Perle, however, was only partly right. As recounted earlier in these pages, Russia has had a long history of acquiring know-how from the West, and U.S. negotiators of exchanges were well aware that the acquisition of science and technology was a principal Soviet objective. Accordingly, the exchanges and cooperative activities were structured to focus on science rather than technology, and, as will be explained later in these pages, they were prescreened by the U.S. intelligence community to ensure that there was no technology transfer that would impinge on national security. As for Perle's charge that the Soviet Union got the "lion's share" of benefits, much of the joint research under the U.S.-Soviet cooperative agreements was of benefit to both superpowers and the rest of the world as well, in fields such as environmental protection, medicine and public health, artificial heart development, transportation, and space. The space agreement, for example, proved useful in preparing the way for the U.S.-Russian space cooperation of later years.

Meetings between the United States and the Soviet Union on space exploration began as early as 1955, when the two sides met in international forums to discuss their contributions to the International Geophysical Year scheduled for 1957–58. Little more was done, however, until 1959, when the National Aeronautics and Space Administration (NASA) received a legislative mandate to cooperate with other countries. NASA shortly thereafter initiated talks with the Soviets, and over the next few years began carefully controlled exchanges in the scientific, but not technological, results of space research.[6]

4. John D. Negroponte, in testimony before the Subcommittee on International Scientific Cooperation of the House Committee on Science, Space, and Technology, Washington, D.C., June 25, 1987 (Current Policy No. 997, Bureau of Public Affairs, Department of State).

5. Richard N. Perle, "Like Putting the K.G.B. into the Pentagon," *New York Times,* June 30, 1987, A-31.

6. The author has drawn here and in subsequent paragraphs from e-mail exchanges, May–June 2001, with Arnold Frutkin, former NASA Assistant Administrator for International Affairs.

In May 1972, President Richard Nixon, as part of his détente strategy, signed a cooperative agreement with Soviet Premier Aleksei Kosygin that provided for a U.S. Apollo spacecraft to rendezvous and dock with a Soviet Soyuz vehicle. The subsequent Apollo-Soyuz project led to the highly visible July 1975 "handshake in space" between an American astronaut and a Russian cosmonaut.

The objectives of the two signatories to the space agreement were political rather than technological. The Americans wanted to draw the Soviets into cooperative efforts, while the Soviets sought recognition as equal to the United States in space, especially after the Apollo 11 mission had made the first successful manned lunar landing in 1969. When Henry Kissinger, as National Security Adviser, asked NASA in 1972 for a space proposal that was more substantive than a mere exchange of data, NASA came up with the idea of parallel launches of manned capsules that would dock with each other and permit reciprocal visits by American astronauts and Soviet cosmonauts. From the start, it was designed as an "arm's-length" project to limit Soviet access to U.S. technology.

U.S. officials and engineers who worked with the Soviets on the Apollo-Soyuz project believe that it was mutually beneficial. The Soviets already knew much about the open Apollo program, while the Americans knew little about the closed Soyuz program. However, American and Soviet engineers found that the Soviet docking device was better than the American, and when they agreed that it should be used for the joint docking, the Soviets delivered their blueprints so the Americans could build one that was compatible. The Soviets also agreed to reduce their cabin pressure to permit transfers of astronauts and cosmonauts without a decompression chamber but they asked the Americans for the flight-suit cloth necessary to protect their cosmonauts against the increased fire hazard. When U.S. export controls denied NASA permission to deliver the cloth samples, the Soviets developed their own and sent samples to Houston, which the Americans found were better than their own. And when the Soviets asked for the American low-light video cameras so they could broadcast pictures during space flight, their request was also turned down, so the Soviets developed their own, thereby probably learning more than if NASA had complied with their request.[7]

Glynn S. Lunney, U.S. technical director for the Apollo-Soyuz project, believes that it taught American and Soviet space engineers how to work together—a considerable achievement for the 1970s—and thus prepared the way for later cooperation in space. The Soviets came to Houston and learned how NASA ran its working groups. The Americans visited the Soviet launch site, observed their docking training, and learned how the Soviets ran their space program at a fraction of the cost of the American.

7. Telephone interview with Glynn S. Lunney, April 30, 2001.

Apollo-Soyuz also opened the way for direct communication between American and Soviet space engineers. The Soviets at first had objected when NASA proposed direct daily communication between engineers and technicians in Houston and Star City, the cosmonaut training center, preferring instead that communications go through Moscow. NASA engineers, however, held firm and told the Soviets that without direct communication between the engineers, the project would have to be canceled. The Soviets relented, and another advance was made in freedom of communication between the two countries.[8]

Another benefit of Apollo-Soyuz was the human element. Altogether, some one hundred elite Soviet personnel came to Houston for two-week meetings of the Apollo-Soyuz joint working groups, and their NASA opposite numbers made return visits to Star City. In addition to the working sessions, the Soviets were invited to homes and saw how their American colleagues lived. And on those visits, the Soviets, like other exchange visitors, loaded up on sneakers, windshield wiper blades, and other items in short supply back home.

The Apollo-Soyuz project was seen by the Nixon and Ford administrations as the start of increasingly close U.S.-Soviet cooperation in human space flight. After two years of negotiation between NASA and the Soviet Academy of Sciences, the Soviet side initialed a draft agreement in May 1977 that called for a multistep approach to developing a bilateral space platform. That agreement anticipated what eventually occurred a quarter-century later—working together with other countries to develop an International Space Station.

The 1977 agreement, however, was not implemented. The Carter administration, in reaction to Soviet human rights violations, chose not to work closely with the Soviet Union, and the Reagan administration, in 1982, as part of its initial negative stance toward the Soviet Union, allowed the 1972 U.S.-Soviet space agreement to lapse.

With the change in the political climate for U.S.-Soviet relations following the accession to power of Mikhail Gorbachev, a new framework space agreement was negotiated in 1987. It did not, however, list human space flight as one of the sixteen areas selected for initial cooperation, and another five years were to pass before such cooperation once again became politically acceptable.

Cooperation under the Science and Technology (S&T) Agreement was mostly in the basic sciences and included little technology. Information made available by U.S. scientists had already been published and was easily available to the international scientific community. Moreover, the bulk of technological research in the United States is conducted by industry or government defense-related institutions, and measures were taken to ensure that visiting Soviet scientists had no contact with such research.

8. Ibid.

In negotiating the program of exchanges annexed to each cultural agreement, State Department officials employed the old diplomatic tactic of trade-offs—give the Soviets some of the exchanges they wanted, in exchange for those which the U.S. side sought. At the top of the Soviet list of priority exchanges were those in science and technology, and at the top of the list of exchanges which the Soviets did not want were the U.S. traveling exhibitions, which gave millions of Soviet citizens a rare opportunity to see for themselves aspects of life in the United States and to speak in Russian with American guides.

At almost every negotiation of the cultural agreement, the language on exhibitions was the last to be resolved, and it was resolved only after U.S. negotiators had made it clear that without the exhibitions there would be no cultural agreement. At one negotiation in the early 1970s, the American ambassador, Jacob D. Beam, had to bring such an impasse to the attention of Foreign Minister Andrei Gromyko before the Soviet negotiators relented and accepted the U.S. language on exhibitions.

But how to square potential losses in science and technology with the U.S. political objective of encouraging exchanges as a means of bringing about change in the Soviet Union? To resolve that dilemma, a comprehensive system of controls was put in place to monitor Soviet exchange visits to the United States and prevent losses in science and technology that might have a bearing on U.S. national security.

From the very start of the exchanges in 1958, a new category of visas for Soviet exchange visitors was created, "Special Exchange," with the acronym SPLEX, which was tagged to the visa of every Soviet exchange visitor. For each SPLEX visa applicant, the field of study and proposed itinerary in the United States were checked out, in advance of visa issuance, with various components of the U.S. intelligence community. A Committee on Exchanges (COMEX), representing the intelligence and technical security communities as well as governmental agencies concerned with exchanges, reviewed the subject of study or research and proposed itinerary, and rendered an advisory opinion to the State Department on whether the proposed visit was in a field considered sensitive to defense interests and whether the visit would result in a net intelligence loss or gain.[9] In cases where the visitor's research was in a field that might affect U.S. security, the visa could be denied. In most such cases, however, the proposed itinerary in the United States was often adjusted to ensure that there was no access to research funded by the Department of Defense. Moreover, the itineraries of Soviet exchange visitors within the United States were monitored, and any deviation from an approved itinerary required advance notification to the State Department.

9. Represented on COMEX, a subcommittee of the Technology Transfer Intelligence Committee (TTIC), were the CIA, FBI, Defense Intelligence Agency (DIA); Air Force, Army, and Naval Intelligence; National Security Agency (NSA); and Departments of Commerce, Defense, Energy, Justice, State, Treasury, and USIA. COMEX was chaired by the CIA until 1982, and by DIA until 1994 when it was disbanded.

As exchange and cooperative agreements proliferated during the détente years, an Interagency Coordinating Committee on U.S.-Soviet Affairs (ICCUSA) was established by the National Security Council in 1977. Chaired by the State Department's Bureau of European and Canadian Affairs, ICCUSA was responsible for monitoring and coordinating all U.S. government activities with the Soviet Union.

To control the travel of Soviet exchange visitors in the United States, U.S. host universities and other sponsoring institutions were requested to inform IREX or the State Department of any travel planned by a Soviet visitor beyond twenty-five miles from the place of study. If the travel was for pleasure, no approval was required. But if the proposed travel was for professional reasons, such as a visit to another university or attendance at a scientific meeting, advance approval was required. This latter restriction was imposed in reciprocity for a similar forty-kilometer travel restriction on American exchangees in the Soviet Union, for professional reasons or pleasure, but also as a means of keeping tabs on the travel of Soviet scientists in the United States. That system of controls worked to limit any intelligence loss.

All Soviet visa applicants traveling on official passports, which was almost always the practice, and declining to appear for an interview with a U.S. consul, also the usual case, were routinely found ineligible for a visa under U.S. immigration legislation in effect at the time.[10] However, a waiver of visa ineligibility could be issued by the Department of Justice if the Department of State, after considering the recommendation of COMEX, found the visit to be in the national interest. As it turned out in practice, few Soviet visitors were found ineligible, and in most of the questionable cases, it was possible to change the place of study or itinerary and find the visit to be in the U.S. national interest. Moreover, no visits to production facilities were allowed. And since pure science is universal and has no secrets, it was in production that the United States was usually ahead of the Soviet Union and where sensitive technology had to be protected.

Perle, however, questioned COMEX's competence, charging that "the Committee on Exchanges, which has some nominal responsibility for vetting exchanges (and individuals coming to America to participate in them), has failed utterly to carry out its assigned tasks with even minimal competence."[11]

That wide-ranging charge could not be substantiated. Perle had overlooked the COMEX determination of net intelligence loss or gain. If the Soviets, through an exchange, learned how far ahead the United States was in a particular area of research, the United States also learned how far behind the Soviet Union was, and that information could be very valuable. Perle also disregarded the fact that his

10. Immigration and Nationality Act of 1952 (McCarran-Walter), as amended.
11. Perle, "Like Putting the K.G.B. into the Pentagon."

own Department of Defense was represented on COMEX, as well as the Defense Intelligence Agency, which of all the government agencies represented on COMEX, generally took a more critical view of exchanges with the Soviet Union.

Moreover, as a sign of confidence in COMEX, on April 28, 1992, CIA Director Robert M. Gates, on behalf of the National Foreign Intelligence Community, awarded a Meritorious Unit Citation to COMEX "for exceptional service." The citation noted COMEX's "outstanding policy leadership, its reviews of proposed scientific and technical projects with the Soviet Union and Eastern European countries . . . [which] were forthright, thorough, and of a consistently excellent quality."

Another objection came from those who charged that the early scholarly exchanges were not of mutual benefit, since the Soviets were sending mostly scientists and engineers in highly sophisticated fields of research, while the United States was sending mostly students and scholars in Russian history, language, and literature. There is some truth to this charge but here again there were significant benefits to the United States, as will be explained below. In any event, the numbers changed significantly in the 1970s, when thousands of American scientists and engineers visited the Soviet Union under the cooperative agreements of the détente years.

In the early years of the exchanges, the Soviets would not accept Americans in fields which they considered sensitive—Soviet history after 1917, political science, sociology, or other fields that dealt with contemporary Soviet society. Consequently, many American scholars in those fields, anticipating a Soviet rejection, were reluctant to apply for an exchange visit. However, some American students and scholars, especially those in Soviet-area studies, changed their fields of study in order to have the benefit of an academic year abroad and exposure to the realities of life in Soviet society. Many American students, therefore, modified their research topics to conform to Soviet sensitivities while nevertheless pursuing their own scholarly interests.

Mark Von Hagen, for example, currently a professor at Columbia University's Harriman Institute, listed his research topic as "Political Education in the Red Army, 1917–1930," although he actually researched a book on the Red Army, a topic the Soviets would not have approved. Similarly, Hugh Phillips, now professor of Russian history at Western Kentucky University, gave his topic as "The Soviet Union, the League of Nations, and the Struggle for Collective Security," although he actually did research for a biography of Soviet Foreign Minister Maksim Litvinov.

American scientists likewise were reluctant to apply for exchange visits under the Graduate Student/Young Faculty exchange because they did not have the Russian language skills that would have made a visit more productive, or they believed—and rightly so in many cases—that they would be denied access to the facilities necessary for their research. American scientists, however, could also participate in the exchange between the National Academy of Sciences and the Soviet Academy of Sciences. One who did was Don Ritter, who had a doctorate from MIT and later served in the U.S. House of Representatives from 1979 to 1992, where he was a strong supporter of exchanges. Addressing Perle in a 1987 hearing on exchanges with the Soviet Union in science and technology, Ritter said: "You are familiar with the tremendous benefit we gained, speaking from personal experience, in spending a year or three months or whatever in the Soviet Union. It is such a closed society. There are so few people in the United States who have spent a period of time there. It is one thing to visit and get a certain impression and it is another to live there."[12]

The controversy over S&T exchanges prompted a number of studies. "There have been more than twenty-five evaluations of various aspects of United States-Soviet scientific exchanges during the past decade," said Dr. Victor Rabinowitch, Executive Director for International Affairs, National Academy of Sciences, in 1987. "These evaluations," continued Rabinowitch, "conclude that carefully managed exchanges can bring substantial scientific benefits to the United States."[13]

The first such study was conducted in 1966–67 by political scientists Frederick C. Barghoorn, Yale University, and Ellen P. Mickiewicz, then at Michigan State University, who analyzed responses from 472 Americans who had traveled to the Soviet Union since the inception of the exchanges.[14] Those polled included natural scientists who had traveled under the National Academy-Soviet Academy exchange; scholars and graduate students in history, literature, and the social sciences who had traveled under the IUCTG exchange; and a number of U.S. government officials, business people, and undergraduate majors in Russian studies. They were described by Barghoorn and Mickiewicz as "an extraordinarily knowledgeable, distinguished, sophisticated, perceptive, and articulate group."[15]

Natural scientists in the survey thought there were only a few areas in which American scientists could learn much from Russians, although several said they had benefited significantly from their visits. Historians and social scientists, on the other hand, felt that experience in Russia could be enormously valuable and even indispensable. A distinguished legal scholar wrote that experience in socialist countries was "so important that I feel what is written by those who have not been

---

12. House Subcommittee on International Scientific Cooperation of the Committee on Science, Space, and Technology, *Hearings to Examine U.S.-Soviet Science and Technology Exchanges,* 100th Cong., 1st sess., June 23, 1987, 68.

13. Victor Rabinowitch, ibid., 74.

14. Frederick C. Barghoorn and Ellen Mickiewicz, "American Views of Soviet-American Exchanges of Persons," in Richard L. Merritt, ed., *Communication in International Politics* (Urbana: University of Illinois Press, 1972), 146–67.

15. Ibid., 149.

in socialist countries constitutes nothing more than interesting hypotheses for examination by others who can make 'field' trips to the East."[16]

Several respondents noted the deep impression made on Soviet people by the freedom of Americans to travel all over the world. Others noted the profound effect of books made available to Soviet students by their foreign friends, including a young philosopher respondent's statement that the entire philosophical outlook of one Soviet citizen was changed "from orthodox Marxism to a devotion to the ideas of Erich Fromm as a result of conversation and reading of Western literature acquired from American exchangees." On balance, concluded Barghoorn and Mickiewicz, "our respondents tended to stress the role of exchanges as catalysts of dissent, as sources of alternatives to established models, and as a factor in strengthening the hand of 'progressive' Soviet intellectuals and scientists vis-à-vis the political authorities."[17]

The most comprehensive and authoritative of the many subsequent reports on U.S.-Soviet science exchanges was prepared in 1982 by the Panel on Scientific Communication and National Security, whose nineteen members included representatives of university faculties and administrations, former federal agency officials, and leaders in high-technology industrial firms.[18] Commonly called the Corson panel, after its chair, Dale R. Corson, President Emeritus of Cornell University, it was convened by the National Academy of Sciences because of concerns that the Soviet Union had gained militarily from access to U.S. science and technology, and that tighter controls should be established on the transfer of information to the Soviets through open channels, including exchanges.

The panel was asked to examine various aspects of the application of controls to scientific communication and to suggest how to balance competing national objectives to best serve the general welfare. That task involved a careful assessment of the sources of leakage, the nature of universities and scientific communication, the systems of information control in effect at the time, and the several costs and benefits of controls.

The panel concluded that

> there has been a substantial transfer of U.S. technology—much of it directly relevant to military systems—to the Soviet Union from diverse sources. The Soviet science and technology intelligence effort has increased in recent years, including that directed at U.S. universities and scientific research. The Soviet Union is exploiting U.S.-U.S.S.R. exchange

16. Ibid., 157.
17. Ibid., 158–59.
18. *Scientific Communication and National Security* (Washington, D.C.: National Academy Press, 1982).

programs by giving intelligence assignments to some of its participating nationals. This has led to reports of abuses in which the activities of some Soviet bloc exchange visitors have clearly extended beyond their agreed fields of study and have included activities that are inappropriate for visiting scholars.[19]

The panel added, however, that

> there is a strong consensus . . . that universities and open scientific communication have been the source of very little of this technology transfer problem. Although there is a net flow of scientific information from the United States to the Soviet Union, consistent with the generally more advanced status of U.S. science, there is serious doubt as to whether the Soviets can reap significant direct military benefits from this flow in the near term. Moreover, U.S. openness gives this nation access to Soviet science in many key areas, and scientific contacts yield useful insights into Soviet institutions and society.[20]

A similar view of U.S.-Soviet scientific exchanges was held by Admiral Bobby Ray Inman, a career naval intelligence officer whose credentials include tours of duty as Director of Naval Intelligence; Vice Director, Defense Intelligence Agency; Deputy Director, Central Intelligence Agency (CIA); and Director, National Security Agency. Inman believed that the United States was getting more than the Soviets from the exchanges, since it was putting people on the ground in a closed society, while the Soviets did not need to be in the United States in order to collect technological information, most of which was published in the open literature.

In testimony for a hearing on technology transfer conducted by the U.S. Senate Governmental Affairs Subcommittee on Investigations on May 11, 1982, Inman, as Deputy Director of CIA, estimated that 70 percent of Soviet bloc acquisitions of Western high technology was made through their intelligence services. Another 20 to 30 percent, he continued, was made through legal purchases and Western published material. "A very small percentage of it," Inman added, "comes from direct technical exchanges conducted by scientists and students."[21]

In the same hearing, Senator Sam Nunn asked Inman about the IREX exchange:

19. Ibid, 1.
20. Ibid., 1–2.
21. *Transfer of U.S. High Technology to the Soviet Union and Soviet Bloc Nations,* Hearings Before the Senate Permanent Subcommittee on Investigations of the Committee on Governmental Affairs, U.S. Senate, May 1982 (Washington, D.C.: U.S. Government Printing Office, 1982), 236.

We heard over and over again about how the Soviets send middle-aged scientists over as students, we send students of Soviet history over in an exchange program. One is after technology, the other is after some form of legitimate literary or historical endeavor. There is nothing wrong with the latter, but what is it you would like to see the scientific and intellectual community do in this regard and I stress voluntarily without Government dictating?[22]

Inman replied:

There are some exchanges that are clearly in our national interest. We are going to need in this decade out ahead scholars and students with genuine area study capability, with language skills who can watch the actions of our adversaries and give us sound advice, whether they are working in the intelligence community as analysts or whether they are working in the Foreign Service or other parts of the Government. And so we should be cautious as we go about assessing the value of exchanges that we don't underplay the value to this country of various area studies and language training as part of the exchange structure.[23]

Inman's views are supported by Andrew and Mitrokhin, who claim that during the early 1980s, some 70 percent of current Warsaw Pact weapons systems was based on Western technology. They add, however, that most of the Soviet S&T collections came from American defense contractors: "For most of the Cold War, American business proved much easier to penetrate than the federal government. Long before the KGB finally acquired a major spy in the CIA with the walk in of Aldrich Ames in 1985, it was running a series of other mercenary agents in American defense contractors."[24] Also noted by Andrew and Mitrokhin was the difficulty that Soviet industry had in making practical use of the scientific and technical information acquired through espionage and exchanges:

The Soviet Union often found it more difficult to use than to collect the remarkable S&T which it collected from American businesses, most of them defense contractors. In 1965 the Politburo criticized the fact that there was a time lag of two to three years before Soviet industry began exploiting S&T. Even the computer technology stolen by the KGB did no more than, at best, stabilize the striking gap between East and West. . . .

22. Ibid., 248.
23. Ibid.
24. Andrew and Mitrokhin, *Sword and Shield*, 556–57.

The continued backwardness of the Soviet computer industry, despite the expertise of Soviet scientists and the remarkable S&T obtained by the KGB, reflected the cumbersome inefficiency of the Soviet command economy, in which technical innovation had to run the gauntlet of a complex and unresponsive state bureaucracy.[25]

What was not known at the time, and perhaps could not have been foreseen, was the prestige that Soviet scientists enjoyed at home and their immediate importance to the economy. Exchanges in the social sciences and humanities were encouraged and promoted by the U.S. side, but in retrospect, the long-term impact of what Soviet scientists saw in the United States, and their political influence at home, was much greater.

Another objection to the exchanges stemmed from the control that the Communist Party of the Soviet Union had over foreign travel by Soviet citizens. As Edward Lozansky, a former Soviet physicist who is now a U.S. citizen, put it: "While we have been sending over our students, artists, and scientists, many of their participants have been identified as party officials, including members of the KGB. For ordinary Soviet citizens to be included in an exchange program they must prove their unequivocal loyalty to the Communist Party for many years. In addition, they must have spotless employment and educational records before being granted [exit] visas."[26]

Lozansky was correct in describing the KGB screening of Soviet citizens before they could participate in an exchange but he overlooked several considerations. One of the ground rules of U.S.-Soviet exchanges was "sending side nominates," and the United States was therefore in no position to tell the Soviet Union whom it should nominate for an exchange nor how such nominees should be selected. Moreover, since the exchanges were conducted on a reciprocal basis, Americans would not have wanted the Soviets to tell them whom to send to the Soviet Union. Lozansky was also correct in noting that Soviet citizens who participated in the exchanges had to show "unequivocal loyalty" to the regime, and that many were Communist Party members, and some perhaps even KGB officers. But to have opponents of the Soviet regime selected by the Soviet authorities would have been as unthinkable as having American communists sent by the U.S. side.

Today, however, with the benefit of hindsight, it can be argued that having communist loyalists participate in the exchanges was exactly the right policy to bring about change in the Soviet Union. Change in Russia has always come from above, as Gorbachev himself has acknowledged: "My years at the head of the territory of Stavropol have made me understand that change can come only from

25. Ibid., 188.
26. Edward Lozansky and Jennifer Joyce, in *Washington Times,* June 16, 1986.

above."[27] Aleksandr Yakovlev agrees, noting that "perestroika took place and originated within the Communist Party of the Soviet Union."[28]

Gorbachev's glasnost and perestroika reforms came indeed from within the Communist Party, from trusted party members who had traveled abroad and become reformers. As Marshall Shulman explains: "Arbatov is a leading example of what I call the within-system modernizers who made the Second Russian Revolution possible. In any study of how all these extraordinary transformations came about, we'll have to pay attention to the part of people who, in different ways and to different degrees, went about their business [while] all the time pressing for a more modern political culture."[29] And Robert G. Kaiser writes, in a similar vein: "The ideas of perestroika were nourished in different fields for a long time, sometimes a very long time, even too long. These ideas have been developed over the years by scholars, cultural figures, and people engaged in political activity. Such ideas have been discussed in the press and in private conversations. All this was background to the growing understanding that it was impossible to live in the old way and many serious changes were necessary."[30]

Travel to the West for Soviet scientists and scholars was a sign of prestige and status, but those who traveled had to pay a political and ideological price. In the social sciences, almost all exchangees had to be party members and hew to the party line. But travel broadened their horizons, and they returned home burdened with books and new ideas. As Igor Zevelev, a Russian political scientist has put it: "Exchanges helped to overcome the ideology of dogma regarding communism and capitalism. We started to think differently, and saw the world as more complex than we had been taught to believe."[31]

But what should be said about the KGB officers who did come to the United States, either on assignment or under various exchange programs? Were they too influenced by their Western experience?

KGB officers assigned abroad were among the best and brightest of the Soviet Union. Intelligence, like science, was where the talent went. As members of the KGB's First Directorate (foreign intelligence, not to be confused with the KGB's domestic directorates), they were often the sons of privileged members of the nomenklatura. As described by Canadian foreign correspondent Eric Margolis:

> The KGBs First Directorate (today's SVR) was filled with the cream of Soviet society. Its senior officers were often pampered children of the

27. Gorbatchev, *Mémoires,* 143

28. Aleksandr Yakovlev, "The Future of Democracy in Russia: The Lessons of Perestroika and the Question of the Communist Party" (Elberg Lecture, February 22, 1993, at University of California, Berkeley, <http://globetrotter.berkeley.edu/Yakovlev/yak-elb1.html>).

29. Marshall Shulman, quoted by Strobe Talbott in his introduction to Arbatov's *The System,* xvii.

30. Kaiser, *Why Gorbachev Happened,* 91.

31. Igor Zevelev, author's interview, Washington, D.C., April 19, 1997.

Soviet nomenklatura, educated in the best schools and universities, raised in luxury, allowed travel to the west, forbidden books, subversive western music, and meetings with foreigners. The First Directorates training schools were the Soviet Union's Harvard, MIT, and Oxford, and their graduates the young aristocrats of Soviet society.[32]

And like scientists, many KGB officers were also reformers. Those who had served or studied abroad were westernized to a certain extent, and able to see their own country and its failings more objectively. "As the best-informed part of the Communist establishment," wrote Dusko Doder, *Washington Post* bureau chief in Moscow during the 1980s, "the KGB was the first to grasp the catastrophic consequences of Leonid Brezhnev's long rule. Yuri Andropov, the ultimate insider, began the reformist course in the early 1980s which paved the way to Mikhail Gorbachev and, later, Boris Yeltsin."[33]

That view is shared by Stratfor, a Texas-based organization that provides global intelligence to private companies and subscribers:

> By the very nature of their jobs, they [the KGB] were forced to confront the degree to which the Soviet Union was falling behind the West technologically and economically. As guarantors of the regime inside the Soviet Union, they knew better than anyone the levels of inefficiency, corruption and cynicism that had gripped the Soviet Union. Along with their counterparts in the upper reaches of the military, they understood how much trouble the Soviet Union was in long before Western experts got a sense of it.[34]

Adds Stratfor:

> The KGB, as the leading reformist faction within the Soviet Union, collaborated comfortably with the new reformers, both in their legitimate and illegitimate activities. But in the final analysis, while they shared much with the reformers, they differed in one fundamental way: they were Soviet men. They believed, if not in the ideology of the Soviet Union, then in its imperial mission. . . . So long as reform held out promise of a greater Russia, they were prepared to give their loyalty to the reformers.[35]

32. Eric S. Margolis, "Son of CIA Meets KGB," *Toronto Star,* June 24, 2001.
33. Dusko Doder, *Baltimore Sun,* May 11, 2000.
34. "Putin: Yeltin's Madness or Silent Coup" (Global Intelligence Update, August 23, 1999, <http://www.stratfor.com>).
35. Ibid.

KGB officers in diplomatic assignments abroad had a reputation for being more outspoken than other Soviet diplomats. In the late 1970s, for example, a senior KGB officer who had served abroad in the West for many years told me at an official lunch in Moscow: "The trouble with our country is that it is run by tired and sick old men who cannot make the changes needed to bring us into the modern world." It was at that time that Brezhnev had become seriously ill and was no longer managing the affairs of state. And although it was still several years before Gorbachev was named General Secretary of the Communist Party and began his policies of glasnost and perestroika, a KGB officer had the courage and conviction to criticize openly the Soviet leadership in conversation with an American diplomat.

The KGB and GRU (military intelligence) saw exchanges as opportunities to train their officers for future assignments in the West and, in some cases, to station them abroad, as indicated by Oleg Kalugin and Boris Yuzhin, discussed above. Indeed, of the Soviet graduate students in the United States during the first year of the exchange (1958–59), Kalugin has written: "Of the eighteen [sic, actually seventeen] Soviets in our group, half were officers of the KGB or Soviet Military Intelligence, known as GRU; the other half could be counted on to cooperate with us."[36] With time, however, as the Soviets learned how useful the exchanges could be for other purposes, and as other Soviet agencies, as well as the Soviet ethnic republics, competed for positions in the exchange quotas, the number of KGB and GRU agents in the exchanges declined.

But Soviet intelligence participation in the exchanges also provided benefits to the West, as Aleksandr Yakovlev pointed out when asked about the usefulness of academic exchanges: "I believe that exchange programs such as Fulbright [sic] had a very positive impact. Frankly speaking, let's take an extreme. It is very well known that most of the people who, back in those years, participated in those exchanges came from intelligence agencies. And even *that* was good, it had a positive impact on them to a certain extent."[37] That "positive impact" reached such an extent that Kalugin and Yakovlev were named by KGB head Vladimir Kryuchkov in 1989 as among the five who had destroyed the Soviet Union.[38]

Also influenced by their stays in the West were many of the Soviet intelligence "illegals"—agents operating abroad under false identities. Unlike their leaders in Moscow and the Soviet public at large, who had no personal knowledge of the world beyond the Soviet bloc, the illegals knew the realities of life in the West and

36. Kalugin, *First Directorate,* 26.

37. Aleksandr N. Yakovlev, in talk at Russia House, Washington, D.C., September 11, 1998.

38. "At Cold War's End: US Intelligence on the Soviet Union and Eastern Europe, 1989–1991" (a compendium of documents prepared by the History Staff, Center for the Study of Intelligence, Central Intelligence Agency, for a conference, "U.S. Intelligence and the End of the Cold War," held at Texas A&M University, November 18–20, 1999), foreword, n. 70.

in the Soviet Union, and they made the appropriate comparisons. As Andrew and Mitrokhin have written, "There were recurrent complaints in [KGB] FCD Directorate S that after postings abroad illegals sometimes returned with an 'incorrect' attitude towards life in the Soviet Union. Occasionally their attitudes were so incorrect that their careers were cut short."[39]

On the American side of exchanges, IUCTG and IREX kept their distance from U.S. intelligence agencies. As Robert F. Byrnes, the former chair of IUCTG, has told us:

> Throughout their history, the Committee and its successor organization [IREX] have remained exclusively interested in scholarly activities and have no ties with the CIA or any other intelligence or security organization, except when discussing KGB interventions and activities with responsible intelligence officers. They have received no funds from any such organizations, they have provided them with no information, and the CIA has had no influence whatsoever on their policies or actions. Because of their determination to prevent any improper contacts, the Committee and IREX have warned every applicant not only to reject any approach that intelligence or other government agencies might make, but to report any incidents that occur.[40]

When an overzealous CIA employee, in the early years of the IUCTG exchange, sought to persuade one of the American scholars to be alert for information of interest to intelligence officers, the scholar rejected the suggestion and informed the IUCTG chair, Schuyler C. Wallace of Columbia University. As Byrnes continues:

> Wallace arranged that a senior scholar explain to Allen Dulles, then Director of the CIA, the necessity that there be no relationship whatever between the CIA and participants. Dulles quickly agreed that the Agency would, under no circumstances, seek to use scholars on this program. This agreement was renewed in 1960, and it was reviewed and renewed annually thereafter until the need for it ended. . . . Both the Committee and IREX have obliged all scholars to report any attempt by an intelligence agency to contact them.[41]

---

39. Andrew and Mitrokhin, *Sword and Shield,* 260.
40. Byrnes, *Soviet-American Academic Exchanges,* 141.
41. Ibid., 143.

25 | THE FUTURE

When it comes to the relationship between great peoples, that relationship is not finished, not complete when it only consists of the military relationship, the economic, and the political. There has to be, and particularly in the case of Russia, there has to be another supplementary dimension to these relations—and that is the dimension of the meeting of people—in the work of the intellect, in the respect for scholarship and history, in the understanding of art and music and in all the intuitive feelings that go to unite us even in the most difficult times to many people in Russia.

—GEORGE F. KENNAN, October 4, 1999

In the early years of the twenty-first century, Russia is in a new time of troubles—demographic, public health, environmental, crime and corruption, economic, and social—and there are some in the United States who believe that Russia no longer matters in world affairs.

True, Russia has lost an empire; its political, economic, and social systems have been overturned; its military power has been much reduced; and all within the space of little more than a decade. Russia is indeed down but it is not out. It still has many attributes of a great power—nuclear weapons and their delivery systems, vast natural resources, rich oil and gas reserves, a strategic position athwart Europe and Asia, an educated and skilled workforce, world-class science, an active space exploration program, a culture that has enriched the world, and a history that Russians are proud of, and its neighbors very much aware of. Rather than neglected, Russia should be engaged, and it should be a long-term engagement that will lead, not necessarily to marriage, but to a better understanding by Russians of their own country and how it should relate to the rest of the world.

Ronald Reagan, in 1984, in what many observers thought was yet another example of his euphoric optimism, prophesied: "It may seem an impossible dream to think that there could be a time when Americans and Soviet citizens of all walks of life travel freely back and forth, visit each other's homes, look up friends and professional colleagues, work together in all sorts of problems, and, if they feel like it, sit up all night talking about the meaning of life and the different ways to look at the world. . . . I don't believe it's an impossible dream."[1] Ronald Reagan's

---

1. Ronald Reagan, in address to a conference in Washington on U.S.-Soviet exchanges, *Weekly Compilation of Presidential Documents* (Washington, D.C.: U.S. Government Printing Office), vol. 20, no. 26, 946.

"impossible dream" has now been realized as Russians are free to interact with Americans and Europeans at home and abroad, and many thousands come to the United States every year under U.S. government and private programs.

Gone are the quotas and strictures of the cultural agreement on who and how many can come and go between the two countries, and as a consequence, the number of persons exchanged each year has greatly increased. The number of Russians studying in the United States has reached new highs. Russian performing arts groups and individual artists have a presence on American stages far exceeding the 1970s and 1980s. Russian exhibitions are shown regularly across the United States, and in cities where they have never before been seen. And Russian hockey players skate for the National Hockey League.

Optimists, in 1991, were predicting a quick transition from communism to capitalism and a democratic Russia. A market, they said, would do it all. Pessimists were predicting a longer period for the anticipated transition—a decade or two. Realists, recalling Russia's history and centuries-old traditions, thought it would take even longer. But however long it takes, there is much that the West can do to facilitate the process, and one of them is to encourage exchanges with Russia, particularly with young people.

The most effective force for long-term change in Russia is its younger people, who are now moving into positions in business and government. They need to travel, break out of their country's historic isolation, visit other countries, see how other people live, and how Russians are seen by other people. As George Kennan counseled, whatever relations exist between Russia and other countries, there also has to be a meeting of the people.

Such a meeting of the people is being facilitated by Open World (formerly the Russian Leadership Program), created by an act of Congress in 1999.[2] Since its inception, Open World has brought more than five thousand emerging Russian leaders to the United States for visits of ten days. The participants, whose average age is thirty-seven, include officials at the national, regional, and local levels; judges; businesspeople; NGO directors; and journalists. They come from all parts of Russia and represent many of its ethnic groups, and one-third are women. They come first to the Library of Congress, where the program is based, for orientation in Washington and then spend one week in a city where they live with an American family and take part in activities in their fields of interest. Themes covered under the program include, among others, the rule of law, economic development, federalism, health, environment, women as leaders, and youth issues. Open World is governed by a board of trustees, chaired by Librarian of Congress James H. Billington, and its nine-member board includes members of Congress and private citizens.

2. Public Law 106–31.

Other American organizations can sponsor meetings of Russians and Americans. As Loren Graham and Andrew Kuchins have suggested:

> American universities, foundations, professional societies, and the government can play important roles and, with relatively modest expenditures, make a significant difference. Whenever a professional society holds a meeting in the United States or abroad, it should invite participation by scholars from the former Soviet Union, and pay their expenses. Universities can establish exchange professorships with universities in the former Soviet Union, and foundations can make certain that their established fellowship programs are available to scholars, artists and musicians from the former Soviet Union.[3]

That view is shared by Condoleezza Rice, National Security Adviser to President George W. Bush: "The cultural changes ultimately needed to sustain a functioning civil society and a market-based economy may take a generation. Western openness to Russia's people, particularly its youth, in exchange programs and contact with the private sector and educational opportunities can help that process."[4]

A Russian endorsement of that view is presented by Irina V. Alyoshina, a former Fulbright Scholar in the United States, who is now an associate professor of marketing at Moscow's State University of Management: "My students are a new generation of Russians, and even for me they seem to be to be too independent. In five to ten years or earlier, the older generation will be retired and the younger generation will take leading positions in government, business, and education. At that time the world will see real changes in Russia."[5]

3. Loren Graham and Andrew Kuchins, "Scholars in Peril," *Washington Post*, November 8, 1998.
4. *Chicago Tribune*, December 29, 2000.
5. Irina V. Alyoshina, in e-mail to author, October 23, 1998.

AFTERWORD

One day, history may tell us who really won. If a democratic Russia emerges—why then, Russia will have been the winner.

—JOHN LE CARRÉ, *The Secret Pilgrim*

SELECTED BIBLIOGRAPHY

Ailes, Catherine P., and Arthur E. Pardee Jr. *Cooperation in Science and Technology: An Evaluation of the U.S.-Soviet Agreement.* Westview Special Studies in Science, Technology, and Public Policy. Boulder, Colo.: Westview Press, 1986.

Aksyonov, Vassily. *In Search of Melancholy Baby.* Trans. Michael Henry Heim and Antonina W. Bouis. New York: Random House, Vintage Books, 1989.

Arbatov, Georgi. *The System: An Insider's Life in Soviet Politics.* Trans. John Glad and Oleg Volkonsky. New York: Time Books, 1992.

Barghoorn, Frederick C. *The Soviet Cultural Offensive: The Role of Cultural Diplomacy in Soviet Foreign Policy.* Princeton: Princeton University Press, 1960.

Barghoorn, Frederick C., and Ellen Mickiewicz. "American Views of Soviet-American Exchanges of Persons." In Richard L. Merritt, ed., *Communication in International Politics.* Champaign-Urbana: University of Illinois Press, 1972.

Becker, Jonathan A. *Soviet and Russian Press Coverage of the United States: Press, Politics, and Identity in Transition.* London: MacMillan Press, 1999; New York: St. Martin's Press, 1999.

Benedict, Robert Chapman. "An Examination of the First Direct Institutional Academic and Scholarly Exchanges between an American University and a Soviet University." Ph.D. diss., State University of New York, Albany, 1981.

Berman, Maureen R., and Joseph E. Johnson, eds. *Unofficial Diplomats.* New York: Columbia University Press, 1977.

Brown, Archie. *The Gorbachev Factor.* New York and Oxford: Oxford University Press, 1996.

Byrnes, Robert F. *Soviet-American Academic Exchanges, 1958–1975.* Bloomington: Indiana University Press, 1976.

Checkel, Jeffrey T. *Ideas and International Political Change: Soviet/Russian Behavior and the End of the Cold War.* New Haven: Yale University Press, 1997.

Chernyaev, Anatoly S. *My Six Years with Gorbachev.* Ed. and trans. Robert D. English and Elizabeth Tucker. University Park: Pennsylvania State University Press, 2000.

Choldin, Marianna Tax, and Maurice Friedberg. *The Red Pencil: Artists, Scholars, and Censors in the USSR.* Boston: Unwin Hyman, 1989.

Cohen, Stephen F., and Katrina vanden Heuvel. *Voices of Glasnost: Interviews with Gorbachev's Reformers.* New York: W. W. Norton, 1984.

Cole, Michael. "The World Beyond Our Borders: What Might Our Students Need to Know About It?" *American Psychologist* 39, no. 9 (1984).

Cooper, John Milton, Jr. "My Mission to Moscow: An American Historian in the Soviet Union." *Wisconsin Magazine of History* 72, no. 1 (autumn 1988).

Costa, Alexandra. *Stepping down from the Star: A Soviet Defector's Story.* New York: G. P. Putnam's Sons, 1986.

Critchlow, James. *Radio Hole-in-The-Head: An Insider's Story of Cold War Broadcasting.* Washington, D.C.: American University Press, 1995.

Dallin, Alexander. *A Balance Sheet for East-West Exchanges, IREX Occasional Papers 1, no. 1.* New York: International Research and Exchanges Board, 1980.

Dobrynin, Anatoly. *In Confidence: Moscow's Ambassador to America's Six Cold War Presidents (1962–1986).* New York: Times Books, 1995.

Doder, Dusko. *Shadows and Whispers: Power Politics Inside the Kremlin from Brezhnev to Gorbachev*. New York: Random House, 1986.

Doder, Dusko, and Louise Branson. *Gorbachev: Heretic in the Kremlin*. New York: Penguin Books, 1990.

Dunstan, John. *Paths to Excellence and the Soviet School*. Windsor, Berks, England: NFER Publishing, 1978.

Eisenhower, Dwight D. *Waging Peace, 1956–1961*. New York: Doubleday, 1965.

English, Robert. *Russia and the Idea of the West: Gorbachev, Intellectuals, and the End of the Cold War*. New York: Columbia University Press, 2000.

Evangelista, Matthew. *Unarmed Forces: The Transnational Movement to End the Cold War*. Ithaca: Cornell University Press, 1999.

Gaer, Felice D. "Soviet-American Scholarly Exchanges: Should Learning and Politics Mix?" *Vital Issues* 29, no. 10 (June 1980).

Garrard, John, and Carol Garrard. *Inside the Soviet Writers Union*. New York: The Free Press, 1990.

Garthoff, Raymond L. *The Great Transition: American-Soviet Relations and the End of the Cold War*. Washington, D.C.: Brookings Institution, 1994.

Gates, Robert M. *From the Shadows: The Ultimate Insider's Story of Five Presidents and How They Won the Cold War*. New York: Simon and Schuster, 1996.

Gorbachev, Mikhail. *Memoirs*. Trans. Wolf Jobst. New York: Doubleday: 1996. Based on the George Peronansky and Tatjana Varsavsky translation of the Russian original published by Siedler Verlag in Berlin.

———. *Mémoires: Une vie et des réformes*. Translated from Russian to French by Galia Ackerman, Michel Secinski, and Pierre Lorrain. Paris: Éditions du Rocher, 1997.

Graham, Loren R. "Aspects of Sharing Science and Technology." *The Annals of The American Academy of Political and Social Science* 414 (July 1974).

———. "How Valuable Are Scientific Exchanges with the Soviet Union?" *Science*, October 27, 1978.

———. *What Have We Learned About Science and Technology from the Russian Experience?* Stanford: Stanford University Press, 1998.

Grigoryev, V. I. *Rem Khokhlov*. Trans. G. G. Egerov. Revised from the 1981 Russian edition in the series *Outstanding Soviet Scientists*. Moscow: Mir Publishers, 1985.

Hearings of the Senate Permanent Subcommittee on Investigations, Committee on Governmental Affairs. *Transfer of U.S. High Technology to the Soviet Union and Soviet Bloc Nations*. U.S. Senate, 98th Cong., 2d sess., May 1982.

Hixson, Walter L. *Parting the Curtain: Propaganda, Culture, and the Cold War*. New York: St. Martin's Press, 1997.

House Subcommittee on International Scientific Cooperation of the Committee on Science, Space, and Technology. *Hearings to Examine U.S.-Soviet Science and Technology Exchanges*, 100th Cong., 1st sess. [No. 26], 23 June 1987.

Hughes, Thomas P. "How America Helped Build the Soviet Machine." *American Heritage*, December 1988.

Jamgotch, Nish, Jr. et al. *U.S.-Soviet Cooperation: A New Future*. Ed. Nish Jamgotch Jr. Westport, Conn.: Praeger, 1989.

Johnston, Eric. *We're All in It*. New York: E. P. Dutton, 1948.

Kaiser, Robert G. *Why Gorbachev Happened: His Triumph and His Failure*. New York: Simon and Schuster, 1991.

Kassof, Allen H. "The Exchange of People and Ideas." *The Annals of The American Academy of Political and Social Science* 414 (July 1974).

———. "Scholarly Exchanges and the Collapse of Communism." In Ian Tickle, ed., *Freedom First: Festschrift für Peter Sager*. Bern: Verlag SOI—Schweizerisches Ost-Institut, 1991. Reprinted in *Soviet and Post-Soviet Review* 22, no. 3 (1995).

Kellermann, Henry J. *Cultural Relations as an Instrument of U.S. Foreign Policy: The Educational Exchange Program Between the United States and Germany, 1945–1954.* Washington, D.C.: U.S. Government Printing Office, 1978.

———. Box 1, folder 247. Washington, D.C.: Foreign Affairs Oral History Project at Georgetown University, Lauinger Library.

Khanga, Yelena, with Susan Jacoby. *Soul to Soul: A Black Russian Jewish Woman's Search for Her Roots.* 1992. Reprint. New York: W. W. Norton, 1994.

Khrushchev, Nikita. *Khrushchev Remembers: The Last Testament.* Ed. and trans. Strobe Talbott. Boston: Little, Brown, 1974.

Kimmage, Dennis. *Russian Libraries in Transition: An Anthology of Glasnost Literature.* Jefferson, N.C.: McFarland, 1992.

Korey, William. *The Promises We Keep: Human Rights, the Helsinki Process, and American Foreign Policy.* New York: St. Martin's Press, 1993.

Lorkovic, Tatjana, and Eric A. Johnson. "Serial and Book Exchanges with the Former Soviet Union." *The Serial Librarian* 31, no. 4 (1997).

Marand, Christine. "Relations Culturelles Franco-Sovietique (1966–1986)." Ph.D. diss., Institut d'Etudes Politiques de Paris, 1989.

Mendelson, Sarah E. *Changing Course: Ideas, Politics, and the Soviet Withdrawal from Afghanistan.* Princeton: Princeton University Press, 1998.

Mirsky, George I. "A Half-Century in the World of Eastern Studies." *Vostok* (Moscow), no. 6 (1996).

Mitchell, J. M. "International Cultural Relations." In *Key Concepts in International Relations,* ed. Paul Wilkinson, no. 3. London: Allen and Unwin, in association with the British Council, 1986.

Nelson, Michael. *War of the Black Heavens: The Battles of Western Broadcasting in the Cold War.* Syracuse: Syracuse University Press, 1997.

Newsome, David D., et al. *Private Diplomacy with the Soviet Union.* Ed. David D. Newsome. Lanham, Md.: University Press of America; Washington, D.C.: Institute for the Study of Diplomacy, Georgetown University, 1987.

Odom, William E. *The Collapse of the Soviet Military.* New Haven: Yale University Press, 1998.

Okenfuss, Max J. "Russian Students in Europe in the Age of Peter the Great." In J. G. Garrard, ed., *The Eighteenth Century in Russia.* London: Oxford University Press, 1973.

Palazchenko, Pavel. *My Years with Gorbachev and Shevardnadze: The Memoir of a Soviet Interpreter.* University Park: Pennsylvania State University Press, 1997.

Parks, J. D. *Culture, Conflict and Coexistence: American-Soviet Cultural Relations, 1917–1958.* Jefferson, N.C.: McFarland, 1983.

Paul, David Mel. "On the Road Again." *Foreign Service Journal* 64, no. 3 (1987).

Potocki, Rodger. "The Life and Times of Poland's 'Bikini Boys'" *The Polish Review* 39, no. 3 (1994).

Raleigh, Donald J. "In Memory of N. V. Sivachev." *Soviet Studies in History* 22, no. 4 (spring 1984).

Richmond, Yale. "A Tale of Two Georges." *Foreign Service Journal* 69 (October 1992).

———. "U.S.-Soviet Cultural Exchanges." *Foreign Service Journal* 65 (December 1988).

———. *U.S.-Soviet Cultural Exchanges, 1958–1986: Who Wins?* Boulder, Colo.: Westview Press, 1987.

Rotblat, Joseph. *A History of the Pugwash Conferences.* Cambridge: MIT Press, 1972.

Rubenstein, Joshua. *Tangled Loyalties: The Life and Times of Ilya Ehrenburg.* New York: Basic Books, 1996.

Ryback, Timothy W. *Rock Around the Bloc: A History of Rock Music in Eastern Europe and the Soviet Union.* New York: Oxford University Press, 1990.

Sagdeev, Roald Z., and Susan Eisenhower, ed. *The Making of a Soviet Scientist: My Adventures in Nuclear Fusion and Space from Stalin to Star Wars.* New York: John Wiley and Sons, 1994.

Schaffner, Bradley L. "Slavic Book and Serial Exchanges." In Kathleen de la Pena McCook, Barbara J. Ford, and Kate Lippincott, eds., *Libraries: Global Reach/Local Touch.* Chicago: American Library Association, 1998.

Schweitzer, Glenn E. *Techno-Diplomacy: U.S. Soviet Confrontations in Science and Technology.* New York: Plenum Press, 1989.

———. "Who Wins in U.S.-Soviet Science Ventures?" *Bulletin of the Atomic Scientists* (October 1988).

Shveitser, A. D. *Glazami Perevodchika.* Moscow: Stella, 1996.

Sivachev, Nikolai V. "The Study of U.S. History at Moscow University." *Soviet Studies in History* 19, no. 1 (summer 1980).

Sivachev, Nikolai V., and Nikolai N. Yakovlev. *Russia and the United States: U.S.-Soviet Relations from the Soviet Point of View.* Trans. Olga Adler Titelbaum. Chicago: University of Chicago Press, 1980.

Smith, E. B. "In Memory of N. V. Sivachev." *Soviet Studies in History* 22, no. 4 (spring 1984).

Sosin, Gene. *Sparks of Liberty: An Insider's Memoir of Radio Liberty.* University Park: Pennsylvania State University Press, 1999.

Spencer, Metta. "'Political' Scientists." *The Bulletin of the Atomic Scientists* 5, no. 4 (July/August 1995).

Starr, S. Frederick. *Red and Hot: The Fate of Jazz in the Soviet Union.* New York: Oxford University Press, 1983.

Stites, Richard. *Russian Popular Culture: Entertainment and Society Since 1900.* Cambridge: Cambridge University Press, 1992.

Stone, Jeremy J. *Every Man Should Try: Adventures of a Public Interest Activist.* New York: Public Affairs, 1999.

Tioussov, Konstantine. "The Institute of the United States of America of the Russian Academy of Sciences." Master's thesis, Central European University, Budapest, 1997.

Treml, Vladimir. "Western Economic Sovietology and Soviet Authorities." In *The National Council for Eurasian and East European Research, 1978–1998: An Annotated Bibliography of Its Publications.* Washington, D.C.: The National Council for Eurasian and East European Research, 1999.

Tuch, Hans N., and Marvin Kalb. *Communicating with the World: U.S. Public Diplomacy Overseas.* New York: St. Martin's Press, 1990.

Voorhees, James. "The Dartmouth Conference: The Influence of a Transnational Community on U.S.-Soviet Relations, 1960–91." Paper presented at the thirty-ninth annual convention of the International Studies Association, Minneapolis, Minn., March 1998.

————. *Dialogue Sustained: The Multilevel Peace Process and the Dartmouth Conference.* Washington, D.C.: United States Institute of Peace and Charles F. Kettering Foundation, 2002.

Yeltsin, Boris. *Against the Grain: An Autobiography.* Trans. Michael Glenny. New York: Summit Books, 1990.

Reports

Barghoorn, Frederick C. "The 'Special Case' of US-USSR Exchanges." An unpublished preliminary analysis of questionnaires filled out by 180 American participants in the IUCTG and National Academy exchanges with the Soviet Union, circa 1967.

Bobrysheva, Alice. "Thanks for the Memories: My Years with the Dartmouth Conference." An unpublished report prepared for the Kettering Foundation, 1993.

Central Intelligence Agency. "Soviet Acquisition of Western Technology." April 1982.

————. "Soviet Acquisition of Militarily Significant Western Technology: An Update." September 1985.

Department of State, Office of Public Affairs. "Cultural Relations Between the United States and the Soviet Union: Efforts to Establish Cultural-Scientific Exchange Blocked by U.S.S.R." Department of State Publication 3480, International Information and Cultural Series 4. Washington, D.C.: U.S. Government Printing Office, 1949.

Garrard, John, and Carol Garrard. "The Organizational Weapon: Russian Literature and the Union of Soviet Writers." Soviet Interview Project, Working Paper No. 17, University of Illinois, Champaign, April 1986.

Joyce, John M. "U.S.-Science Exchanges: A Foot in the Soviet Door." Paper no. 11 in "Soviet Science and Technology: Eyewitness Accounts." Cambridge: Russian Research Center, Harvard University, 1981.

Kadushin, Charles, Bogdan Denitch, and Louis Genevie. "An Evaluation of the Experience of Exchange Participants, 1969–70 Through 1974–75." Washington, D.C.: International Research and Exchanges Board, 1977.

Kaysen, Carl. "Review of U.S.-U.S.S.R. Interacademy Exchanges and Relations." Washington, D.C.: National Academy of Sciences, 1977.

Kennan Institute for Advanced Russian Studies. "U.S.-Soviet Exchanges: A Conference Report." Washington, D.C.: Kennan Institute for Advanced Russian Studies, Woodrow Wilson International Center for Scholars, 1985.

Klosson, Boris. "Survey of U.S. Educational and Cultural Exchanges with the Soviet Union and Eastern Europe." A State Department report obtained under the Freedom of Information Act (FOIA). Washington, D.C.: Department of State, June 23, 1978.

Kubbig, Bernd W. "Communicators in the Cold War: The Pugwash Conferences, the U.S.-Soviet Study Group and the ABM Treaty." PRIF Report No. 44. Translated from the German by Gerard Holden. Frankfurt am Main: Peace Research Institute, 1996.

Kupferberg, Herbert, ed. "The Raised Curtain: Report of the Twentieth Century Fund Task Force on Soviet-American Scholarly Exchanges." New York: Twentieth Century Fund, 1977.

Lapidus, Gail. "The Impact of Soviet-American Scholarly Exchanges on the USSR." A paper prepared for a joint review of IREX programs by the Ford Foundation,

National Endowment for the Humanities, and the International Communication Agency, December 1979.

Panel on Scientific Communication and National Security, Committee on Science, Engineering, and Public Policy, National Academy of Sciences. *Scientific Communication and National Security.* Washington, D.C.: National Academy Press, 1982.

Richmond, Yale, and Robert Hawkins. Ed. Rick LaRue. "U.S.-Soviet Exchange: The Next Thirty Years, A Conference Report." Washington, D.C.: The Eisenhower World Affairs Institute, 1988.

"U.S.-Soviet Exchanges: A Conference Report." Washington, D.C.: Woodrow Wilson International Center for Scholars, 1985.

INDEX

ABM system and defenses, 86, 99, 100, 101, 167
Abrams Irwin, 59 n. 87, 60
Academy of Sciences, Russian, 146
Academy of Sciences, Ukrainian, 79
Academy of Sciences, USSR, 30, 67, 68, 71, 81, 213
    and Commission on Humanities and Social Sciences, 55, 77–78
    and IREX, 23, 91
    and Pugwash, 100–101
    and "Praguers," 170
    and SADS, 98
ACLS, 21, 23, 55, 68, 77–78
ACTR, 24, 58
ACTR-ACCELS, 116–18
ACYPL, 113–16
Afanasyev, Yuri N., 35, 38–40
Afghanistan, xiii, 20, 31, 103, 106, 144, 176
    and exchanges, 70, 122
Africa, 103
Aganbegyan, Abel, 78
Agency for International Development, U.S., 118
Agriculture, U.S.-USSR Agreement on, 46, 55
Aitmatov, Askar, 154
Aitmatov, Chingiz, 154, 157, 159, 160
Aitmatov, Sanjarbek, 154
Akademgorodok, 203
Akhmadulina, Bella, 155, 156
Akhmatova, Anna, 37
Aksyonov, Vasily, xiv, 139, 155, 157, 159–60, 167
    and jazz, 206–7
    and Metropol, 175–76
Alabama State University, 145
Albee, Edward, 153–54, 157, 158, 176, 210
Albright, Madeleine, 84, 105, 107
Alexeyeva, Ludmilla, 143, 189
Alferov, Zhores I., 75–76
Aliyev, Geydar, 114
Allen, George F., 114
Alley Theater, 113
Alliluyeva, Svetlana, 37, 138
Alvin Ailey Dance Theater, 126
Alyoshina, Irina V., 228
American Academy of Arts and Sciences, 91, 98
American Association of Museums, 120
American Ballet Theater, 126
American Bar Association, 113

American Chamber of Commerce, Moscow, 174
American Conservatory Theater, 113, 126, 160
American College of Cardiology, 113
American Councils. See ACTR-ACCELS
American Council of Learned Societies. See ACLS
American Council of Teachers of Russsian. See ACTR
American Council of Young Political Leaders. See ACYPL
American Economics Association, 113
American Embassy Moscow, x, 138, 149–51, 152
American Field Service, 113
American Friends Service Committee. See Quakers
American Library Association, 113
American Philosophical Society, 146
American Russian Youth Orchestra, 121
American University, 199
Amerika Magazine, 148–51
Ames, Aldrich, 37 n. 42, 220
Anderson, Martin, 114
Anderson, Raymond, 162, 168
Andover, 105
Andrew, Christopher, and Vasili Mitrokhin, 88, 220–21, 225
Andropov, Igor, 89
Andropov, Yuri, 29, 82, 223
Angola, 106
Anti-Ballistic Missile Treaty. See ABM
anti-Semitism, 8, 29, 168
The Apartment, 128
Apollo-Soyuz Project, 212–13
Arab-Israeli dispute, 112
Arbatov, Aleksei, 86, 107, 114, 174
Arbatov, Georgi, 18, 77, 81, 87, 169, 222
    and Dartmouth Conference, 83, 85, 95, 105
    and ISKAN, 82–92
    and Progress Publishers, 144–45
    and Pugwash, 95, 100
    and SADS, 98
    and UNA-USA, 108
Arbatsumov, Yevgeni, 169
Ardis Publishers, 140–41, 175
Arena Stage, 126–27, 154
Aristova, Irina, 173